AN UNEXPECTED JOURNEY

Life in the Colonies at Empire's End:
A Woman's Role

MARGARET REARDON

Published in October 2015 by Catherine Armstrong
Bourn Cambridgeshire England CB23 2SU
cfm.armstrong@gmail.com

ISBN: 978-0-9934010-0-8
eISBN: 978-0-9934010-1-5

A CIP catalogue record for this book is available from
The British Library

Typesetting and design by Head & Heart Publishing Services
www.headandheartpublishingservices.com

Cover design based on an idea by Jackie Taylor

Dedicated to the wives of Colonial Service Officers and Foreign and Commonwealth Officers who accompanied their husbands wherever they went on lonely and often difficult postings – always a long way from the comfort of home.

Official recognition has yet to be given to the many spouses who dedicated a significant part of their lives in service, albeit indirectly, to the Crown.

'I regard wives who supported their husbands in Africa as being as important as those they were supporting.'

Sir Rex Niven
Commissioner for Special Duties, Sokota, Northern Nigeria
(With a long and distinguished career
in the Nigerian Administration)

CONTENTS

PREFACE

These memoirs are based on the diaries kept at the time giving day to day life experiences abroad with my husband, Patrick Reardon, on his many postings throughout the world on behalf of Her Majesty's Overseas Civil Service. By their nature and, given the sensitive political times we lived in, they are not as detailed as they might be – which is entirely intentional.

It is hoped that this account of my life, during the twilight years of the British Empire, will be a source of reference for future historians as well as of some interest to the general reader and my own descendants.

The original diaries, memoirs, official documents, photographs and supporting papers are stored in the collection of Margaret Reardon in The Bodleian Library, Weston Library, Broad Street, Oxford OX1 3BG.

INTRODUCTION

Margaret Reardon was born in Mayfair on 16th February 1920. Her parents were both in service, her father as butler to Lord Londonderry and mother as lady's maid to the wife of a Belgian Financier. Her father then took up the position of Chapel Clerk (and subsequently Assistant Librarian) at Trinity College and the family moved to Cambridge. She was educated at St Augustine's Primary School and the Central School in Cambridge from 1925 to 1937.

At the outbreak of the Second World War she joined the Civil Defence organisation in Cambridge. In 1942 she enlisted in the Women's Auxiliary Territorial Service (ATS) and served until 1945 in the Isle of Man, attached to the Royal Signals Corp 'Y' Branch (an outpost of Bletchley Park). Her war work connected to Bletchley Park has recently been recognised.

On 27th October 1945 she married Captain Patrick William Reardon of the Essex Regiment, son of George Reardon and his wife Florence of Ilford, London. Shortly afterwards, Patrick was posted overseas as part of the army of occupation and administration of the former Italian colony Eritrea and was joined by Margaret a few months later. As Civil Affairs Officer they lived in various areas of Eritrea for the next five years. Margaret accompanied him on his duty safaris into the bush, visiting schools and clinics while Patrick was attending to tribal and civil matters, courts and administration. Their son Timothy was born in Asmara in May 1950.

After the handing over of Eritrea to Ethiopia by the United Nations Four Powers Commission, Patrick was retained as Advisor to the new government. He and Margaret remained in Eritrea until 1952. Patrick returned to England and applied to join the Colonial Service, attending the Devonshire Course at the University of Oxford, while she remained in Eritrea. He was appointed to the District Administration in Tanganyika. In November 1957, Margaret gave birth to their second child Catherine in Dar-es-Salaam. In addition to raising a young family under difficult conditions, she continued to carry out her official duties as hostess, organising women's clubs, clinics and other social work, as was expected of her and other wives of serving officers.

In 1961, when Tanganyika attained self-government, Patrick and Margaret were posted to the Bechuanaland Protectorate. Here they got to know Sir Seretse and Lady Ruth Khama and their family well and were acquainted with Lady Mitcheson, the author. When the territory became independent, Patrick was appointed Permanent Secretary to the Ministry of Commerce, Industry (Mines) and Water Affairs and they remained there until December 1971 when he retired, after localisation of the position.

Patrick was awarded the Order of the British Empire for his services to the Crown in 1968. Margaret remained with him throughout their twenty-five-year-life in Africa in sometimes unpleasant places with poor housing, only seeing her son for a few weeks each year while he was in England at boarding school. Latterly, changes in government policy meant it was fortunately possible to have both children nearer at Boarding Schools in Swaziland and South Africa.

In 1973 Patrick left Africa when he was appointed by Her Majesty's Overseas Civil Service to take up the position of Deputy Financial Secretary of the Gilbert and Ellice Islands. Margaret joined him shortly afterwards. Living in Bairiki on the Gilbert Islands was a very happy time, despite its remoteness and the thirty-six hours of flying time from England. Their daughter continued her studies initially in New Zealand and then in England, returning to the islands for her main holidays.

Their son, Timothy had by this time married and was living in England. When Patrick became Financial Secretary and Deputy Governor in the late 1970s there was plenty for Margaret to do, with VIP visitors and local dignitaries to entertain. Eventual independence of the two islands and separation into Tuvalu (Ellice) and Kiribati (Gilberts), meant that by 1979 it was time to move again.

After a few weeks back in their home in Sussex, Patrick left again for another overseas posting; this time to the Turks and Caicos Islands in the West Indies where Margaret again joined him. His job as Government Secretary and Deputy Governor was not the happiest of postings. The house was atrocious and the work of the British Administration was complicated by the attitude and corruption of local ministers. There were other political issues, widespread drug smuggling and several international crises involving the islands. Despite these difficulties, they made many friends in the expatriate community, including those on the American Air Force base, and enjoyed a good social life there.

In 1981 Patrick was appointed Governor of the British Virgin Islands. On the afternoon of 19th September 1981, at fifty-seven years of age, he died instantly of a heart attack. Margaret returned to England and tried to come to terms with the loss of her beloved husband and their extraordinary way of life.

Margaret, in her ninety-sixth year as this book is published, often looks back on her thirty-seven years of life in the colonies with fond memories. Grateful for the many experiences she shared with her husband, for the opportunity to meet so many interesting people from diverse cultural backgrounds and the friendships she made along the way. This book vividly describes a woman's perspective on this important chapter in Britain's final years of Empire.

AN
UNEXPECTED
JOURNEY

PART 1

The First Seven Years

ERITREA

1945–1952

BRITISH MILITARY ADMINISTRATION

1

A Journey to Foreign Parts

After our marriage on 27th October 1945, we managed to get some leave from our respective battalions in the Women's Auxiliary Territorial Service and the Essex Regiment and spent a few days having a brief honeymoon at a pub in Maldon, Essex. We were greatly entertained by a party of airmen and WAAFs, who spent their time creeping stealthily in and out of bedrooms during the early part of the evening, in the manner of a French farce. Three days later Pat left to go back to Warley Barracks in Essex and I returned to camp in Shrewsbury, Shropshire. Although WWII was officially over, we were still on a war footing. Not long after our return from honeymoon, Pat left for Northern Ireland where he thought he was to join a draft of men destined for the Western Desert. However, on arrival he discovered that they had already left the previous day – one of those life-changing events. He took a few hours off to sightsee and then returned to Warley Barracks and asked for some more leave, which was granted on compassionate grounds. With me being granted further leave on the same grounds, we met up in London and had a few more happy days together, staying at the Great Northern Hotel at Liverpool Street Station. It was our favourite place, a lovely old-fashioned hotel with good service and comfort. We both returned to our units wondering what our next moves would be. Within a few hours Pat was on his way to the Middle East, travelling the Medlock route. This involved journeying across Europe by train, finding a ship bound for Cairo at the other end; entailing much delay and time.

I received the odd letter or two from him, but communications were difficult in those days. Once in Cairo, he and the other officers that he had been travelling with enjoyed themselves swimming, sailing and relishing the sunshine; before being directed to embark upon a Nile Valley steamer to Khartoum in the Sudan, where they caught the train to Kassala and on to Tessenei in Eritrea. Thence they went by truck to Asmara, where they were to be billeted in the Officers' Mess. Surprisingly, Pat found that he was to be Acting Superintendent of Prisons with a workforce consisting of a mixed bag of the Italians and the British. He was just twenty-two years of age, an Army Captain, with the original intention of making the Army his career as his forefathers had done so before him.

A small house had been allocated to him not far from the centre of Asmara. After moving in, he applied for permission for me to join him and for company he also bought a working Pointer Braque puppy, Bobby. Whilst Pat was enjoying settling in to his new life and job, I waited in England for demobilisation organised on a point's system which was dependant on length of service, age, and so on. The only way I could have left earlier was through being pregnant or as a result of ill health. It was all done that way to simplify matters; a preferable alternative to hundreds of people pouring into demobilisation centres to be issued with ration books and clothing coupons at the same time. The men were given 50/- suits, with broad stripes, which most of them hated and many refused to take them. The girls were allowed to keep their uniforms. I remained at Shrewsbury until my demobilisation number came up on the 15th December 1945. I had applied for earlier release, in order that I could join Pat as soon as my Movement Orders came through. I returned to my parents' home in Cambridge to await the call. It was pretty quiet after the excitement of wartime life on the Isle of Man for several years. Most of my old friends had also married and left the area. I returned to my job with the Cement Marketing

Board, which was mandatory for returning services personnel. I worked in the Analysis Department dealing with costings, sacks and cement which was not very stimulating. Many of the people I had worked with previously had gone; either killed in conflict, married or emigrated as G.I. brides. The remaining original staff were mainly older women and thought me very odd to be considering going overseas at all; amongst 'savages and insects' as one woman put it. She thought I should wait until Pat returned to England. I stayed with the Cement Marketing Board until 1946, when my visas, tickets and Movement Orders arrived.

As with most young women of my era, I had over the years been getting my Hope Chest ready for married life, which was a large wooden trunk made for me by my father. It contained various items, sometimes handmade or given to me as gifts. There was linen, hand embroidered tablecloths and matching napkins together with other household items some of which were given for birthdays and Christmas. There were also useful household items such as tea towels, potato peelers and spoons. All goods were rationed still, so there was no going out to the shops to stock up on items. My mother generously put in the family silver and the canteen of cutlery that had been their own wedding present, together with some knick-knacks. I also added a few personal items. My box was despatched to the docks filled with my precious long playing records and the special record case, given to me by the office staff at the Cement Marketing Board.

I visited my in-laws in Ilford to say goodbye and my mother-in-law joined in the desperate search for suitable clothes for me to take overseas and wear on the journey out there. Although I had heard that it would be much easier to buy things when I got to Eritrea, the problem was what to wear on the ship. In those days there were no boutiques or chain stores apart from the Co-op and everything was still rationed. I had been given some extra coupons when I left the ATS, but they actually bought very little. I still only weighed seven and a half stone, so fortunately could still wear the clothes I had before the war. I packed everything into my army kit bag, a canvas style bag with a string top, which had to be slung over your shoulder. Despite receiving my Demob

Orders, I was still legally in the ATS and would continue to be until General Demobilisation, which took place some years later. This meant that I had to also take my uniform and gas mask. My father wanted to come and see me off, but it would not have been easy for him, as I had to report to the Rail Transport Office at the docks in Southampton. So, I made the journey alone. In August 1946, I boarded the P&O liner Strathnaver which was then in use as a troop ship and was going to the Far East, calling in at Egypt where I was due to disembark. There were about fifty civilians, and the rest of the passengers were British troops who were accommodated below deck.

My cabin had originally been a large suite which, for war purposes, had been fitted up with ten bunks. There were nine women, one of whom was travelling with a small boy of about four years. The child fell out of bed regularly screaming loudly with fright, so in the end we dealt with it by putting piles of pillows and anything else we could find beside his bunk. He still fell out, but less noisily. Air conditioning was unheard of in those days, and we had one small porthole, which remained closed for most of the time if the weather was bad. The situation must have been rather grim, but I do not recall being too worried by it. We were all used to hard times in those days. There were no private bathrooms, so you had to use the nearest one to the cabin on a rota. The Indian steward on duty would call you when the bath was free, once you had indicated to him that you wished to wash. He would have filled the bath with seawater and across the bath on a rack there would be a bowl of fresh non-seawater. It was tepid. You soaped yourself down in the seawater which meant that the soap did not lather properly, rinsed with fresh non-seawater and then plunged down into the seawater to clean off. This left you feeling sticky but refreshed.

It was a troop ship and therefore 'dry' with no alcohol served on board. However, I discovered quite quickly that everyone had brought their own small supply. My table companion was a tea planter on his way back to India, and he introduced me to Glenmorangie Whisky which was a drink much favoured in those days. An orange juice was ordered from the steward and when his back was turned, out came the hip flasks. We all said it was medicinal given the sea was pretty rough from time to time. There was a small shop on the ship where everything was off ration so we could buy as much as we liked which was wonderful. We bought cigarettes and various items such as chocolate bars, which had been strictly rationed for so long in England. Life on board the Strathnaver was very relaxed. The non-military passengers were wives and children of armed forces personnel, others were Indians returning to their homes, planters and business people. Life was still pretty basic. There were no deck chairs, so we had to sit on the deck. No cups of Bovril or tea brought round at 11 o'clock, as they did on later journeys we made on other ships. Each day we consulted the lounge map to confirm our whereabouts and the old hands were always there to give us a geography or history lesson on just about everything. I learned a great deal about life abroad on that voyage. Not many working class people went on cruises or overseas in those days, and to me it was a terrific adventure. Even the Spartan conditions did not trouble me after nearly four years in the ATS. It helped that I had good company too. We did not call into any ports because Europe was in turmoil still, so it took us just nine days to go through the Mediterranean Sea.

Our arrival at Port Said in Egypt was not very dramatic. Those of us who were disembarking went off the ship with our hard rations, which consisted of doorstep sandwiches filled with cheese or meat, wrapped in greaseproof paper as plastic bags had not yet been invented. Everything dried out in the heat and over the next hour or so we lost them all: they were pilfered by small local boys. We checked that all of our heavy baggage was unloaded and then the ship sailed off and left us on the quayside. Then the Rail Transport Officer took the half a dozen of us to a hut in the middle of the dock. The dock was criss-crossed with train tracks and there was much activity going on such as unloading and shunting. It was about midday and the heat was at least 90°F. The hut was fortunately a canteen and a kindly elderly Egyptian staff member wanted to cook us a meal of fried eggs and chips. Given the heat, we declined, but accepted the tea he offered. It was getting hotter and hotter by the hour, and several hours later we were still waiting to be collected and taken elsewhere. The old cook did his best to keep us supplied with refreshing cold drinks or tea. By about 3 o'clock we were getting anxious, especially as there was a fretful two-year-old child with us. We were then approached by two German prisoners of war who were working nearby. Speaking excellent English, these very handsome twenty-year-olds in their brief shorts asked anxiously why we were there and when we explained the situation, they immediately volunteered to go and find out what was happening. They thought that perhaps we had been forgotten, which we probably had been. One of them said that if we had not been collected within the hour, he would find a Jeep and take us himself. In the meantime, they chased away the pestering small boys. Later in a letter home to my parents, I wrote that ironically we were protected by the enemy from our supposed Allies.

Eventually, around 5 o'clock the Rail Transport Corps collected us from the hut and took us back to the dock area, where we were taken to the railway station and put on the train to Cairo. The journey, which was interesting with lots of local colour and noise, took several hours and the train stopped at a lot of small stations. We were in a First Class carriage, much to the disdain of a middle-aged Egyptian and his wife who clearly were from a fairly wealthy background judging from her jewellery. It probably was a bit of a shock to have a group of rather crumpled, unaccompanied women disturbing their peace in the comfortable compartment. After such a hot and arduous journey, we were all more than ready for the comfort of our hotel. An army truck picked us up from the railway station and deposited us at the side door. The Grand Hotel was a lovely old building with large rooms and ceiling fans, the top floor of which had been taken over by the British Authorities as an officers' leave camp. It was occupied by men coming in from the Western Desert who were having a few days rest. After we were shown to our rooms and had freshened up, we went down to the dining room for dinner, much to the excitement of the officers already there. Someone said the word 'Women!' which made us all laugh. We all gratefully accepted various kind offers of sightseeing trips around the ancient sights. A very nice young Army officer took me for a lot of wonderful tours of the area and of Cairo itself, including the Pyramids and Sphinx. We had tea at Groppi's, a glamorous hotel that was a must in any well-heeled tourist's itinerary, and had dinner in their famous Roof Garden. I also saw all the famous mosques and had a private viewing of the ancient treasures of the Cairo Museum, including the Tutankhamun wonders, which the Army officer was able to arrange. The museum was at that time closed to the public because of continued troubles in the area and many exhibits were stored in its basement for safekeeping.

I spent about two weeks in Cairo and then bade goodbye to one of my fellow travellers, the woman with the young child who was on her way to Libya. The rest of our party was sent down the coast to Alexandria and we stayed at the YMCA hostel there, which was efficiently run by some Egyptian ladies. The nearby canteen served delicious home made cakes and a good cup of tea; after all our wartime deprivations and rationing, everything seemed wonderful. As usual I did some sightseeing before we were once more put on the train; this time we were headed again for Port Said. When we arrived we were piled into Army trucks and travelled a further fifty miles to Lake Timsah near Ismailia, which was a military camp for the British garrison in the canal area to rest and recover. Here we were allocated a Nissen hut to sleep in with a sand floor; the temperature was over 90ºF. They put thatched jackets made from reeds over the top of the huts in the hot season to help mitigate the heat of the sun and these were just being erected on the day we arrived. There were a few ATS girls on the staff and I was pleased to meet one I had known briefly in the Isle of Man ATS Camp. The ships were passing through the canal all the while and we could see them from the camp. We hoped that at least one was carrying our baggage.

We swam every day in the designated area of the canal that was clean. On our first visit to the local bazaar, I bought fruit which was still such a luxury for us at that time. I put it on my locker beside the bed. Despite sleeping under a mosquito net I woke in the middle of the night covered in small ants; my first lesson of tropical life. The canal area was malarial and we were taking Paludrine, a new anti-malarial drug which had replaced all the others like Quinine which was awful and Mepacrine which turned people yellow. The canal was known as the sweet water canal and there were date trees all over the camp; we only had to shake them for the ripe dates to fall down. The tropical fruit available in the area was wonderful. I was quite sorry to leave Timsah when the time came. We were there for only a week, so we relaxed as best we could for this short transit break, before our respective onward journeys. All this time we knew where our husbands were but getting to them was the problem; there were no passenger ships, no railways and only military aeroplanes. They were having quite a problem with getting us to Eritrea.

2

ASMARA

Eventually, they managed to sort it all out. In September 1946, I left by air, but not before having to go back to Cairo by road. It was a small plane holding eight to ten people, mainly military and VIPs. Being in a Moslem country, the unveiled British women on board the aircraft were an object of great curiosity. There was no airline steward; instead on a rack at the back of the aircraft there were about six Thermos flasks holding tea or coffee. I had been given the usual hard rations and the man I was sitting next to kindly fetched me cups of tea when needed. It was quite a long journey and we had to stop to refuel. Small boys mobbed us as we sat in the airport terminal of sorts. The airport was provincial and near pens full of livestock, which added a somewhat unpleasant aroma to the surrounding area. Temperatures were well over 100°F.

Towards the late afternoon that same day, we landed in the city of Asmara which lies on a plateau about 7,000ft above sea level. The terrain was very bleak and always windy, but thankfully that meant it was much cooler. There were rows of tall trees planted at the end of the runway, probably as a windbreak. On first impressions, it did not look very interesting or inviting. As there were no airport buildings in those days, Pat was amongst a group of people stood on the edge of the airfield. Fortunately we did recognise each other after all those months apart. I had only my small hand luggage, so it was easily loaded into his

Fig 2.1 *Patrick with his Army Police Issue 327 Fiat* Topolino *(little mouse).*

small police issue car (see Fig. 2.1). He had managed to find a small villa for us and had been able to move out of his original house allocated to him by the Army which was in the cantonment (military quarters) area. Our address was 103 Viale Roma, conveniently close to his office. We had one bedroom, a sitting room, a kitchen and a bathroom with all mod cons. A small servant's bedroom was just off the hall, which led out onto the small patch of garden at the back. All of the furniture (see Fig. 2.2) had been made by Italian craftsmen in mahogany; it was very heavy, stylish and solid-looking. The chair cushions were hard and they were stuffed with horse hair. The floors were stone and covered in sisal mats. We would have enjoyed using the fire, but it smoked like mad and we never managed to cure it; a pity as the weather was very cold and at times it hailed and snowed. When my Hope Chest arrived by sea, I was able to make the villa look quite homely. I put the chair back covers I had laboriously embroidered at school on the chairs to cheer them up. Although between us we had a few pots and pans and kitchen basics it was hardly a well-stocked kitchen, but as I could not cook it did not really seem to matter. Luckily Pat was quite handy in the kitchen and we ate out a lot as there were so many lovely Italian bars and restaurants. I began trying to learn some Italian.

The other household members included Bobby the large Pointer Braque, then just a few months old. His long and enthusiastic tail swept things off our low table at regular intervals and constantly needed bandaging up as he was always damaging it. Bobby was devoted to Pat and went everywhere with him including the office. I missed him around the house as I was quite isolated at the villa; the other wives were across town in the military quarters at the cantonment. One evening Pat came home with something tucked into his battle dress (army uniform), which turned out to be a small puppy. She was a two months old Alsatian cross, which was going to be destroyed if no home was found for her, so of course we had kept her and I named her Judy; she became my devoted shadow.

We had a very nice maid called Gabriella who was a Coptic Christian. It may not have been her real name as it was the custom to adopt an Italian name and many girls were called Gabriella. She was clean and quiet, using all our facilities including the bathroom, which was the custom there. On her day off, she bathed and put on a clean dress and a traditional white muslin *shama* (shawl) and went to church. She then visited her mother on the outskirts of town. She came back by 6 o'clock and never stayed out late. The young unmarried Coptic Christian girls were very modest (chaste) and there were no boyfriends hanging around. Her duties were house cleaning, washing the floor and doing the laundry. She did not do the cooking. I did get the cookery books out and tried my hand at some things, and got better at it in time.

Pat was in the Army of Occupation administering Eritrea, which was thankfully a more benign one perhaps than would have been the case had the shoe been on the other foot. The Italians had fought on the side of Britain in the WWI but changed sides under Mussolini in WWII and Eritrea, being one of their colonies, came under occupation at the end of the war as a result. Once the troops had fought their way to Asmara over the challenging countryside and mountains; now however life returned to something like normal despite the area being under British military rule. The British Ambassador took over and set up various departments, one of which was the Prison Service that Pat was assigned to. So as the war was over, military personnel like Pat found themselves directed to civilian jobs in the Occupied Enemy Territory Administration. With the help of fellow officers, he ran the Police and Customs in Asmara and the surrounding districts. Unfortunately, while he was at the Amba Galliano police station in Asmara, he did not earn much pay. As I was fortunate in having no domestic ties, I decided to look for a job and got one in the Chief Justice's office as a typist (the one finger variety). This job could only be done by a *Britisher* because it was dealing with restricted or secret information. My work consisted mainly of typing up proclamation notices for the local population announcing curfews and prohibitions, to be printed and displayed in public places as they were under Marshall Law. For the first year we were there a non-fraternisation order was in force. This meant that any contact with the former enemy was to be kept at a purely 'need' or 'where necessary'. The rest of the staff in the office was made up of Italian men who worked as translators or in general office work. Of course this made nonsense of the non-fraternising and we quite quickly behaved in a friendly way. They liked having a young girl in the office and used to bring lovely cream cakes in for me at coffee breaks. I learned a lot about Italians and their way of life during the months I worked there, and started to learn to speak the language.

Initially the non-fraternisation order was not difficult to uphold, as I knew no Italian and could just point to groceries in the store, always being polite of course as we were ambassadors for our country. Not many of them spoke English either. Quite a number of Italians had left the country as soon as it was possible, fearing for their safety. I discovered later that they had been told that the British Troops would mistreat them. The poorer people who had not had the finances to leave were understandably very worried. It must have been awful especially for wives and daughters, as occupying armies were not known for their civilised behaviour. I am proud to say that to my knowledge nothing unseemly took place.

Fig 2.2 *Asmara 1946: Dining room furniture in our first home, Viale Roma, produced by Italian craftsman.*

We were kept quite busy with official entertaining for various dignitaries, including a memorable Tea Party (see Figs. 2.3 and 2.4) in Gezabanda on 3rd May 1947 in honour of the Magboul, an important official of the Sudan Government. The various notable Eritrean and senior military administration officials who attended included a senior Coptic Priest.

Pat also started to teach me to drive. The traffic was not too great in Asmara, but I could have done without having my lessons in rush hour. He devised various military-like tests for me, such as having to drive down the steep mountain roads, through native villages where dogs chased the car. Once when I had to drive through yet another herd of goats, unfortunately in all the confusion I ran over one and had to recompense the owner. He was a real taskmaster. In those days, fortunately we did not have to take a Driving Test at the end of it all. Throughout the years in the territory I drove a Lancia, an Alfa Romeo and eventually Jeeps and a large lorry across deserts, rivers and escarpments. Every three years, we visited the UK when we were on leave to catch up with our families. At one stage we brought back a Morris Minor, which was the latest model available. We eventually sold it for a good price – such was the interest in it.

Asmara was a lovely place to be stationed in. The climate was good with warm days, cool nights and not much rain, when it did rain it was very heavy and arrived in brief downpours. We had a small garden with a few tropical plants in it. We could have grown quite a lot in the garden, had we been so inclined, but we knew our stay would only be temporary. As time went on the shops re-opened and more stock appeared. One could buy most things, although cooking oil remained rationed, as were one or two other commodities which I expect were imported from Italy. But the wonderful delicatessen Tagliero's was full of food we in the UK had not seen for a long time. It was the first time I had seen butter in its natural colour and was unused to seeing housewives buying it by the ounce as they required it. Surprisingly, many of the expatriates were so insular in relation to the different life style to which we were being exposed and refused to try any foreign foods. Many moaned about it all being so different to the UK and some even returned home. Pat and I were enjoying it all as fortunately we were very similar in outlook. We ate out a great deal usually at a bistro called Mario's and often at the Officers' Mess. Sometimes we drove six miles out of Asmara to an Italian café, down a precipitous road with the valley floor falling away thousands of feet beneath us. There we ate *zigany* which is a very hot, spicy local dish served upon heavy sour bread called *ungero* and was usually eaten with *tej*, a local fermented drink. One kept away from it when behind the wheel. The café was run by an Italian man and his Eritrean wife; Eritrean women were very attractive and number of European men ended up marrying them.

Once in a while we would drive down to the coast to Massawa on the Red Sea where at times the temperature was 100°F or more. We would stay at some quarters at the old Italian naval base; it was pretty basic but adequate and used as a rest house for the military. We usually went with friends, and enjoyed swimming in the netted area of the sea that formed the port. We climbed out rather quickly though on one occasion, when a local man arrived to tell us that the net was broken and sharks had been seen in these waters.

We found Asmara very comfortable, cool and interesting with a civilised, almost continental lifestyle. There was plenty of sport, including tennis, golf, football, polo and motor racing. We went shares with an Italian for a small racing car, mainly I believe on account of our being able to get the petrol. It was fun for a while and gained us entry into Italian homes and society, which helped us to get to know them and improved our language abilities. By now we had become quite fluent, in a way. Mr Corbi, an elderly Italian who was in charge of Public Works, was a very dignified man who had married an Eritrean woman. They had two daughters in their twenties. They used to make the most delicious ice cream and some years later I loved to treat my son Timothy to it. I used to spend time chatting with them as they used to do some dressmaking for me too. His wife remained in the

Fig 2.3 *Gezabanda in Asmara 3rd May 1947: Patrick (2nd from left) and Margaret (3rd from right) hosting Tea Party in honour of the Magboul, Political Official of the Sudan Government.*

kitchen and did not come into the sitting room at all. Life must have been difficult for them as racial prejudice against mixed blood offspring was quite strong then.

There was a NAAFI where we did some shopping and also a military hospital and doctors. A number of British wives had arrived, while the number of men marrying Italian girls grew. We had an acquaintance who was courting a young Italian girl, Gabriella Gasparini, who became a great friend of mine. As a respectable married woman, I had to promise her parents that she would be chaperoned by me. It was a big responsibility and had to be taken seriously. Another friend was Babs Abbot, the daughter of one of Pat's fellow officers. She always came to stay overnight with me when Pat went away; it being considered inappropriate for me to be left alone, even with a servant. We always purchased some delicious real cream meringues made by the local Italian baker. This was such a luxury to us after wartime Britain. Babs always kept most of the cream on her last mouthful of meringue. This proved too much for our dog, Bobby. As she bent over her book, with fingers aloft, he rose up and snatched the whole lot in one gulp. A few days earlier he had eaten a chocolate cake that I had made, which was most annoying as I had really struggled to make this cake after a number of failures; I did not know that at altitudes one must alter the proportion of certain ingredients. Someone from the American Radio Station kindly put me right. On this occasion, I had placed the cake on the tea table and went to greet Pat on his arrival home from the office. As we came back into the room, the cake was disappearing down Bobby's throat. The next day he came out in bumps all over his head, which the vet said was allergic rash. Pat told me later that he did not really eat cakes. Bobby was constantly wanting to go in and out of the door to the garden, so I taught him to open it himself by pressing the handle down and visitors were quite astonished when he used to close it behind him. It took me quite a while to teach him do the latter. Judy took her guard duties seriously and would try to bite anyone, especially the local population, that she considered a threat to me. Because of the rabies threat, I had to be very vigilant as any bite had to be reported. Unfortunately one day when we were out the puppies, Bobby and Judy, tore Gabriella's *shama* into minute pieces. When we got home it was like a snowstorm in the villa and they must have had a lovely time doing it. Naturally, we apologised and gave her a brand new one in its place.

I should perhaps mention something about the people of Eritrea and will start with those in the Hamasien or the Asmara area, which was mainly agricultural and part of the Central Highlands. The word Asmara means forest of flowers, but it was not clear why. The city of Asmara was surrounded by smaller native villages, some of which were quite large and the people of the area were Coptic Christians. The women wore their hair in plaited styles. For a married woman, these plaits were all over their heads from back to front; for an unmarried girl, there was a shaved area in the centre of their head and their hair was plaited at the sides. These beautiful hairstyles were dressed with rancid butter pomades, which unfortunately attracted flies. At intervals their hair required redressing. A skilled hairdressing woman came to the house and the hair was unplaited, washed with a soapy infusion made from Neem tree leaves, and carefully re-plaited and anointed with this special butter product. The whole process took hours. Just as the smell of the rancid butter began diminishing and it was becoming possible to live with it, they redid their hair and the strong smell started again. The men wore their hair in a tangled bouffant, but many had adopted the European style of short back and sides. About 50 per cent of the people of Eritrea were Trigray-Tigriny and about 34 per cent Tigre from the lowlands or coastal regions, the remainder being made up of smaller ethnic groups. The indigenous population was quite friendly towards us with the women making a trilling sound as a welcome, although it could be quite alarming when one was not expecting it

Pat and I were pretty healthy, eating well and putting on rather too much weight. The wartime rations in the UK had clearly kept us all slim. Pat played polo regularly and I used to find myself timing the chukkas. The other wives had got wise to it and timed their arrivals after the start. Watching the games was not always very exciting, but at least it was warm and sunny. I had to time the ball if it went off the field and this time needed to be added to the overall chukka time. There was always someone disposed to argue, so I know something of how the football referees feel. We got used to the Italian music, their way of dancing and songs like Santa Lucia and other Neapolitan tunes dominated the music scene. No one seemed interested at that time in American Jazz or Big Band music, especially in Keren and elsewhere. It was only later, after the American Radio Station opened in Asmara and broadcast their late night music, that we heard this type of music and other more modern songs; the station was called Radio Marina.

I had to give up my job after a few months because Pat was transferred to Adi Ugri for temporary duty. We were allocated a villa; everything was called a villa or a palace in Eritrea. The house was plain with ugly windows which were typical of its type for that era. Neither Pat nor I were too bothered by the nature of our new quarters, with its usual

Fig 2.4   *Gezabanda in Asmara 3rd May 1947: Maghoul Tea Party with Coptic Priest and Maghoul with Patrick (on right).*

Public Works Department issue of ill-matching furniture and some sisal mats on the stone floor. The furniture (one adult bed, wardrobe, lounge chairs, wooden stove and kitchen table) was piecemeal and shabby. No refrigerators or iceboxes were provided. We had an ammunition box, which had a thick lining; it was about the size of our usual tin trunks, though thinner and longer in shape, which doubled up as a cool box. We used to buy a small ice block from an Italian man who owned a small electricity plant. In order to keep food chilled, we wrapped it up in newspapers and shut the lid of the box, with the ice keeping all of our foodstuffs cool. We often used the box to chill our Mellotti's beer or keep butter cool (it often came in tins from the NAAFI) and to prevent any game we had shot from going off. We shot for the pot, usually eating guinea fowl or buck, though occasionally when a local animal was killed we would receive some goat or sheep. From time to time, we were also able to have milk from a local cow when she was in calf, which had to be boiled immediately and then stored in the icebox. We had very few vegetables apart from tinned ones, but fruit was a little more readily available as sometimes local farmers had some to spare. Perhaps we had so recently been in the Army that anything was deemed comfortable. Ordinary people's homes back in England were fairly basic too in those days. We took all the furniture we had had made for our first house with us. My favourite item was the dressing table, made in art deco style by an Italian cabinetmaker in two colours of wood and inlaid. The local man who made it was an Italian friend of ours and was my friend Gabriella's father. In any case, life was pretty exciting, lots of travel and new sights for which people pay a fortune today.

Our maid Gabriella came with us and we had a resident gardener-caretaker whose job it was to sweep, tidy and to fetch wood for the kitchen stove, which was our only means of cooking. All that grew in the garden were some poor looking zinnia and bougainvillaea. Water was very expensive so there was no lawn. We did not do much official entertaining in Adi Ugri, which meant we ate out a lot instead. However small the villages were, there was always some bar or other serving good Italian or Eritrean food. Adi Ugri was just an outpost overlooking the Asmara to Massawa road; perched on the edge of the mountain about 7,000 ft up with fantastic views across the countryside, which in the most part was made up of more mountains and very little vegetation. There were only four other villas and some police barracks in the form of 'beehive' huts. The villas were occupied by British Police Officers and there were also some Italian officials with their wives. There was only one other English woman in the village, with her small children, whose husband was a Senior Civil Affairs Officer. Unfortunately, their poor little children suffered constantly with conjunctivitis; a terrible thing which every Eritrean child suffered from caused by the clouds of flies which clustered round their eyes. Adi Ugri had probably originated as a means of guarding the pass, which it was still doing. There was a problem with armed bandits in Eritrea, who were called *shifta*. They usually made short sharp raids on farms and small Police posts; the object being political harassment in most cases. They were almost impossible to catch and melted into the local scene. Sometimes pursuing Police would find embers of fires still warm and then only some herdsmen with their goats in the vicinity, so it was difficult to tell if they were the *shifta* or not. They regularly attacked cars travelling along the roads to the remote farms, held up and occasionally killed the occupants. We too could have been raided and killed in our beds; it would have been relatively easy although we were usually armed. We got to know the Italian families, including some brave souls who farmed in nearby areas, who always had to be alert for *shifta*. We always travelled with a Police escort, whether going a few miles or back to Asmara for a weekend. Everyone was armed. I also used to do short visits with the patrols, with a machine gun resting across my lap while Pat drove.

Pat and I took up riding in Adi Ugri. The groom used to bring the horses up to the house for us each day. As it seemed to be a different one each time, I never really got a chance to bond with any of them and to get to know their temperament. No one gave me a lesson, I was just shown how to get on the horse and given the reins, told where to put my feet and off I went. The horses were used by the Police who did patrols over the difficult terrain on horseback. I managed to learn enough horsemanship to be able to ride over to the nearby village store, tying the horse up to a post – much as in the Westerns. Although I continued to ride up until we left the country, it was never really my thing.

After six months in Adi Ugri, we were transferred back to Asmara and got our old villa back in Vaile Roma and I was able to return to my previous job. Things must have been desperate, as they seemed keen to have my one finger typing skills. Once again everything was piled onto big Army trucks with Gabriella tucked in amongst it all and the dogs on top of the baggage. Over the years we got used to these frequent moves, some at very short notice; invariably moving into another none too clean villa and trying to make it into a home. Usually there was a dirty blackened kitchen, which luckily I did not have to clean. No woman today would have accepted the conditions, but back then you just got on with it. Back in Asmara, we settled into our usual routine, with Gabriella in her room at the back of the house. I was doing some cooking by then. One day I touched her meat with the fork that I had just turned my pork chop with and she refused to eat it. Up to that point, I had not realised that Coptic Christians had the same religious issues about Pork as the Jews and Moslems. I had to quickly give her money to get some more meat for her dinner. We had no manuals to instruct us about these sort of taboos, and had to learn as we went along.

By this time I had been given a beautiful horse, called *Ungaria* (Italian for Hungary) who had belonged to the daughter of an Italian General, rumoured to be a relative of Count Antonelli. She hated men and would turn round to kick if any man approached her. Getting her saddled was a bit of a problem, but as long as I was there holding the head collar we managed. She was very gentle with me but took an extreme dislike to camels. She was a pretty bay mare, with one white sock and was a thoroughbred cross. She used to turn her head and nibble at my foot when we were walking along, and I discovered that the General's daughter had fed her chocolate as they went along. She had my NAAFI chocolate supplies from then on. She was quite old and sadly went very lame after someone took her out riding without my permission one day. The vet suggested that we retired her at the Vaccine Institute and she seemed to live out her life there quite happily. I used to go up to see her regularly with chocolate treats until we left the area.

Rabies was endemic in Eritrea and there were human cases all the time. The Vaccine Institute had cages full of goats, dogs and cats that were suspected of having the disease. They were waiting out the two-week incubation period which was necessary to enable owners or people who had been bitten or scratched to have the preventative injections. These were twenty-five injections into the stomach. During my stay in Africa I had to have them twice; initially after my cat had bitten me under my arm before disappearing over the wall screeching, never to be seen again. The second time was when a dogfight took place under the table at the club after a stray dog had wandered in and picked a fight with the owner's dog. This resulted in me getting my ankle nipped and no one knew which animal was responsible. Pat had to have them too a few years later after someone else's dog had gone rabid just after he had stayed at the house. The vet insisted that this was done although he had not been bitten, in case he had been licked on an open cut. One of the Senior Veterinary Scientists at the Institute told me that they had had a 100 per cent success rate with the vaccine so far, but that it could not possibly stay that way which was an awful thought. Several Europeans died of this terrible disease while we were there, including a child. It left me with a lifelong fear of contracting it.

3

KEREN

Towards the end of 1947 we were transferred to Keren in the Western Province. We had all piled into an Army truck for the journey, the dogs balanced on top of the baggage, a procedure which would be followed on our moves around Eritrea in the months and years to come. We drove about 105km from Asmara, along the winding routes down the pass and along the dusty plain (see Fig. 3.1), to our new home. It was a large house and Italianate in design, surrounded by an iron fence in a fancy style with big gates. It was quite obviously the house of an important Italian official or maybe an affluent former Italian resident. It was however empty, except for the usual meagre Public Works Department issue of furniture. There were two wicker chairs and a settee in colonial style with removable seat cushions but without padded arms or back, a desk, a sideboard and a dining table with six chairs. The beds were a plain iron framed hospital type. My Hope Chest came in handy as an additional piece of furniture and was used for storage in the bedroom. Luckily I had my own Italian made dressing table from Viale Roma, which I refused to be parted from. Apart from the bedding, some linen and basic kitchen equipment, we also had a few books, knick-knacks and some coffee tables, but nothing else. Sadly, we had to leave the other pieces of furniture in Asmara, as they were strictly speaking Government Issue furniture and not ours to keep. So in in the spacious rooms, we only had sprinkling of rather quaint odds and ends of furniture, which did not quite go with the more grandiose style of the house. The arrival at a new house was always the same. After a quick inspection to take it all in while the baggage was being unloaded, we were then busy sweeping out the sand and dust that had accumulated after the last owners had left the house. Finally we made up beds and put up mosquito nets. In an effort to make it all look like home again, we always put out our books and personal knick-knacks on the shelves. The driver would be helping to take our boxes of pots and pans into the kitchen, which we always hoped was free from cockroaches and other undesirables, but seldom was.

On this occasion, Gabriella came with us (see Fig. 3.2). Unfortunately after a month or so she went back to Asmara. The two additional members of staff we had employed were men of the Moslem faith and this was not considered a suitable arrangement for a single Coptic Christian woman. We appointed a cook for the house and a second houseboy cum safari-cook. The latter would be cooking for Pat as he travelled around the region for his work camping safari style, under canvas in the bush. It was quite a different life to our Asmara one. After we settled in, we had a very nice young boy called Omar as a house-boy. He was the son of a local Chief and as such had never worked in a European's house before. Sadly he only lasted six months as he lacked any proper training and fell foul of the other servants, who could be awkward when they wanted to be so. We engaged someone else who might well have been a relative of the cook which could have been the issue in the first place, but from our stand point you could never get to the bottom of these disputes. Tribalism was very strong and this, coupled with religious issues, meant there was no mixing of peoples except where necessary.

We were very happy in Keren as it was quite a pleasant little town, with a cathedral and lots of Italian style bars where one could sit outside and have a coffee. We could get a certain amount of fresh fruit, vegetables and tomatoes. The Arab *Souk* (market), though small, was fascinating and one could buy spices, rice and onions there. I often

Fig 3.1 *Keren 1947: Our car on the dusty old road to Keren.*

used to wander around the shops and would be asked in for coffee as everyone spoke Italian and I had a good working knowledge of it by then. Here they had silversmiths making ornaments from melted down Maria Theresa Thaler, which were the silver bullion trading coins. Eritrean women tended to carry their wealth upon their person in the form of jewellery such as earrings, bracelets and so on. There was an Italian sports club and a hotel that by all accounts had once been a brothel for Europeans. We quickly settled in and joined the local activities, playing tennis, swimming in the hotel pool, and going to the Saturday night dances at the sports club. We went to dinner parties at other people's houses and we gave them ourselves. There were about six families from the British Administration in Keren, the rest of the population of Keren were Italian or Eritrean. In time I made friends with several Italian women, and used to join them for coffee or sewing parties.

Of course it was not all fun and games there was a serious reason for Pat being there. His duties as part of the remit of the British

Military Administration were to tour the district which covered hundreds of square miles. The country had to be governed, criminals caught and dealt with, and various other important matters had to be taken care of. He was out on safari tours for a great many days each month to the different villages to sort out problems and when it was possible, I accompanied him on his visits. As I was the wife of a representative of the ruling establishment, I was tolerated at most male gatherings but never directly addressed. However, I was fortunate in being able to visit the women's quarters in the Moslem villages and took the opportunity to learn more about their lives and customs and sometimes share some delicacies.

We would prepare for the safari tours carefully. Into one box would go bedding and medical kit, such as was available in those days. Another box would contain foodstuff, there were boxes filled with lamps and the paraffin to put in them, not forgetting the matches of course. Next came the camp beds, chairs, tables and a folding canvas bath and of course the mosquito nets which were very necessary because we were in Malaria areas. We also took a certain amount of water to tide us over for a few hours, specially boiled and filtered. This had to be done to all water daily to ensure it was uncontaminated for use. We had a full complement of staff, interpreters and the two dogs which always came along too.

Once everything was loaded up, we would set off early in the cool of the morning in the Army 15-cwt truck, with the two *Askari* (armed native soldiers). The two dogs were always somewhere on top of all the baggage. Poor Judy was regularly car sick as the vehicle lurched and swayed over the rough unmade roads and Bobby usually shot over the top of the cabin every time we halted suddenly to negotiate a bad piece of road. This was usually just tracks which sometimes had to be cleared of bushes or dried riverbeds and sometimes we sank into deep sand, which caused quite a pantomime. At this point the cook would leap down to brew up some tea, taking the box with the kettle, cups, a jar of sugar and the tea with him. In a matter of minutes, he would have the fire burning, kettle boiling and a couple of chairs ready for us to sit on. The dogs would rush about chasing things, stretching their legs and so happy to be free. Pat would perhaps stroll off looking for Guinea Fowl to shoot for supper or maybe a Gazelle for the evening meal. We would be feeding our whole entourage that night on the kill. If he had not found anything on the tea-break or when we were digging ourselves out of the deep sand, which could take up to forty minutes or so, there would be a further stop if a Gazelle came into sight. It was always expected of us to bring a good kill into the camp. If we were to camp at a village, it was the local custom that these kills would be offered as a gift of meat for the Chief and his people.

If we were staying at a village, a campsite would have to be prepared by the villagers a discreet distance away and a thorn bush barrier, called a *Zareba*, was cut and placed around it. A donkey rider would be despatched to the nearest water hole for supplies. Our tents would be pitched quickly and the inevitable tea brewed up on the fire, which would have already been prepared. Ample supplies of wood were piled up and the cook got busy with roasting the afternoon's kill, hot water would also be produced for our welcome baths after the dusty journey. Water for bathing was quite often muddy and not filtered. We would be covered in sandy dust from the journey, but sometimes if a wind was blowing the sand would be whipped up into clouds. If you were caught out in the open in one of these sandstorms, however mild, the grains hitting bare flesh were like needles. The desert winds were called *Khamsin* and could be very severe where there was deep sand, but fortunately in the lowlands of Eritrea it was not such a big problem in the dunes. While we were camping, I was always very grateful for the *Zareba* that had been put up very thickly around our party. At night we could hear the leopards and hyena packs, which would have been likely to take the dogs as they were very partial to dog meat, especially the leopards. The local people seemed to sit up all night, talking around a huge fire designed to keep the wild animals away. There was always plenty of evidence that they had been around though when we looked

Fig 3.2 *Keren 1947: Gabriella the excellent house maid from Asmara was a young unmarried Coptic Christian. Omar, the son of a local chief lacked experience as houseboy and for various reasons did not last long in the post.*

for tracks and pugmarks in the mornings. At other times, we would camp in the bush in the vicinity of several villages and then our servants would put up the *Zareba* themselves. Even though we might be several miles from habitation, as soon as you stopped a few people would appear, goodness knows where from. They would then be pressed into service collecting wood or water. It was probably the most exciting event for them, especially as I was present and they were not used to seeing European women. Ticks, flies and mosquitoes were troublesome everywhere we went, and it was a nightly ritual to de-tick the dogs; first covering them with oil to loosen their grasp, then pulling them off and burning them. I always did this last thing at night, even in camp. I used to have the area of the tent and surroundings swept as a preventative measure, but it seemed quite useless as the following day they would have just as many.

Each time we came back to our villa, it was good to get away from dusty roads and have a real bath and wash my hair. Pat and I slept outside on the veranda under nets each night as it was so hot in the house, nearly always 80º–90ºF during the day and slightly less at night. Looking back on it now, I wonder why we were not eaten by something. The flimsy fence would not have kept out a determined lion or leopard and, as the dogs slept under our beds, this might have been quite a good additional snack for them. The fenced garden was quite big and full of cages as the previous owner had had a private menagerie (see Fig. 3.3). They came in useful as we used to put Judy in one at times when she was in season. The locals were very keen to mate their animals with good new breeds. In fact Bobby always managed to escape frequently and must have fathered many offspring for them. They used to parade their bitches in season near our house, which was very dangerous with so much rabies in Eritrea. Both dogs were regularly inoculated with anti-rabies shots. One of our cages was always filled with guinea fowl; live ones most likely caught by the locals using nets. They were wonderful guards and would set up quite a noise if a stranger or snake was anywhere near. The garden was dry, had a few struggling bushes and a tennis court, which was unfortunately in a poor state of repair with no net so we played tennis at the club or hotel.

As well as the dreaded malaria, other perils we had to contend with were Jiggers (which burrowed into the toes) and Hookworm (which also burrowed into the feet and ended up in the intestines causing a debilitating illness). No one ever walked barefooted. At night we put on

Fig 3.3   *Keren 1948: Margaret with dogs Judy and Bobby on the veranda with previous occupant's menagerie cages in background.*

slippers if we got out of bed, having placed them upside down on the bedside table to avoid a scorpion or spider crawling into them. Even so, we tapped them out first before inserting a foot. We had scorpions, spiders, sugar ants that came after any food that was left out; white ants that ate everything including the window frames, ceilings, and once my silk bedspread which slipped onto the floor while I was resting from the heat one afternoon. In desperation we used to put the legs of our food safes into large tins (usually those used to store cooking fat) which we filled with a water and paraffin mix, but it did not always work.

In Keren we had ceiling fans on regular electricity and water from a tap. The water was always boiled and filtered by me daily. It was put through an aluminium double filter with a 'candle' which allowed the water to drip slowly through. It was then deemed to be safe, which it must have been as we never suffered any trouble. It was all very well until we had to put a clean 'candle' in when the old one got so dirty. It could be scrubbed clean, but eventually got too bad and had to be replaced, all the water tasted strangely scented for several weeks and was horrible to make tea with. Our servants were very good and the cook could produce a decent plain meal. Local meat was tough, so stews featured regularly on our menu. Everyone had at least one servant, including the high status Eritrean government officials and even the poorest Italian. Pay was very poor by our standards, but we fed and housed them and their families. It was considered undesirable to have a servant who spoke English, in case they were able to listen to conversations and spy. I was advised not to keep a very detailed diary for the same reason, a fact that I very much regret. This was perhaps because of the war and the fact that we had spy-mania by then. Being in Eritrea was a very happy time in my life and I have written these memoirs from my diaries kept at the time.

Fig 3.4   *Asmara 1951: Sudan Defence Force March Past taken by Brig Hardy Spencer.*

Pat worked at the government office when he was not out on safari work. It was about 100 yards from the house. He started work at 6 o'clock when it was a little cooler as this allowed him to get through the mounds of the paperwork and administration with which he was landed. Dozens of people used to arrive at the office not long after he and the other officers got there. The villagers always had some problems, such as land grievances or needed advice or permits for this and that. Our breakfast was at 9 o'clock, when he came home again for an hour before returning to his desk until 1 o'clock. After that we took the *grande siesta* like the rest of the town. As we would lie on the bed with the swaying ceiling fan on, I always wondered if the screws had ever been properly checked. The villa had heavy shutters which were closed in the early morning and remained so until nightfall, in true Italian fashion. They were most effective and certainly kept the hot air out. The bedrooms had doors out onto the veranda. In fact there were doors onto the veranda everywhere, which made it easier to move all the chairs, small tables and lamps outside in the early evening when we sat out to have a pre-dinner drink. The servants were on duty all of the time, so this furniture moving routine was carried out smoothly each day. After dinner and when we retired, the furniture was put back into the sitting room. It sounds strange to modern ears, but that was the way things were done at the time. The servants would not have thought it unusual, and would have been quite shocked had we not kept these high standards. Although their hours were long, it was not hard work and there were quite a few rest breaks. The cook only cooked; he did not chop the wood for the stove, this was done by a young boy. The houseboy's daily routine including light dusting and sweeping, laying the table and bringing and serving food from the kitchen. The laundry was done by another member of staff and so on. A large part of their day was spent sitting or resting. Their living quarters were private and at the end of the garden, a little away from the house. We were a small community of twelve to fifteen people or so and there was always a lot of activity going on. Their wage was about £2 a month plus food and accommodation. This compares quite favourably to England at that time, as the working man was paid a similar amount but he had to provide food and rent from that income as well.

There was a small military presence in Keren of the Sudan Defence Force which consisted of Sudanese soldiers with the officer ranks mainly of Europeans. Their Commanding Officer was Hardy Spicer (see Fig. 3.4) who usually attended the various military events (see Fig. 3.5) taking place there.

We were pretty poor in those days and any pay we had was spent on food, the servants and official entertainment. We were very happy though and were getting to know the population well, receiving invitations to Arab feasts and Coptic weddings which we enjoyed. We became very friendly with a Yugoslavian doctor, Leopold Sentochnik, who was later joined by his brother Albert. They were anti-communist and had escaped from Tito's regime. Eventually Albert was joined by his charming wife and baby son, who had to escape over the mountains under the cover of darkness. The little boy had been drugged, so that he would make no sound and give them away. They had to travel all the way through Italy first to get to Eritrea, which was a terrible trip. We did unfortunately get some hostility from certain Italians.

Pat's senior officer was Kennedy Trevaskis who, with his wife Bunty, lived in a lovely house at the top of the hill above us. It was quite nicely furnished and comfortable. He had been a P.O.W. in Italian hands, captured during the fighting in Eritrea. Kennedy and Bunty Trevaskis did not mix with the Italians, except where necessary. His Eritrean jailer had subsequently been engaged as his houseboy cum valet after the British Victory. He was much liked by the locals. Later he became High Commissioner in Aden, and survived an assassination attempt at Aden airport. He wrote a very long report presumably to the Foreign Office, on the Eritrean people and their tribes and customs, which I typed up for him. A great many years later, I threw my tattered copy of these papers over the reef while living in the Pacific, which I now rather regret. They had their first child in Keren while we were there. There was great excitement as the local people awaited the birth. However, as far as the Moslems and other locals were concerned, the arrival of their baby daughter Jennifer was not considered as auspicious as having a boy and the event was quietly ignored. They did go on to have two sons, which seemed to restore their standing in the community. I was considered an even greater failure as a wife, as we had no children at all at that time. The Italians, who live for babies, were lighting candles and sprinkling holy water to help the situation. As I was enjoying my time swimming, riding, socialising with friends and so on, I was not too bothered about it. Pat battled on with his court cases in a very noisy style, as there were always crowds of people outside the office, with the *Askari* trying to control the situation. Most of the cases were very long-standing and often ended up in the High Court and were often concerning various things such as assault and theft of stock.

Keren, which means highland, was about 2000 ft lower than Asmara. The surrounding countryside was drier and more arid, with a covering of native bush and scrub which the goats ate. The temperature was about 80°F plus most of the time with not much rain at all. We were lucky to have adequate water there, thanks to the Anseba River. We made several visits to the former battlefields above Keren, about ten miles down the mountain pass. It was at Fort Dologorodoc that the Italians fought bravely against the British on the road between Keren and Agordat in the highland Anseba Region of Eritrea, known by the British as the Cameron Highlands. General Lorenzini had been killed there and in the early days there was a lovely iron cross erected in his honour at the top. Sadly it had disappeared by the time we returned to Keren on our next transfer; melted down to make bullets, I expect, by the *Shifta* who also took railings and other metal work from the cemetery under the cover of darkness for similar purposes. The Highland Light Infantry had painted 'HLI – Scotland For Ever' in white paint, and we kept the letters repainted while we were there.

In the earlier days before the *Shifta* became too active we sometimes returned to Asmara for weekends, driving up in our Alpha Romeo. We stayed at either the Ciao Hotel with friends or at Government House in the guest apartment. Brigadier Drew was the Governor and he and his wife made us very welcome. The rule was that we ate our first and last meal with them, otherwise we were free to do as we pleased. We usually went dancing at the Moulin Rouge nightclub or the slightly posher Mocambo as both had good dance bands. Sometimes there were cabaret acts and one that I rather enjoyed was the mud wrestling; two blonde very big German girls writhed in a large container of mud – an amazing sight. They were successfully touring Africa and the Middle East with this act. We would also return to Asmara for special events. The road was quite a good one with tarmac all the way; the last few miles were quite a stiff climb up the escarpment. Large vehicles had to do three point turns on the hairpin bends to get onto the next stretch of road. The drop was quite frightening, but the view was spectacular and made up for it. There were many accidents; the Military erected a sign with skull and crossbones at every accident scene, which served as a good reminder. Pat did the driving and we usually had an armed *Askari* in the car with us, because of the serious risk of *Shifta* on this road.

Sometimes, Pat would do a safari on horseback to more inaccessible areas, but it was not over great distances. This always necessitated even more planning than taking vehicles. Fodder had to be added to the baggage, as there would have been no guaranteed natural grazing for the horses en route or at the destinations. I did not accompany him on these horseback safaris, neither did I go on the camel ones; the latter of which made Pat feel queasy due to the motion of the camel stride. Where possible, he used a truck instead. The camels they used seemed particularly nasty animals with a tendency to kick or bite and spit.

On our safaris we saw mainly aggressive and noisy baboons which I disliked, much preferring the dainty and pretty gazelles. There was not much to entice other creatures into the area; there being little to eat and even less water. There were hyenas, which could be heard soon after the sun had set. They often came into the townships in search of food, foraging in the dustbins and rubbish dumps and sometimes taking livestock, dogs and cats. The screeching noise they make will

Fig 3.5 *Asmara 1951: Margaret (3rd from left) and other officers and their wives attending SDF March Past.*

always evoke Africa for me. Buzzards were a frequent sight rising on the thermals and circling over carrion. There was a very small antelope (12–16 inches) called a Dik-Dik. One of the Italian women had an orphaned one as a pet. It used to leap up onto her piano when guests came, its tiny dainty legs balancing there. I did not see any big game in this region.

One of the safaris I enjoyed most was to Nakfa which was 150km north of Keren in Sahel Province, stopping at Afabet on the way. Pat would always have business to discuss with the Chiefs and he would be waylaid by anxious groups of people. The problems were usually the same; land disputes, stolen camels or wives, government laws or taxes, and sometimes an assault or murder. He had to deal with them all, and was still only twenty-three years of age. The only assistance he had was a native clerk and me. It was at about this time that I started to take an interest in schools and I used to visit any that were nearby. They were very basic, with children using slates or the sand outside to draw on. Educating the natives was a very high priority for the Italians. Where there were some, I was also was asked by the doctor to visit the basic clinics and report back to HQ in Asmara. There were a few drugs, aspirin and bandages and perhaps some kind of antiseptic cleanser. Penicillin had not long been discovered and was not in general use; the other wonder drugs had still to be discovered. Two of the worst illnesses that were rife were Venereal Disease and Tuberculosis. If you add the various skin diseases, Smallpox and parasites, life was tough for the Eritrean peoples. We were protected by our injections, inoculations and modern hygiene methods. It was difficult to keep clean if you had to walk long distances to collect water as the women did. They had a hard life, but seemed to keep cheerful.

While we were in Nakfa we stayed at a lovely little cottage that had been the Government Rest House; it was thatched and had a lovely open fireplace that we used as it got quite chilly at night. Of course the furniture was the barest minimum of old beds and even older chairs and tables. The view was of the village below and you could see beyond it for miles. We always loved it up there; it was such a break from the heat down in Keren. We had our safari cook, so all the work was done by him and the place was always full of people fetching water or wood for the cook's stove. Unfortunately the Anseba region was mosquito ridden, especially the valley through which we had to travel to Nakfa.

Initially, we only had a little Brownie box camera in those days and the photographs we took were not up to much. The better sorts of cameras were used by professionals and too expensive for ordinary people like us. Later I had my father's Zeiss Ikon folding type with which I managed to take the photos in the album. Getting film was difficult. If kept too long it began to deteriorate in the climate and obtaining new film meant having to send for it from Asmara, several hours ride away.

One of the difficulties in Eritrea was the number of different tribal languages. Although Italian was used as the *lingua franca*; each time we moved over a tribal area we would need an interpreter, sometimes two or three, each explaining the problem. It was like the Tower of

Babel and a wonder anything got sorted out at all. One of my greatest memories of Eritrea was the early morning sounds. Everyone was up at sunrise. The air was so clear you could hear every household in the African villages grinding coffee in their pestle and mortars; a thumping noise repeated everywhere. When visiting villages, coffee was always served before any business was discussed. It was served in tiny cups from a pot with a straw sticking out of the spout to filter it. I always wondered if the straw was clean. It was brought to the boil several times, cooled and served heavily sugared.

Sometimes we would be invited to a feast of stewed goat meat, which was very strong smelling and today I still dislike any goat products, including cheeses. We preferred the guinea fowl and gazelle we shot ourselves. If goat was used, the Moslems had to kill it the Halal way, blessed in the name of Allah, slitting its throat and draining the blood. Generally, I tried to remove myself as far as possible from either of these processes.

As an English woman with her military officer husband, I was just about tolerated by the Moslems. Few Italian women toured with their husbands into the places I went. I tried to keep a low profile and sit quietly somewhere near the back or visit the women folk. When I look back now, I am only too aware that perhaps I should have worn more covering garments. I also had two dogs with me wherever I went, one of whom was very suspicious of Africans. It was not the custom of Moslems to keep animals as pets; using dogs for guarding duties with goats. These seemed to be poor half-starved things with every rib showing. Young boys would be sent out with the guard dogs to take the flock of goats in search of food and water. You would see them all sitting under the thorn trees, beside empty *wadis* (waterhole) some way from the village. They would only go to school when the youngest male child had reached the right age around six years old; by that time the oldest boy would maybe be fourteen years old or more, that is if the intervening babies had been girls. Every Moslem village had a small mosque. The mosque in Keren was rather a nice one and I have an oil

41

painting of it by Doris Duke in my collection.

The principal tribe in the area was the *Beni-Ame*, who were *Beja* people from north east Sudan. There was also the *Hadendoa* tribe, who were Moslem and mainly nomadic. They dressed their hair with beautifully carved wooden combs and rancid butter and camel urine, which smelt really high (awful). A lot of raiding went on between these tribes of both animals and women. So, there was plenty of work for the Civil Affairs Officers in this area, one of whom was Pat. The other tribe of interest were the *Hausa* from West Africa who were descended from people making their way across Africa, taking years to attempt to reach Mecca for the obligatory lifetime visit which would give them the title *Haji*. Some died in the process, others were born on the way and some successfully made the trip.

It was while we were living in Keren that I gave up horse riding for good. We used the Police horses, which were rather lazy and under-exercised beasts. I had a rather tubby grey mare called Europa, who napped and hated leaving her stable. Worse still she hated camels and used to shy if she met any, which was quite often. Pat rode on a very large black stallion called Black Jack. He always set rather a fast pace and poor old Europa tried to keep up. The police officers also rode out with us so I usually brought up the rear with a groom. On one particular occasion we rode along the top of a bank bordering a quite deep ditch full of muddy water. The horses in front decided to jump the ditch and canter to catch up with the others that had gone ahead. I fell off when Europa tried to jump the ditch dividing us from the other horses and misjudged it, falling back into it. Both the poor horse and I had to be rescued. We were both pretty shaky and it was quite difficult to remount, so we made our way slowly back to the stables. There was also a deep ditch dug around the stables to keep out wild animals. Usually when we approached it, the mare always quickened her pace over the narrow three-foot wide access plank, which let her into the stable yard. This time she continued straight into the stable too quickly and I nearly hit the wall, and that was the last time they could get me onto a horse.

4

TESSENEI

Early in 1949 we were transferred to Tessenei which is an outpost on the Sudan border. It was a desert; just sand and more sand, with small African villages and some Italian peasants eking out a living. We stayed with Ken and Bunty Trevaskis overnight and then all our possessions and the dogs were loaded onto the three ton Army truck. There were always boxes of office papers and equipment to cart around and medical supplies for onward transmission. Pat and I travelled in our Alfa-Romeo Tourer.

The servants only came with us to help us to settle into our new home. Once again, they did not want to leave their traditional tribal area and live in a new one. We drove down the escarpment, past the old battlefields and down to the plain at the bottom – it was very rocky, dry, dusty and hot. We passed the rock on which the words "HLI Scotland For Ever" had been painted; it was at the end of what was known as 'Happy Valley', a misnomer if ever I heard one. The famous Cameron Ridge was away in the distance.

Although the road was tarmac for 75km as far as Agordat, it was a very long journey for us in the dust and heat to this our first stop; then through Barentu which was a small village and on to Tessenei, a further 100km away. It was a five-hour journey at least in an open car. I drove for part of the way and we adopted a rather dangerous idea of changing over while still in motion when Pat was driving, I would slide in behind

Fig 4.1 *Tessenei 1949: The house about 20 miles from the Sudan border.*

him while he moved over. We thought it cut down the time, anything to get the journey over with. On our first stop in Agordat, which was a lot better than Keren, we were able to go into the small town and have a cold beer at one of the bars. Our clothes were sticking to us, our hair was full of sweat and dust and it was too hot and sticky to wear a hat. Our truck with baggage and dogs was travelling behind us. When this arrived, we were able to take the poor dogs off the truck to give them water and walk them, while the driver and the *Askari* went to a nearby native bar; they preferred to be separate from us. After our welcome stop, we had to set off again once the dogs were back on the truck. It was dreary desert-like scenery; not dunes, just miles of sand with sparse bushes to break up the landscape, sometimes goats, a camel or two, the odd native and perhaps a truck going in the opposite directions. As we had left the tarmac behind at Agordat, it was a corrugated dirt road all the way. In time we reached Barentu and stopped for another beer in a tiny bar and to walk the dogs again and stretch our legs. We drank beer as it was safer than drinking water. These dirt roads were kept in order by a gang of native workmen who tied heavy branches to the back of a truck and then drove up and down flattening out the ridges that formed. Otherwise, the corrugations shook vehicles to bits; one's hands became numb from the vibrations.

Relieved, we drove into the outskirts of Tessenei, the temperature was over 100°F and we had been about six hours on the road. It was a bit of a shock, just a flat desert and very little else. We were directed to our villa, which was really a bungalow. In the distance, there was a lovely building which should have been Pat's office, but had recently been condemned as the faulty foundations were causing it to collapse. Another temporary building had been put up for use as an office about 50 yards away from our house. Somewhere over in the distance, there was a bungalow for the Police Inspector and also a two-storey house for other staff. All of these buildings were dotted around in a moonscape, with some scrubby bushes here and there. The nearest African village was some two miles away.

Our home had an imposing gateway and a dried up garden of practically nothing but edging stones. We had two small bedrooms, a sitting room and a dining room which was in the centre of the house. The veranda at the back enclosed the house and it was very airless as a result. However, there was a nice wide veranda at the front of the house (see Fig. 4.1), well mosquito-netted and we ended up sleeping and spending most of our time there. The furniture was the biggest and the heaviest imaginable; no doubt it was there because it was too heavy to have been carted away by anyone. We had brought our small personal bits and pieces with us. We managed to rid ourselves of the worst pieces in the house by sending them back on the truck when it left, however quite a few remaining pieces were in poor repair. Tessenei had its fair share of creepy crawlies of course; lizards that climbed all over the walls and sometimes fell off onto the floor or the table. Fortunately, they never did so into our food or drinks. The larger ones used to give loud barks which were quite unnerving.

The kitchen was about 15 yards from the house and like a black hole, very cell-like and grubby; our first job was to get it cleaned up and whitewashed. Going into it after dark was quite an experience, as dozens of cockroaches would scatter up the walls to safety making a rustling noise. Everyone who has lived in the tropics will recognise the scene. We took on a Yemenite cook called Abdu. He was employed as cook and safari boy. Unfortunately, he was an unpleasant man, who became very troublesome. We also had another servant called Teclai, who was a Coptic Christian and had been in the same area since birth. He and Abdu did not get on. One day when Pat was on a short safari and it was Teclai's day off, Abdu became very threatening and accused me of not paying his wages. I was afraid, as I thought that I was alone in the house, but suddenly Teclai appeared behind me to defend me. He chased Abdu off. I have always wondered how he knew what was brewing up, but one could never get to the bottom of it all. After that, Pat never left me alone with Abdu, who was from then on confined to the kitchen. He was quite a reasonable cook and they were hard to find. If Pat went on a safari after that without me, he always took Abdu with him. In the end we had to dismiss him and found another cook called Mohammed, who was a much nicer man.

I tried to do something with the barren garden, but everything that was put in it seemed to be eaten by white ants. It was well over 90°F in the shade and much more so outside; no grass would ever grow. We had piped water, but if I turned on my tap to water for very long, the pressure dropped all the way down the line and people came and complained. In the end, I just gave up and used the water from our baths to try and revive the flowering bushes like Bougainvillea, which someone had planted long ago.

In the bathroom, we had a dangerous looking *Scaldabagno* boiler; it had to be lit to heat the bath water. Fortunately, it was so warm that we were glad to have cold baths and showers. When we were terribly hot, we used to put an ice block in the bath and take turns to sit on it. The Italian who owned the electricity plant used to make the large ice blocks and would deliver them to us every day. We needed them because we had no refrigerators. Instead we had to use an old ammunition box as a cold box, with the ice block inside of it. It was not a problem, because we did not have a lot to put in it, except butter or beer. Apart from onions, tomatoes and potatoes, we rarely saw anything more exciting unless visitors brought us fresh vegetables or salads. The only meat we could buy was tough old goat meat or sometimes stringy beef, which had to be stewed up and eaten that day though this never went to waste as the servants always welcomed the leftovers which they used to add to their traditional dishes. If he went to any outlying villages during the day, Pat always brought something back for the pot for the household, including the staff. On other occasions we would arrange trips out with friends (see Fig. 4.2) to shoot for the pot always accompanied by armed *Askari* for added protection against the *Shifta*. Bread was brought up from the baker in the village two miles away daily. The servants had to walk and fetch it if no transport was available. Sometimes our guests would send us a tin of butter from the NAAFI when they returned, but unfortunately it was always rancid by the time it reached us. I used to try to clarify it, but in the end it was still rancid. Otherwise, we got our supplies from a tiny Arab store. The owner sold cotton materials in small amounts, candles, matches, pasta, rice, and paraffin. We were his best customers for tins of peas when he had them in stock.

I still went out with Pat on longer safaris and the routine was the same as I have described earlier in previous chapters. We had to remember not to camp in riverbeds for fear of being washed away in a flash flood, when rain fell in the highlands and came down in a bore in a matter of hours. At such times, the Gash River was just a muddy, thick flow carrying everything with it, though it was dry riverbed for most of the year. Some of the journeys we made were right down to the Ethiopian border. We used to camp on the bank of the Setite River that formed the natural border between Eritrea and Ethiopia, taking the servants and dogs with us. We used to paddle in the shallows and sometimes the dogs swam in the river. The dogs used to chase the crocs, making them slither into the water on the far side of the banks. It was not until years later that I realised that crocs are quite at home on land

and that we might well have found them in our tent eating our dogs, but sometimes ignorance is bliss.

Pat regularly held meetings with various Ethiopian officials. One day a higher-grade Ethiopian official requested a meeting on their side of the river, which was crocodile-infested. On the day we were to meet the Ethiopian officials, we all assembled along the banks of the river and took off our shoes. There was a Welsh Police Inspector, our various interpreters, the Chief Clerk from the office, translators and other officials in the entourage. The only place one was able to cross was in one shallow part where the cattle went over, as the crocodiles used to lie out on the mud banks in the centre. We had to wade about 30 yards across under the interested gaze of the officials, who sat on chairs with a servant holding over their heads the very ornate umbrella they favoured. Our party battled across, keeping a wary eye out for the crocs, then we had to stand at the edge of the water, replacing socks and shoes while trying to look dignified. All the time the Ethiopians stared impassively. Pat and the British party had to approach and try to regain our self-respect, before business was started as always with a cup of coffee. I was tolerated, just. I asked to be taken to the *Souk* (native market) and it took over half an hour for permission to be granted. I was closely guarded on my visit, not for my safety but in case I saw anything I should not have, such as guns. The Ethiopians officials were suspicious and unfriendly, and always were on the many times we had to meet them. We were pleased to get back on our side of the border on each occasion.

In Tessenei, Pat worked from the same routine as before; he was always on call and the clerk would come to either fetch him or inform him of any incident. The problems were always the same as they were in other districts; land claims, assaults and all sorts of administrative problems. He also acted as a magistrate, although anything serious went to the High Court, as before. Some of the staff who worked with him were Eritrean, but many were Sudanese in the Tessenei area.

We had some sandstorms and many mosquitoes. There were a lot of

Fig 4.2 *Tessenei 1949: Margaret (in hat) with Helen Murphy and Taffy Saunders on shooting trip for the pot in SDO Western Province jeep, accompanied by* Askari *for protection against* Shifta.

snakes about and they tended to get into the woodpile near the kitchen door. A local villager brought me two young semi-feral cats which I called Zodi and Mitzi, and it was their job to catch the snakes. They would stalk the snakes, sneak up behind them to whack them on the head, and then throw them in the air and pounce, killing them as they landed. They never missed. It was their source of food and I did not have to feed them at all. Zodi never came into the house but Mitzi did sometimes, braving the dogs. She was quite fierce and strongly feral. I had reason to be grateful for her visits. The electricity generator had to be turned off and on manually each day. It used to start up quite noisily, so we always knew when to put the lights on. One evening it was late starting up, as the man who owned and operated it was delayed. Pat was away and the dogs were patrolling the garden outside. I was alone in the house apart from Mitzi, who was paying one of her visits. She had come through the double doors, after one of the servants had passed through and let her in. It was getting quite dark, so I decided to go to the back door and ask someone to bring in an oil lamp. As I started to walk through the dining room, there was a loud hiss. I was frightened and not able to move a step; it was dark and I could not see anything. Earlier I had thought I had seen a movement in the sitting room but decided I was seeing things. All I could hear was crashing and spitting from the snake. I yelled loudly for someone to bring the light quickly. Then I realised that Mitzi was on the sideboard, inches away from me and things were hurtling to the floor. Mohammed came with a lamp and we could see that the cat had a snake by its head. Eventually, it was despatched outside. The servants said it was a poisonous one, which it may well have been.

I had lots of adventures in Tessenei, in one way or another. I regularly used to walk the dogs in the grove of trees which had been planted around the electricity plant, as it was not very far away from the house and quite pleasantly cool around there. One evening just before sunset, I met the Italian engineer who had come up to start the electricity supply up. He told me not to come again as the workmen told him they had seen a leopard there the day before. After that I never ventured there unless accompanied by Pat and his gun. We never saw the leopard, so hopefully it had just gone away. The garden at the house was not much safer. Pat, the Welsh police inspector and the doctor had all gone off together on a shooting expedition for the pot, so I was alone again. After watering the struggling garden bushes, I walked down to where the water tap was, some 20 yards away from the house, to make sure it was turned off properly. We always allowed passing local villagers to come in to collect water if they needed it and sometimes they did not turn the tap off properly, which then dripped into the concrete trough put there for horses or livestock. To my horror, I came face to face with large fierce looking male and female warthogs with their young drinking from the trough. They can be very unpredictable creatures at the best of times, and I fled. Even the dogs had the sense to bolt and we all squeezed through the front doors together. The amusing part was that Pat and the shooting party had hoped to come across some warthog and ironically never did.

Not long after we had newly arrived at the house, I went to take a shower in the dark as the lights had failed to come on. As I turned the water on, suddenly all these strange objects started hitting my legs. When Pat brought the light in we discovered that there were lots of tiny frogs. After that, before we got under the shower water, we had to collect them up in a small bucket as they came up from the drain. They were not poisonous, but could have attracted snakes, so we put them into the outside drains instead.

As the time went on we managed to make ourselves more comfortable. We acquired an old fashioned icebox with a heavy door just like a safe, which was lined with zinc. It did not hold much more than a few bottles of beer. We used to tie our dog Bobby to it to keep him from wandering off at times. Our cook learned to make excellent bread and the milkman (see Fig. 4.3) called reasonably regularly with fresh milk, complete with debris floating on top. After it had been strained and boiled, it was safe to drink or use in cooking. The man was a local tribesman with a very wild appearance; his hair was a rancid-buttered fuzz adorned with large combs. Most of the men who were not westernised looked very similar and one got used to it after a while. The cook cleaned all the pots with sand, collected from the ground outside the kitchen door. It was surprisingly effective. No scourers there, but we could buy pumice sometimes which the locals ground down and sold by the pound. Water boiling and filtering was a daily chore which I always supervised. All of our clothes went into the wash at the end of the day and the laundry was done for us. It was bashed around in a stone sink with a washboard, coarse soap and cold water. Starch was used in Pat's shirts which used to crackle as he put them on, as they were very stiff, but luckily this soon softened especially in the heat. By now we had acquired another Coptic Christian girl called Gabriella who did the laundry and some housework, but she only stayed a few months and then went back to her own district.

Our social life was quieter here, but we still had friends to visit for dinner or drinks and we often returned the hospitality. We were also invited to the simple homes of the Italians who were living in the area still and we occasionally attended native feasts. Once in a while we would drive all the way back to Keren for a few days respite. Even a few thousand feet up the mountain would give us a break from the heat. Sometimes we went to the small village called Barentu, which was part of Pat's district; it was in the charge of an English Non Commissioned Officer (NCO) who had the rank of Police Inspector. We stayed in a house which had been divided into two, half was for the NCO and the other half was kept for the Civil Affairs Officer, in this case Pat. We were all sure the house was haunted; even the dogs were unsettled by

Fig 4.3 *Tessenei 1949: Outside the kitchen block Abdu the Yemenite cook with the milkman who regularly called with fresh milk with debris floating on top.*

it. Strange noises were heard, the WCs would flush themselves, doors opened and shut. There may of course have been a feasible explanation. I made some enquiries and heard that an Italian administrator had thrown himself off the rock on which the house stood and died, after his wife had left him. The people who took over from us never heard a thing and were very scornful about there being ghosts.

It was even nicer when we went over to Kassala in the Sudan for a weekend break. About fifty miles away over some pretty barren bush, it was like going into another world. The houses were built in the Colonial style and the gardens were lush, with green lawns. There could not have been a greater contrast from our side of the border. The time was one hour behind Eritrean time, so 5 o'clock was a cool and pleasant time. Tea was served on the lawn under a shady tree and the servants were dressed in spotless white Berber traditional robes *Djellaba* with cummerbunds. The china was delicate, the jugs silver, and there were cakes and scones. It was so civilised.

We usually stayed at the guesthouse but sometimes with the Deputy Governor, Philip Broadbent and his wife. She was unusual in that she stayed in Kassala for the whole length of their tour of duty and had her small daughter with her. All the other wives went back to the UK with their children during the hot season and only visited when it was cooler. They missed such a lot, and it was a lovely life for a child. On our stay I was the only other white woman in the whole province, which was rather fun. Surprisingly, the houses were made of mud and wattle only, like old English cottages were years ago, but they were really lovely and nicely furnished. We used to drive over the no-man's land area between the two territories in a 15-cwt truck, the dogs with us as usual. We could not have left them behind, as they would have run wild and probably have been stolen to act as herd dogs. There was seldom another vehicle to be seen on the journey. On one of our trips over to Kassala, we broke down and were stuck on the road in scorching heat with no shade, which was very worrying. As far as they eye could see, the only shade was a small bush. There was no telephone or any other way of getting help. While the driver tried to mend the fault, we got out of the truck to try to get any breeze there was, but the sand was so hot that it burned our feet through our shoes. We thought a vehicle was approaching once, after we had been there for about two hours, but it turned out to be an aircraft going over. We remained by the lorry for three hours and I wondered if we would ever be found, until by chance a lone camel rider appeared drawn by some unusual activity. He was despatched to get help and set off at a gallop. In due course a lorry arrived from Kassala to rescue us. The beer they gave us on our arrival had never tasted so good. After this experience, we always travelled with two vehicles and telephoned our expected arrival time to our hosts in the Sudan. It fortunately did not happen again.

There were always some interesting dinner parties, or drinks parties at the Sudanese Defence Force (SDF) officers' mess. Sometimes the SDF would be giving a special evening for their native soldiers, a sort of 'letting their hair down' event. There would be a feast, followed by skits performed by individual soldiers; little jokes about the Commanding Officer or other officers which caused great mirth. The people who were the butt of the laughter would take it in good part and enjoy it. These had to be explained to us, as it was all in Arabic which all the European serving officers also spoke. Natives, whether Arabic or African, are keen observers and can pin point one's habits and idiosyncrasies very well. (Later on in another part of Africa, a friend's servant faithfully mimicked the way I turned my head to the left if I called on her when she was out, as she could not remember my name.)

In Tessenei our lifestyle was rather different, as I have explained earlier, but it did not make us unhappy. We still had good friends and quite a lot of visitors, official and otherwise, which we always appreciated. They brought newspapers and books, or sometimes other treats from the NAAFI like tins of peas. There were no other English women for several hundred miles. The two or three Italian women who lived there were from the southern part of Italy and always seemed to be clad in black, as presumably they were mourning some relative or another, as was their custom. Unfortunately, we had little in common. On one occasion, one of these women asked me whether I was a Christian as she had heard me talking about Christmas. Apparently, she had no idea that there were other varieties of Christianity than the Catholic faith and seemed oblivious of the other religions practised in the area including Coptic Christians. It was in a way quite lonely, but I formed a warm friendship with the Egyptian wife of a Sudanese Chief Clerk. She was about twenty years old and already the mother of two children. He drank heavily and had beaten her up several times. I would like to think her life may have improved after we used to see each other regularly for coffee. He knew I would have noticed her injuries and reported him to Pat. Not long before we left, he came home inebriated and broke all the furniture up. However, long before this happened, she and I had to sit on the bed quite often and drink our coffee, as all the chairs were minus their legs from previous episodes. She was an excellent cook, making delicious cakes and when we dined with them, she made a wonderful meal. She always did things in such style. On these occasions, she would borrow furniture, glass and china. A while later, I was not sorry to learn that he had died, probably of liver failure and that she had gone back to the safety of Khartoum and her family. In those days, I had no feeling of racism; I liked or disliked people in the ordinary sense. It was purely cultural.

Pat was required to visit his district regularly as representative of the British Military Administration, covering hundreds of square miles and most of the time I went along too. Quite often we were accompanied by other officers who had other roles to play, such as the Welsh police inspector who inspected police posts and outstations and the Yugoslavian doctor from the hospital who visited dispensaries and held surgeries. If there were no other medical staff with the doctor, I would assist him at his clinics. Seriously sick patients would be dispatched back to Tessenei by one of our trucks. The most terrible injuries we saw over and over again were of children who had fallen into fires; the poor things in unspeakable pain and so many of whom would not live despite the treatment. It was most upsetting to us. On these high-powered safaris, in the evening Pat always wore white trousers with a cummerbund around his waist. I had a black silk housecoat, which covered me from my shoulders to my feet. This display of over dressing was entirely for the benefit of the chiefs and local dignitaries, who expected us as representatives of HM Government to behave like superior beings. Being on safari, it was easy to become sloppy and despite opinions to the contrary today, the local people did not like standards to slip as it made them feel devalued. We always had a great affection and respect for the people in the Western Province of Eritrea. In the villages we visited, I was of great interest to the women who seldom appeared and were veiled. In nomadic villages, they were screened away from men and visitors. I knew that I was being watched from behind some curtain or other. Sometimes the chief would invite me into the tent to meet his favourite wife. No men had this privilege of course. Even on one occasion when the chief's wife was dying of cancer, the male doctor was not allowed to personally give her a morphine injection or see her. The man said casually that she would die and that he would get a new wife.

While in Tessenei we saw the occasional film, put on by the Italian owner of a bar. He had put up a brushwood enclosure and charged a few cents admission. We sat on backless benches or brought our own chairs. We ate pumpkin seeds which the locals fried and sold in small packets at the door. They were delicious. The films were quite often silent, the Buster Keaton sort. I loved going there when they were showing because the audience was as interesting as the films. Some of the local tribesmen who attended the film show, had traditional matted hair styles dressed with rancid fat decorated with ornaments in it and sat watching the film holding their 6ft spear. They always sat impassively and I wondered what they made of it all. The more westernised locals appreciated the jokes and applauded and laughed.

In December 1949, we were told that Pat would take over the town of Agordat with its larger districts in the New Year. I had also discovered that I was expecting a baby and this announcement was greeted with great excitement by everyone. I prayed that I would do the right thing and produce a son when the time came, so that Pat would not lose face with the local population and chiefs. A woman who produced daughters was considered a liability, as dowries of cattle and jewellery were then required for marriage.

5

Agordat and Return to Keren and Asmara

We moved to Agordat in January 1950. The house we had there was huge; it had been one of the Kaiser's hunting lodges and was a mix of baronial and Arab styling, with one enormous ballroom-like central room. All around the outside of this were smaller rooms, each one opening up onto the so-called garden. The garden consisted of sand, more sand and the odd Bougainvillea struggling for existence, along with a small plant called Vinca which has pink flowers and seems to generally thrive in the African climate. The kitchen and stores were on the ground floor and very large. Upstairs, there was the same room arrangement, but the centrally placed room was divided into one third and two thirds by a partition of wood which was 6 inches off the floor at the bottom and only seven feet high. These were our sitting room and bedroom – hardly private. There was an awful old fashioned bathroom with one of those continental wood-burning stoves for heating the water. This caused the room temperature to reach well over 100ºF, but we did have plenty of hot water. The water was piped into the house and we had electricity all day. From outside, the house looked like the average British town hall and inside we had the usual Public Works Department allocation of furniture; a wooden settee, three matching chairs with cushions and removable covers, a bookcase, sideboard and a dining table with six chairs. In the sitting room section the furniture was lost up one corner. Had we had a Badminton set, we could have put up an indoor court and comfortably played at the other end of the partitioned room. This was the only time we had a double bed and we soon found out why. The springs had sunk in the middle, creating a trough. We tried to get a replacement, but none were forthcoming. In desperation we strung the wires up as best we could and had an extra mattress made in the market to go underneath. We certainly slept in some terrible beds over the years. Our boxes with our personal items came with us as usual.

Shortly afterwards I went for my one and only antenatal treatment. Our Yugoslavian doctor friend, who by now was in charge of the hospital in Agordat, said he would rather not have the responsibility of my case. In any case, he was a general surgeon and not an obstetrician. We always joked that he would rather have amputated than done a delivery. So, I was driven up to Asmara by an Indian trader who was going there on business. He had the only private saloon car in the area. It was a long and very hot journey. I stayed in Government House with Brigadier Drew and his wife and saw the doctor at the military hospital, who pronounced me fit and well. He prescribed me some iron tablets which I was to collect later that day. After doing some shopping for the baby and visiting friends, I went back to the dispensary to collect my pills only to be told that someone had collected them. All my protests were in vain and I never got my tablets. I have often wondered who took them and what effect they might have had, good or bad. After a few days of rest in the cool of Asmara, I made the long hot return journey back to Agordat in an Army truck going in the same direction. After this experience, I did not bother to make any further visits to the doctor.

While I had been away, Pat had managed to get the place re-decorated and the walls whitewashed. I got busy with preparing the nursery, which was to be a small room off the balcony, running down one side of the upper part of the house. No doors were ever closed, everything was open plan. In England my mother kindly did all of the necessary layette buying of things like bottles, nappies and clothes and everything that might be needed for the baby and myself. All their parcels arrived by sea over the months ahead and miraculously nothing was lost. I did a lot of sewing myself too. My parents had obviously had a lot of pleasure adding extra things for the baby, including a knitted bonnet – the temperature in Agordat was over 90°F day and night.

Somewhere about this time Pat was demobbed from the Army. There was no need for the huge numbers of officers anymore. Despite his original intention to become a regular soldier, he had to make a career change at this point. He chose to take the two-year Foreign Office Contract instead, continuing in Eritrea in the same job. No decision by them was being made about the future of Eritrea. I think at this moment we could have taken some UK leave, but in my condition it would have been very tiring. In fact, neither of us wanted to do so, as we were happy where we were. Pat was involved in his job and doing lots of safari work. There were lots of problems in the district and the *Shifta* (see Fig. 5.1) were still very active.

I was no longer going on safari or bumping about in the truck, for obvious reasons. Instead, I stayed at home supervising the rest of the Public Works Department decorating. It all looked splendid when it was finished. They painted the nursery in dark green. Perhaps it was the only paint they had, but the workmen would not budge when I asked them to change to a lighter colour. I was only a woman of course and as Moslems, they did not rate my opinions too highly. Later on they did offer to change some of the paint for dark brown or canary yellow but I settled for the green colour, as it was cooler. There was general uproar while the partition was repaired and repainted. In our quarters upstairs, there were seven sets of double inner doors, seven sets of large double shutters, six odd doors and six odd shutters; all of which needed a new coat of paint. The walls and ceilings needed three coats of whitewash, which would in time flake and fall off. Downstairs, it was a similar story. It took about six weeks and it was no wonder I felt nauseous from the paint smell in my condition. In addition, all the lights were brass chandeliers and had to be taken down and looked so lovely when they had been cleaned. How thankful we all were when it was finished, including the servants as they had been brewing up coffee for the workmen all of the time as well. In Africa there seemed to always be three times as many people than are actually required for the job; there were always some hangers-on and the servants would join in as well. The noise was deafening. One afternoon I had taken refuge in one of the smaller rooms to rest, when loud screams wakened me. I rushed to the balcony to find dozen or more men and women climbing over our very high fence. The servants were pulling people over our fence and our dogs were busy snapping at their ankles. Whatever was outside was obviously much worse than our savage dogs. It proved to be a rabid hyena, snapping, squealing and howling. The poor beast ran past the house, towards the hospital where it ran down the corridor and was eventually cornered and shot by the police. We were kept busy bandaging cuts and bruises from the frantic scramble of the escape for some time. The workmen started decorating the outside of the house. By the end of March, the decorations were finished. Judy had bitten one of the workmen as well, so I was pleased to see the back of them. One of things that upset me at the time was that my little parrot Coco was stolen. He disappeared with the workmen on their last day. They said the cat had broken into the cage and got him, but I doubt that it was true, as he had fascinated them all.

We found some congenial company in Agordat, especially at the army transit camp. I suppose Pat and I tended to gravitate to Army messes having both been so lately in the Forces ourselves. We used to have dinner there and watch old films. Pat and I joined a book club, which was quite a new idea then, and received regular choices of the latest books sent out from the UK. I kept busy most of the time. Apart from organising the household and entertaining official visitors, I sewed curtains for the nursery and trimmed a baby basket ready for the baby things. I had not realised that all nappies in those days had to be sewn around the edges and were not finished, so that was a job to be done too. I celebrated my thirtieth birthday on 16th February 1950 surrounded by sewing, with just another three months to go for the big

Fig 5.1 *Keren 1952: Captured* Shifta *with Eritrean District Officer.*

day. El Amin our new houseboy embroidered a tablecloth for me in a pretty cross-stitch. It was beautifully done and such a lovely surprise. I was now well over seven months pregnant and the temperature was always over 90°F day or night. I kept very fit and well, apart from a terrible desire for fruit or fruit juice. No doubt it was some vitamin deficiency or other. Pat sent out the word and every visitor or passer-by from wherever would kindly arrive with a gift. There were tins of juice, bottles of squash, the odd orange or sometimes a lemon or dates. I was very grateful. Thank goodness it was not coal or some of the other strange things that women sometimes crave at these times.

Our cook, Mohammed, was excellent. He produced good quality plain food and he made good bread. We took on a man who had been a houseboy to the Sardinian Duke of Aosta, whose name was El Amin. He still had his beautifully made and embroidered jackets with the ducal crest on it, which he wore around the house and looked very smart. We must have been a poor substitute, but we were the top dogs of the area and native servants are terrible snobs. All the staff wore spotless white garments (see Fig. 5.2) called *Djellaba* and turbans, which we provided. We also employed a house girl, partly as a sort of chaperone for me and to be a nanny to the expected baby. It took us some time to find a suitable girl, but after a few false starts, we managed to find an older Coptic Christian woman. Her name was Lulu. The two girls who applied earlier were vetoed pretty quickly by the other staff members, one on account of her morals and the other was said to be light fingered. It was pointless ignoring the feelings of our own staff, if you hoped for peace in the household.

In February 1950, we had a United Nations Four Power Commission going around the territory. Its duty was to find out the views of the population regarding their future. To help conduct this process, some Foreign Office officials arrived from London. A previous such survey had been done by the British Military Administration prior to this. This Commission toured the villages, interviewing local chiefs, elders and various VIPs. There was rioting in Asmara and we heard that forty people had died and that 150 had been injured. Troops and police were busy trying to keep order. Many of the highland peoples wanted a union with Ethiopia, who were pushing hard for this idea; conversely the majority of lowlanders wanted British colonial status, which was never on the cards. Pat was very busy with the backlash of all this activity. The Asmara riots were quelled by March, which was a relief as I was due to go up there for the birth of the baby. Over this busy political period we had a lot of official visitors, but fortunately the staff was able to cope with minimum supervision from me. We always used the very large room downstairs for official entertaining which was about 50ft x 50ft. The dining table was equally enormous. When it was laid with the white china and linen, with a mass of Bougainvillea flowers in the centre of the table, it looked magnificent. Everything had to be provided by us including all the glasses, linen, china and cutlery, which was a severe drain on our finances as it needed to be of a certain standard for official entertaining. I was lucky in that my parents had given me all the linen and cutlery they possessed when I left the UK. We had some extra silver salt and pepper sets made by a local silversmith. A kind official coming down from Asmara brought me some huge salvers in plated silver, which had once belonged to Lloyd Triestino and some similar vases. They had been in a store in Asmara somewhere. Additional cutlery and cut glass was also found for us. When we left Eritrea, we returned it all. I have always wondered what happened to the original contents of these houses. Pat's pay at the time was very poor. We had a very high standard to keep up. We could save nothing at all, but I do not think we were thinking much about the future at that time in our lives. If it sounded as though we were living in the lap of luxury, that assumption would have been quite wrong. Nothing was easy. Our living quarters were very basic and, as I have said earlier, the furniture was even more so. We had native made mats for the floor and sitting room lamps were made from Chianti bottles and the wires trailed out of them. I had the lamp shade frames made in the market and covered them myself. The floors in all the rooms were either plain concrete or sometimes tiled.

The weather was very hot by April 1950 with no rain at all. The only water we saw was in the rivers where flash floods coming down from higher ground swept away cattle and people. It happened very quickly and it was always dangerous to be in a riverbed at times like these. We always chose the riverbed to drive along if possible, because it was so much easier, smoother and more direct, but we had to be very aware of what was happening further up river and this was not always an easy thing to do.

For some reason Agordat had a large number of hyena in the immediate area and at nights they would make screaming and laughing noises outside our fence. Standing on the balconies, we could see rows of gleaming eyes if we shone a torch. Sometimes, the noise was so loud that it kept us awake for nights on end. In the end we employed a watchman who used to throw stones at them to chase them away. Once he told me the pack was fifty strong. I do not know what brought them into the area. Perhaps lack of game due to the drought conditions, or maybe locally there were goats or other livestock they could plunder. As a consequence, there were a lot of rabies outbreaks. We used to put camp beds up on the flat roof when it was very hot and airless with our mosquito nets draped over us, but the mosquitoes were very busy. Eventually, Pat had a special net cage put up there and beds remained in place there permanently. The trouble was though that the sun rose very early and, by 6 o'clock, it was too hot to remain up there and we had to come downstairs. So our days always began very early.

There were other English wives in Agordat with their husbands who were with the police or army. We held coffee and tea parties to pass the time, as it was not really possible to do any charitable or good works for the locals, as there were strict tribal customs to take account of. I was also very busy making uniforms and aprons for the staff. I had the use of a 15-cwt Army truck for transport, but climbing into it was quite a problem in my condition and so I preferred to walk if I could and a servant always accompanied me. I tried to do something with the garden that just had shrubs in it. I had a nice patio prepared overlooking the surrounding countryside, as we were on a slight hill, but even with its palm canopy it was just too hot to enjoy sitting on it during the day. At night I preferred to stay upstairs on the balcony. The servants clearly thought I was mad. We were always considered a little bit eccentric whatever we did. I used to walk the dogs down to the palm grove about 100 yards from the house in the cool of the evening for exercise. Usually I went with a servant, but one evening I went alone and was met by a wild figure that approached waving his heavy stick at me, a rather frightening sight, his matted hair with ornaments sticking out. I thought he was going to attack me and the dogs were agitated too. He made me retreat back up the hill, which was most fortunate as it transpired that he was turning me away from the danger of a probable rabid hyena, which was lying down further along the path. Lula had seen what was happening and came running. When all was explained, the tribesman was taken into the kitchen for coffee and he saw the funny side. I never walked to the grove again alone, unless I was with Pat and his gun.

Pat was still travelling with the UN Commission, and I began to wonder what would happen if I went into labour suddenly. I decided to prepare my case for a hasty departure. A truck coming down from Asmara brought us a very ancient refrigerator. That was a relief and it would prove essential when the baby arrived. Pat came and went, usually collecting clean clothes, fresh stores and mail, or instructions from HQ. There was not much in the way of communications in those days, except on the telephone. In the middle of all this, he was probably licked by a rabid dog belonging to the Police Inspector with whom he was staying. It was too risky to ignore, so they both had to go to Asmara (with the dog's body on ice for examination) to see the Medical Officer and start their 25 injection regime. The dog was proved to have died of rabies, so he had to remain at home and go to the hospital daily. At the same time, he also had to do his safari jobs whilst travelling in the heat of the day, driving for miles each day. There was also some local trouble, which he had to sort out. Unfortunately, some British troops still in the area were angered by something done by local prostitutes and as a

Fig 5.2 *Agordat 1951: The staff wearing white* djellaba *and turbans (left to right).* *Houseboy El Amin,* Askari, *Mohammed the Cook, Nanny Lulu, Safari Cook.*

consequence set fire to their huts, which injured several people. A lot of anger was felt about this in the village.

When Pat finished his course of anti-rabies injections, we went up to Asmara. On the way we stayed in the Guest House in Keren for two nights, but sadly a lot of our old friends, both Italian and British had left because of the uncertainty of the country's future and unrest. We arrived in Asmara, complete with my dog Judy, who had an uncertain temper and could not be left with the staff. We stayed with friends for a day or two and wined, dined, shopped and enjoyed the cool climate at 7,000 ft above sea level. I also had a check-up at the hospital. We both had hair cuts, which was a bit of a luxury as usually I had to cut both of our hair. Although there were local barbers, it was not considered safe to go to them for fear of contracting ringworm and other skin diseases.

Pat left to go back to Agordat on 10th May and as the baby was due around then, I stayed on in the guest wing at Government House with

Sir Freddie Pearce and Olwen his wife. We waited and waited, everyone getting a bit fed-up, including me and my hosts. I used to make the driver go over all the cobble stones in an attempt to hurry things along. He however said that nothing would happen until the next full moon and amazingly he was right. It was so embarrassing, but you just cannot hurry nature. Early on the evening of 26th May I went into labour and was admitted to the Military Hospital and Timothy was born at 10 o'clock. The hospital was in the middle of an epidemic of gastroenteritis and I went down with it quite quickly and became quite ill. The hospital denied that it was enteritis and just said that it was normal after childbirth, which I knew not to be the case. I was very worried for us both and remained there a week before I discharged myself. I booked into a hotel and sent for an Italian doctor I knew, who gave me some strong drugs to clear up the bug. I was subsequently unable to feed the baby myself and had to get tins of baby food from the NAAFI which always seemed to be out of date. Pat rushed up from Agordat to see me and his baby son. Later in the day, he was given a party at the Officers Mess to celebrate. Having had a drop too much, he returned to his hotel where he fell over a chair in the bedroom. The next time I saw him, he was sporting a black eye. I remained at the hotel for about a week, gathering my strength for the long journey back and plenty of visitors came to see us. The baby was very placid and the hotel provided me with a young Eritrean girl as a baby sitter, whenever I went to the dining room for my meals.

I did the return journey to Agordat in stages, in order to acclimatise the baby to the heat. On 10th June, in Keren I stayed at the house of an Italian acquaintance whose weekend cottage it was. In the meantime, Pat was travelling to and fro, sometimes to Asmara or Keren for conferences and instructions; backwards and forwards on the dusty road, so we were able to meet regularly. A friend from Asmara came to stay with me, with her maid and brought her children. We all ate at the local hotel once a day and swam in the pool and relaxed. My old Italian friends in Keren were delighted to see the baby. They thought he was like a doll as he was so small, just 6.13 oz. Pat had some wonderful letters from local chiefs and dignitaries. Others came to see him to congratulate him on his son's birth and also on having a wife who bore sons, which was very important to Moslems. My stock was quite high as a result too. I was still a bit weak from the enteritis attack and the few days in Keren helped put me on my feet again. Timothy, as we had decided to name the baby, was not doing too well on the baby food. Pat made great efforts in Agordat to find a cow that had recently calved and finally found an Italian with a small holding who had one. He agreed to bring a daily supply of the milk for us, which continued for the rest of the time we were in the area. The milk had to be strained, boiled and skimmed to make it the correct strength but whatever it was that I concocted it was the right mix because he thrived. All this had an odd fallout. Sometimes the Italian women would be unable to feed their infants and inevitably these poor babies died because the mixture was too strong or too weak, and they did not seem to know about sterilising the bottles. As soon as Timothy started to thrive, the news spread fast and I was asked to teach mothers who had lost their previous babies how to proceed. I drew up charts and instructions for the doctor, for whom bottle-feeding was a mystery too. It was wonderful to see how many babies lived because of it; even if I had to battle to get them to boil the bottle, as they thought a good wash would suffice.

We all returned to Agordat at the end of June 1950. Timothy, who by now was being called *Nini* (small one) by the servants and Italians, settled down well in his nursery despite the heat. He lay with just his nappy on, under the net and was very placid. It took me quite a while to get back to my old self; probably as a result of the stomach bug which had weakened me, but also from lack of sleep with all those broken nights and three-hourly feeds which Timothy had to have to keep his weight up. He used to lose weight alarmingly, if I tried to lengthen the time to three and a half hourly feeds. I suppose there was not much substance in the skimmed milk, but if I tried to alter the mixture he was immediately ill, however gently I did it. In the end I put a sort of rice-based, baby food called Farex into his feed, which helped fill him up a bit better. It was a worrying time.

We had a lot of rain that year in the autumn and the local tribesmen nicknamed Timothy *Saidi*, the rain bringer. They had all been delighted at his birth and congratulated Pat. Roads and bridges were washed away, but no one minded because it meant that the wells filled up and there was grass and foliage growth for the animals. I nearly lost Judy when she jumped into the flooded river for a swim, but we managed to rescue her. I took up swimming at the Transit Camp pool and played tennis there too in an attempt to get the weight off which I had gained over the pregnancy. It did not help and I never quite got back to the 8st 4lbs I used to weigh, but perhaps I was too skinny then.

Pat was still going away on safaris quite a few nights each week. I was quite safe with my loyal servants around me and never lonely. It is impossible to be alone in Africa, there are always people in the servants' quarters, chattering and often singing. People were visiting from Asmara, bringing treats, or game that they had shot along the way. There would be great excitement from the servants; skinning the animal and cutting up the parts, usually a leg for me and the rest for them. During the wet season, Pat got stranded several times and he was unable to cross swollen rivers for several days and return home as planned. I was always pleased that he took tinned goods with him as you could not always rely on getting game to eat at such times.

After a few months or so, we decided to make a trip to Asmara which thankfully provided some respite from the heat. I also needed a check-up at the hospital, but it was mainly a shopping trip. As usual we stayed at Government House. During this visit, we started to make arrangements for Timothy's Christening. The Army Padre agreed to come to Agordat to perform the ceremony. It was quite important to make an occasion of it because the local people, both Italian and Moslem, would have expected it of us. I had already remarked just after our first arrival in Agordat, what a wonderful room the downstairs area

Fig 5.3 *Keren 1951: Timothy with his nursemaid outside Mohammed the cook's family home with goats.*

would be for a party, but at the time had no plans along those lines. Now we started thinking what a good idea it might be. Like all these plans, this one seemed to have a life of its own… The officers at the Transit Camp organised a band for us; it was the dance orchestra of the South Wales Borders Regiment no less, which we paid for. As soon as the invitations went out, the Italian guests offered to do the decorations which they did magnificently, using palm leaves and Bougainvillea. The room looked absolutely wonderful. People were having evening suits brought out of mothballs, all over the area. We bought dozens of pigs, which were slaughtered and cooked by local people for us. Mohammed our cook prepared salads and fresh fruit. Crates of wine appeared from everywhere as gifts. I had nothing to do really, but enjoy myself helping to get the party co-ordinated.

On the morning of the important day of 26th August 1950, Timothy was christened by the Padre. About thirty Italian guests attended and some British friends. Unfortunately, Moslems were not able to attend the Christian baptism. After the ceremony, we had cakes and wine in the garden in an Italian style. The stand-in godmother was a friend, Helen Murphy the Palestinian wife of the Police Officer, who was a Christian. The other two godparents were not represented. The Padre retired to the camp for the night, and we had a quiet night. The next morning the Padre held a Communion service for seven of us in the anteroom of the hall before leaving for Asmara. In the meantime, the house was a hive of activity with all the food preparation. I do not remember where all the cutlery, plates and glasses came from, but were no doubt borrowed from all around the district. That evening, about seventy guests of various nationalities arrived all in their finery. It was the biggest event held in the area for ten years and certainly the largest such gathering since the war in the area. The band played until midnight and after they had left we played music on an old gramophone. Eventually it broke up at 2 o'clock and people drifted away after that. I went to the kitchen at about 11 o'clock to thank all the staff and lock any alcohol away in the store. I found the kitchen thronging with people and dozens more outside; the staff and their families, others from the office, drivers, *Askari* and anyone who had even the remotest connection with us all were sitting down eating and celebrating. It was lovely to be part of such a community celebration. In the morning everything had been cleared away, cleaned and the place was spotless. I expect those two days were talked about in the district for years. Timothy received some nice presents, mainly things which people had in their possession such as sets of cake knives or local bangles and gold jewellery. The Europeans were very poor and just scraped a living in small holdings.

Life eventually returned to normal. I had started making weekly visits to the local clinic just before Timothy's birth, not for myself but to help the doctor who was having a problem, as most of his patients were Moslem women. They could not tell him their symptoms directly and had to do it through another woman. Between us we set up a system. I noted in my diary that on one day we had ninety children there. He decided to start a childcare programme to try to treat people before they reached an acute stage. We started a school inspection of the local schools, and found that of the 140 children present most had ringworm, TB and a whole host of other illnesses. (This was only a small percentage of the local children, as most did not go to school at all, either because they were girls or because they were herding goats.) I used to do the notes and give encouragement. My presence just ensured that everyone came to the clinic itself or agreed to treatment. It was the way things were done in tribal life and the chief was paramount. Pat had wanted to start the clinics and I was able to support him in this, as I too was very interested. I don't know what happened to them after we left the area. Later on, Pat extended the inspection to include regular visits to schools and also to the *Banda* Camp. The *Askari* (or *Banda*) were a native army attached to the administration office. They lived with their families in an encampment close to the offices. Another one of the duties I found myself involved with was the local schools. I was concerned particularly that girls were not receiving education. I felt there must be something I could do about this and obtained permission from HQ in Asmara to start a small school, and was allocated a teacher. I was sure there was something these girls could learn without breaching the Moslem rules, but all they were allowed to learn was the Koran, sewing and cooking; they were not allowed to read or write at all. I wonder if things have changed much in the intervening years.

I started accompanying Pat on short safari at times, leaving Timothy in the capable hands of his nursemaid Lula, who had far more experience of babies than I had. She had worked for some important people in the past. Lula was already doing the bottle sterilising herself and was feeding him under my supervision. She loved to dress him up and changed his clothes several times a day to show him off. Under her careful supervision, Timothy enjoyed playing with the cook's children Sara and Asta (see Fig. 5.3) and sometimes ate meals with them. I think that Lulu would have remained with us for a long time.

Fig 5.4 *Halhal 1952: Elections had to be held in readiness for self-government and Pat and teams of fellow officers toured the area carefully explaining the concept to the local population.*

Sadly at the end of 1951 the doctor said that she was showing signs of TB and that I must dismiss her, which I did. The disease may not have been active, because fortunately no one else became infected. I then took on a girl call Amati in her place, who was to remain with me until I left Eritrea. She was not a skilled nursemaid, so I used to take Timothy with us on safari while she was in our employ. I always enjoyed my safaris and the villagers loved to see the baby, with his blue eyes and blonde curls. It meant a mountain of baggage and there were always the two dogs with us of course. Timothy never came to any harm and I would have been unhappy not being able to go with Pat. We used to travel for miles in the trucks, right into the desert.

In one area, we always came across nomadic tribes on the move. These people wandered from area to area for various reasons, taking all the families and goats with them putting up rough tents wherever they decided to remain for a while. All the women travelled in a type of tent on the backs of the camels, which were very effective. It kept them sheltered from the sun which was blistering. As usual there were plenty of children. We would come across these families, either on the move or encamped. They would always welcome us and insist that we joined them for refreshments; offering goat stew with native bread and coffee. When they could get it, they also offered camel milk to drink. In return, we would give them gifts of tea or coffee. I have to mention here that never once were Pat and I offered sheep's eyeballs or any other oddities, which so many people report eating. In all the years that we travelled under these circumstances, none of us suffered any ill effects. I would stay in the background while Pat discussed matters with the men through an interpreter. Sometimes it was necessary to use more than one interpreter, as there were so many languages and dialects in use. We always seemed to have someone in our entourage who could make himself understood. We could have about twelve or more local people with us including clerks, police, *Askari* and drivers. There was usually more than one truck. We would also be taking supplies such as school desks, books and clinic supplies. The women were very interested in and me and were fascinated by Timothy with his beautiful golden curls. On one of our safaris, we joined a local chief for dinner in his tent just outside a village. It was a lovely meal of chicken. When I remarked that I had enjoyed it, he told me that it was his ex-wife who was cooking. He said that when she got too old, he divorced her and married another young girl. He went on to say that he had kept her on as a cook because she had nowhere to go; he remarked, rather shockingly, that she was lucky to be in this situation. Women had no protection under these circumstances and I must have seemed to be a creature from another planet, with my face uncovered and bumping around the countryside in a truck with my baby and husband. Many of the men had VD, but it was considered a sign of manhood. The doctor told me that when he confirmed it was VD, they would raise their spear in the air and say "Thanks be to Allah!" never worrying much about the treatment. The wives must have been infected and the children. It was a vicious circle and caused many women to become barren. The poor things would be sent packing if no children arrived.

As usual, on safari I was kept busy inspecting schools and at the clinics, checking drug cupboards. We brought with us Aspirin, Bismuth and worming medicine for the clinics. There were no other drugs in those days, although sulphur drugs were starting to appear and would be miracle cures in their time. We were still digging ourselves out of ruts, and setting up camp in the way I have described earlier. At one stage I was also able to utilise a skill learned in the ATS, and made myself useful by producing maps of certain off track areas as there were none available. After the heavy rains, the mosquitoes were very bad, so we had to start giving Timothy Paludrine, the anti-malarial pill which we all took. It was a terrible job as he would not take it willingly. I solved this by crushing his ¼ tablet in a small amount of milk and inserting the milk into the side of his mouth when he was asleep. Then I would have to wake him quickly and give him a drink before he realised what had happened. It worked and he never contracted malaria.

Pat had to take over another area while someone was on leave, so more travelling back and forth. By this time the Red Locust Control people had arrived and more people meant new conversations and news from outside of Eritrea. The Western Province had a terrible plague of locust while we were there; it was an amazing experience. They were in clouds like a hailstorm, as far as the eye could see and in swarms several miles wide. They got in your hair and your clothes. When you ran over them on the road it looked just like it had rained. They ate everything and then moved on. The Locust Control people's job was to find the breeding ground and destroy them before they could take flight.

By mid April of 1951 we decided we had better think of some UK leave and show our son to his proud Grandparents. It was almost five years since we had left home after the war. We flew home via Cairo, as was the system in those days. There were no long haul flights, so we stayed overnight outside the city at the Heliopolis Palace Hotel. This was the hotel used by airlines; it was some distance from the bustle of Cairo and had big airy rooms opening out onto large balconies. The planes (Argonaut) were slow and no proper meals were served on board, only coffee and sandwiches. Disposable nappies were unheard of then, although at a later date I did try some which were little more than a tissue width and not much good. In addition to all of our luggage, we had a carry-cot filled to the brim with items required for the journey including clean nappies, tins of baby food, bottles, mixing jug and spoons, teats, and on top of all this an eleven month old baby. Of course, we had no seat allocated for him, but in those days they usually gave you the front seats and the carry-cot could be put on the floor at your feet. We were travelling First Class with lots of room fortunately. In those days, there was a circular lounge at the back of the aircraft with magazines to read. The WCs had complimentary Elizabeth Arden toiletry items in them. We flew

Fig 5.5 *Halhal 1952: British Military Outpost.*

on from Cairo, via Benghazi in Libya and then Rome, stopping off at both airports for a hot meal. The journey took two and half days, during which I had to keep filling up my thermos flasks with boiled water for Timothy's feeds. He was only just being weaned and I was afraid to feed him anything doubtful which might affect his tummy. What a nightmare journey and we were very pleased to see London Airport (now called Heathrow).

We spent three months in England, dividing our time between both our parents' homes and then went to Switzerland to see Pat's brother, Geoffrey, who had been living with his Aunt and Uncle in Montreux. We took Pat's mother with us and drove across France in our new Morris Minor, landing at Dunkirk on the ferry. Even in 1951 it was very battle scarred, looking exactly as the photographs show – only one tall building still standing and the rest just rubble. It was quite shocking. On our drive across France, we saw some more of the destruction and some of the many soldiers' graves. I had left TJ (as we were now calling Timothy) with my parents for the ten days we were away, which meant that we managed to have a bit of break away from parenting. He was very happy with my parents who enjoyed having him, playing contentedly in their garden. He clearly seemed not to have missed us both when we returned.

Pat had decided in the meantime to accept a new Foreign Office appointment, which had been offered to him. It was back in Eritrea, where we wanted to be, and was what we had been given to understand was likely. This meant that all our baggage and servants, plus the two dogs, were in situ as hoped. He then had to fly back to take up the job in August 1951. I remained at home with my parents in Cambridge for a week or two longer, waiting for the passage out to Eritrea to be arranged for the items we had bought in the UK all of which had to be shipped out there. These included household goods, TJ's toys and the precious Morris Minor. I flew back in September, the same journey all over again but this time with no one to help me. TJ was now eighteen months old and still there was no seat provided for him on the aircraft, so I had to have him on my lap. Fortunately, he was rather an engaging little tot and several passengers very kindly helped amuse him from time to time. Having stopped over in Rome for breakfast, we arrived in the late afternoon in Cairo and stayed again at the Heliopolis Palace Hotel overnight. It was here that, desperate for some clean water for TJ to drink, I had to resort to very weak local beer, which meant that he slept very well! It was the safest option, after boiled water. I was still carting the usual supply of nappies, and boiled water in the thermos in the carrycot. I did eventually manage to get some boiled water, after a struggle. Fortunately, I managed to arrange to get the soiled nappies washed and dried, ready for the onwards journey.

When we landed in Asmara, I found out that Pat had been posted back to Keren, not to our old house, but one that was located on the hill above the town. It was the usual Italian type of villa, all windows with shutters and tiled floors. We had the usual Public Works Department furniture ration of basic items. After the long journey, I was relieved to get to the villa as all the servants were there and the household was running smoothly. What a relief it was to hand TJ over to Amati and to relax for the first time in three days. Mohammed continued to produce his lovely meals. We still had various friends in the area, both English and Italian. Our life went on much as before.

Pat went out on safari as usual and most of the time I went with him taking the baby with us on those long and dusty drives across country. On one very memorable trip we went to Mersa Gulbub on the Red Sea coast in the South of Eritrea. It was a fair distance to travel over on rough dirt tracks. We camped on the sands on the edge of the ocean and ate fresh fish brought to us by the fishermen of the nomadic *Rashaida* tribe who were camped about 50 yards away. The women completely covered their faces with black cloths which were sewn all over with pearl buttons, only their eyes were showing. While the men fished, the women were in tents made from skins stretched over the branches of trees. All their household items and tents were carried on the backs of camels. One of the drivers from our party, who was able to speak their

Fig 5.6   *Halhal 1952: Margaret and one of the staff on official visit with Patrick.*

dialect, came over to me and said that the women would like me to go over to their tent. I quickly agreed and went over with him. There was not much communication between the women and me outside the tent, especially with a man present. But when they invited me inside and he had gone back, there was a lot of sign language and we made ourselves understood quite well. They were very interested in Timothy of course. I had coffee with them, served the traditional way. They used water taken from a well somewhere that they stored in special goat skinned bags. Later on, before we left two days later, I went back with some onions which they had asked for. I could not believe my eyes when the tiny children tucked into them raw.

Conditions were comfortable in Keren, we had regular supplies of electricity and water. Cooking still had to be done on a wood stove in a smoky outbuilding. The new villa we had been allocated had only two bedrooms, a bathroom, and a dining room/sitting room, which all opened out onto a veranda. One of the features of this villa was the long flight of steps leading up from the road, rather like those in a museum.

One night one of the dinner guests who was feeling somewhat over confident after a glass or two of wine, drove his jeep all the way down the fifty or so steps. Luckily, he came to no harm.

The usual way to leave was the road at the back of the villa. There was the usual complement of insects, cockroaches and scorpions, plus this time large rats. If we left the bedroom door leading to the veranda open to get air during the night, rats came into the bedroom. One night one climbed up onto my dressing table and chewed half of my pretty Victorian mourning jet brooch despite the two dogs and Mitzi the cat being present. This was a shame as it was a favourite of mine and had quite a lot of sentimental value, as it had belonged to my grandmother. From then on, all the doors remained closed. We had lost one of the cats, Zodi, who sadly disappeared while we were on leave and we never did find her despite us calling for her. She was part wild Ethiopian cat very similar to Abyssinian cats, whereas Mitzi was much more like a domestic cat. Unfortunately, some time later Mitzi gave a large yowl and disappeared over the wall. As she may well have contracted rabies, I had to have another course of anti-rabies injections. The threat of rabies was ever present. Sadly a young local Italian girl contracted rabies from a calf she owned which had been ill. She had been trying to feed it, not realising that it had been bitten by something and they both died.

Pat, just twenty-seven years of age, was still very busy with his job which meant he had a lot of responsibility. We were both speaking Italian fairly well, and often spoke to each other in the language by mistake.

Because of my commitments at home with Timothy, I did not have time to get involved in the various clinics again. Instead I was asked by a friend of ours, Bert Hodgeson the Headmaster of a nearby school, to help out at the secondary school where he taught male pupils from twelve to sixteen years of age. The school was part of the Military Administration's remit. He had a very broad Yorkshire accent and he thought my accent-less voice would do nicely for the English Literature classes. The boys were due to take their British School

Certificate and my job was to do the Shakespeare plays with them. Fortunately, I had always enjoyed these plays and with a Teacher's Copy of the play we got to the required examination standard. It was great fun and rather amusing at times. The boys were fascinated by me and half the lessons seemed to be taken up with questions such as 'How old are you?" and "How does an electric light bulb work?" The former one I answered by telling them that one should never ask a lady her age! On the more technical questions, if Pat did not know the answer, I wrote off to my father for the answers. As a result of this, I was approached by the Aga Khan community to teach their girls accent-less English.

Timothy had a very devoted young Eritrean called Ibrahim (Ib as he fondly called him). Ibrahim used to sleep on the veranda across his bedroom door and when TJ woke at about 5 o'clock he would call out to Ibrahim who would go and dress him, taking him out into the garden to play. When Pat was away, Ibrahim would be very much on guard. Timothy enjoyed playing with the children in the servants' quarters, where he was one day when a large snake came out of the woodpile. It was quickly killed, but after that the woodpile was relocated some distance from the house and servants sitting out area. Timothy was about two years old by now and quite a handful.

I also had another guard, an older Ethiopian man. He was rather a character; always carrying an ancient gun and a bandolier of bullets around his chest. He was an ex-Italian native army-trained soldier. He was rather terrifying to look at with his traditional hair style and his weapons. One of the things I have regretted since is that I was unable (because of the Moslem etiquette regarding such things) to photograph many of the interesting people I was fortunate to have met in my time in Eritrea. We were so heavily guarded because of the bandit problem which was getting worse at that time. These *Shifta*, as they were called also raided towns. Long after we left Tessenei and Agordat, I discovered why we were never attacked on our long journeys to and from Asmara, when other people travelling on the same roads were. I had always put it down to the fact that we always had guns, but in fact Lula's brother was part of a notorious *Shifta* band and we only found this out when he was captured and she appealed to us for help. No doubt all the servants knew about him and the office staff, but we were completely ignorant of the fact.

While we were at the end of the second period in Keren, there was a lot of political agitation, and the local people began to change in their attitude to foreigners in their land. Unfortunately, Mohammed our good cook started drinking heavily and we had to dismiss him. We took on a new man called Waldenkeil, a Coptic Christian, who acted as cook and safari-cook. Although he was a good cook, he was unpleasant to deal with and Pat always took him with him on safari. Amati found him nasty too and sadly left to go back to her own village not long after he joined us. Thankfully, Lula, who had been given a clean bill of health after her TB scare, came back as nursemaid and house girl.

In 1952 the British Government started to set up a 'Whitehall form of government' in readiness for self-government and elections (see Fig. 5.4) had to be held; a new idea for the local population as Eritrea had been an Italian colony since 1886. The proposed democratic system had to be very carefully explained to everyone in all corners of the country. To this end, every district and outpost (see Fig. 5.5) throughout the country had to be visited by teams of British Officers, many of whom had not been into the bush before. Every available official was drafted into the service for this purpose. With them went an army of interpreters and clerks. As one would expect, Pat was part of the team. As with his various other official trips, I accompanied him when I could (see Fig. 5.6) and quite frequently ended up taking the notes.

After the elections were held and the House of Assembly was set up, many of the British personnel began to hand over their responsibilities to the local appointees and departed from the country. On the 9th June 1952, Pat received a letter which said he was being given three months' notice, and it went onto thank him for his valued service. We were very sad indeed to have to be leaving Eritrea. Shortly thereafter, he received another letter inviting him, in the light of his experience and reputation, to become an Advisor to the new Government of the Western Province. Only six Advisors were to be appointed and he was very honoured to have been chosen. We were both delighted to be able to stay on. However, because the Ethiopians were to take over Eritrea as a designated self-governing province, there was a general feeling of unease all round. The Eritreans would have preferred self-government and not being under yet another country's rule and this point was made to the UN Four Power Commission by local chiefs. They would though in reality have much preferred to have become a Territory of the British Empire, but this option was no longer possible as most British Territories all over the world were starting to be in the process of being prepared for independence.

The UN Four Powers Commission's plan for the Ethiopian take over was a very unpopular idea for the lowland Moslems, who disliked Ethiopians as they were largely Christian. They would have preferred to have joined the Sudan. Not all the Coptic Christians welcomed it either; there being a historic animosity between the two countries. Added to this, there was the fact that Eritrea had long been independent of Ethiopia since the late 1880s. Because of the unsettled and possibly inflammatory situation, Pat decided to send Timothy and me home to the UK. I sadly packed up our house and left. At this point, he moved up to Asmara where the Eritrean Government had decided that all the Advisors should be based. Sadly we had to put Bobby, our old pointer, down as he had had cancer, but Pat still had the company of Judy our other dog. The official handover of Eritrea to Ethiopia took place with much ceremony on the 16th September 1952 (see Fig. 5.7). His Imperial Excellency Haile Selassie, Ethiopia's Emperor visited various places on an official tour in October that year including Keren (see Fig. 5.8), where a parade was held in their honour (see Fig. 5.9).

Fig 5.7 *Asmara 16th September 1952: Notables, Foreign Officials and South Wales Boarder Regiment at the lowering of the Union Jack and Handing over of Eritrea to a Federation with Ethiopia.*

Pat took up his new duties and received a letter from the Eritrean Chief Secretary Designate, Tedla Bairu, welcoming all the Advisors and saying that he would rely on their advice. He was a very nice man and was quite sincere, but within weeks the Ethiopians were in full charge. Things changed very rapidly, everyone was forced to carry identity cards with photographs and no one could enter or leave the country without the required permits. Nothing was done without reams of paper work. Finances were restricted and no funds were allowed to go out of the country. From being a happy relaxed place, it all became a bureaucratic nightmare. Pat moved into his Asmara flat, none too happy at the turn of events. There was a certain amount of work for the Advisors to do, but it was soon obvious that they were not being listened to, and after a few months quite a few of them resigned. The Ethiopians had clearly never intended to run things as proposed and agreed by the UN Commission. Although we still found our social life pleasant, Pat decided to write to the Colonial

Office to ask for an interview. In January 1950, he was told his services as an Advisor were no longer required and he returned to the UK for further instructions and attended interviews at the Colonial Office. Because of his relevant experience in Eritrea at a senior level, Pat was accepted quite quickly into the Colonial Service. However they could not decide which rank he should be appointed, because traditionally everyone started at the bottom and worked their way up the ranks of the service. While they mulled this over, he was staying with both sets of parents, turn and turnabout.

Pat got a permit for me to return and Timothy and I and settled back in. Timothy suffered very badly from Otitis-Media (Glue Ear) and despite repeated doses of Penicillin, which was then being administered by injection and a spell in hospital, the condition became quite painful and acute. The doctor decided to operate to remove his adenoids. Because a few days earlier a child had died after a similar operation under anaesthetic at the hospital, the doctor decided to operate without using an anaesthetic as apparently the altitude was affecting the recovery from anaesthesia. I had to hold him on my lap

Fig 5.8 *Keren October 1952: Ethiopian Emperor HE Haile Selassie and Empress touring.*

for the procedure, which took just a few minutes and he was given ice to suck. He recovered quickly and had no further trouble. All the medical people I have related this story to, have been incredulous.

I was advised not to go back to the UK, as if Pat was appointed to the Colonial Service, the likelihood of my being able to join him on his first tour was not certain at all. As we had no home base in England, it seemed a good idea to stay put. The thinking was that I was in Africa already, and that I could plead my case. We also thought it would help that I was in what was then hostile territory with a small child. I had to get a Residence Permit to enable me to stay on in Eritrea, which I managed to do so through contacts and old friends. I was also supposed to put down a Government Bond, which I managed to avoid again through acquaintances in the old Government. It was quite a worrying time in Eritrea and I was considering moving to Kenya, but then the Mau Mau trouble began there and it certainly was no place to be going. Fortunately, I still had friends in Asmara and the Secretary to the French Embassy put me on the invitation list which was a nice surprise, so I had lots of parties to go to. One thing led to another, before I knew it I was invited to the American Embassy events too. It was quite a busy diplomatic scene then. I quite often met up with the Count and Countessa de la Porte, an interesting and well known couple on the social scene

I was expecting to move off shortly to wherever Pat was sent to and had packed up all our baggage ready to send on. So, I was just living out of a small safari box of old stuff. In the meantime, the new Government gave me notice to get out of my house, going back on their promise to let me stay there until I left. I was fortunately able to find a small cottage at a reasonable rent and moved there. Thankfully I was getting regular money into my bank account from Pat and living quite frugally. Timothy started nursery school, run by an expatriate woman for international children. I was told by an Eritrean acquaintance that the Ethiopians thought that I had been left there as a British spy. Whether this was true or not, I never found out. Pat was getting frantic and worried about the situation for me in Eritrea, not helped by the fact that the mail took so long. The owner of the little cottage I was renting decided to sell it and return to Italy, so I then had to move out into a hotel. There I met an American girl, Shirley Eilola, who had come out to do work for an Agency called Point 4, which was some sort of US Aid Programme. Through her, I got to know some lovely Jewish families and went along to all their celebrations too. She had been allocated a villa, but was too frightened to move in by herself, so she asked me to join her and we both moved out of the hotel and joined forces. They had given her a large station wagon vehicle as part of her job and this meant we were able to go for drives out and down to the coast, as the *Shifta* troubles had abated at that time. The car was a great novelty, as no one had seen anything like it before. In addition an American PX (similar to a NAAFI) had opened up, and we got all of our supplies there with some new types of food for Timothy and me to enjoy trying.

One of the events that made me decide to move in with Shirley was something rather frightening that happened to Timothy. I was sitting in the busy waiting room of the hotel, with Timothy one minute quietly at my feet playing with a toy and the next he had completely vanished. The police were called, guests in the hotel went rushing around the gardens and general panic ensued. About forty minutes later he was returned to the hotel by two shoe-shine boys whose pitch was outside the café, where we always went for coffee and ice-cream. They knew him and eventually realised that he was alone. It transpired that one of the hotel guests had apparently given him ten cents to spend on sweets and he had decided to go and buy himself some, crossing two busy roads in the process. He was only two years and five months old at the time and how he remembered the way, I just cannot imagine. Anyway, the two boys were very handsomely rewarded. It was a classic example of the way in which people in Africa are good observers of people and somehow seem to know all your secrets when you live amongst them.

Fig 5.9   *Keren October 1952: Mounted welcome for the Emperor and Empress.*

Shirley and I lived quite happily together. She went to work and I kept house and cooked dinner; we also gave cocktail parties. We both had our own social circle which occasionally overlapped. The arrangement worked very well until she fell in love with an American Major, a handsome rotter, who let her down very badly. Not long after I left Eritrea, Shirley flew out to America to get married to him. Sadly, he failed to meet her at the airport and had given her a false address. She never heard from him again. She was a dear friend and we kept in touch for many years.

About that time I was offered a very highly paid job in Saudi Arabia as a Personal Secretary. Apparently they were not allowed to employ single women. They even offered to fly me and TJ over, complete with my maid and dog. Although it was highly paid and I was quite tempted, I knew I could not commit myself as I was waiting for news of Pat's new appointment through the Colonial Service. Also, at this time I was asked if I could run a small hotel for its Indian owners.

Suddenly, my instructions from Pat to depart arrived. He had been posted to Tanganyika on 4th June 1953 as an Administrative Officer. I arranged for my dog Judy to be sent down to him and she flew out on East African Airways under the care of the steward whom we knew when he was a waiter at the Italian Club. He took her to his hotel in Aden for the night and delivered her to an acquaintance in Tanganyika until Pat was able to collect her. I was so grateful for his help, and all those other people who were such good, kind friends, when I needed them so very much.

In the meantime, I had to get an exit permit to leave and all my heavy baggage was inspected. Goodness knows what they thought I was taking with me. Another family leaving at the same time had written railway bridge on their lists (part of a child's toy set). The customs officials made them unpack and produce this bridge. Surely they really did not think the family could have packed away a real railway bridge in their boxes. I was also told to fill in a form stating exactly how many cases I intended taking. Knowing that one can never really tell so far in advance what you need to take for a child. I said two suitcases and a bundle. I put all the leftovers of clothing into a travel rug, so I had my bundle and roped it. When I got to the airport and had to show all my forms, permits and ID, I had to unroll the bundle for inspection. By the time the officious Ethiopian official had passed me for exiting the country, the aircraft which had been diverted especially to pick me up was already half way down the runway already taxiing to take off. I had to run after it, with a stream of porters carrying the baggage and a small child, to the foot of the steps which had been dropped down from the aircraft for me. I was hauled aboard and it took off quickly. I think they were afraid of being impounded. The cabin of the plane was packed with pilgrims on their way back from Mecca who were sitting in the gangway cross legged, not on the seats. They hawked and spat all the way. We were the only Europeans, apart from the pilots. There were no refreshments on board, but when we briefly landed in Addis Ababa we were given some.

It took about an hour or so from there to get to Nairobi. I then took a taxi to the hotel. The streets were eerily deserted, because it was in the middle of the Mau Mau trouble. In the elegant foyer of the New Stanley Hotel, I felt like a refugee with my bundle. I stayed there two nights, but we were not able to leave the hotel or go into the grounds because of the risk of being shot at by the Mau Mau. The glass front doors had been damaged and boarded up, so one had to leave and enter by a very narrow side door. I took all my meals in my room and I could not leave Timothy, even though the hotel staff remaining on duty was from the *Kikuyu* tribe and not involved in the Mau Mau uprising. Under the circumstances, I was very relieved to leave Kenya.

POSTSCRIPT: THE ERITREAN LEGACY

My memories of Eritrea are very fond ones. I liked the people. They were happy days which I will remember for ever, and the places we saw there are ones I will never forget. Patrick's hard work there was clearly appreciated by those he served and before he left, he was very

Four Power Commission – Front Cover picture.

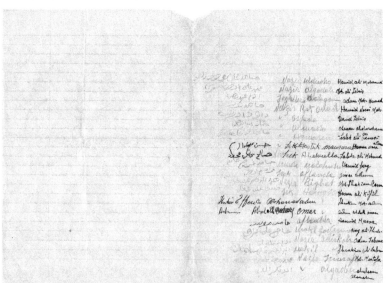

Signed letter of appreciation from Moslem League of the Western Province Eritrea to Patrick (in Arabic with translation).

touched to receive a signed letter of appreciation from members of the Moslem League of the Western Province Eritrea on behalf of all the Party members. The translation reads thus:

'To: P.W. Reardon Esq
After Greetings.

Before explaining anything we would like first to ask you to excuse us for taking the liberty of writing to you personally, but it is beyond our control to keep in secrecy such a gratitude.

Now that all political activities have come to an end, we, the members of the Moslem League of the Western Province on behalf of ourselves and all members of the Party, hereby pass to you our thanks and gratefulness of the esteemed assistance and good deeds which you gave to us and which, we dare say, was the main route which lead us to success and made us reach very calmly our aims. Such an assistance and help could never be forgotten by any of us.

We are, therefore, see ourselves [sic] compelled to confess of such assistance by which we are indebted to you and beg that the Almighty God bless you and appoint you to be the helper of all.

7/5/1950   Yours faithfully'

Moslem League of the Western Province 1950

After our departure, Ethiopia tightened its grip on Eritrea and embraced Marxism. The Emperor Haile Selassi was deposed in 1974 and he and his family were either imprisoned or killed. Eritrea started to fight back in 1975, as they believed in a different type of communism. Nakfa then became a terrorist training area. There was a severe famine in 1985/6 and it was thought that Ethiopia had a deliberate policy of withholding food from Eritrea in order to bring them to heel. Thousands of Eritreans have died from the famine and in the process of fighting for the freedom of their country.

The terrible things that happened after the British left have been repeated over and over in other parts of Africa since. Eritrea fought a terrible war to free itself from domination by Ethiopia and is still trying to rebuild its country today, despite the regular incursions by Ethiopia. I often wonder whether things would have been any different, if we had in fact allowed them to become part of the British Commonwealth as they had so clearly wished.

PART 2

The Next Eight Years

TANGANYIKA TERRITORY

1953–1961

COLONIAL SERVICE

6

Arrival in Tanganyika

Timothy and I flew into Dar-es-Salaam on 19th September 1953, leaving our beloved Eritrea behind. Someone met us at the airport and took us to the hotel Chez Margot. Pat was at this time about 600 miles away up country. The hotel was comfortable, cosy, friendly and right on the beach. The temperature was about 80°F day and night, with a slight sea breeze. The town was quite small with a chemist and just a few other shops mainly owned by Indians. One could buy very little other than carpets, brass ornaments and some dress materials. The main meeting place for Europeans was the New African Hotel, which was an old colonial style building with high ceilings and large rooms. In the ground floor courtyard sitting area, a huge palm tree had grown and grown until it eventually lifted the roof. Everyone congregated in this area and one always met someone familiar, either from the same area or old friends from previous stations. During the first few days I went into the town a few times and visited the New African Hotel. I bought some more kitchen equipment and for Timothy, a bicycle. Although the choice was limited and I could only find beige curtain material with a brown and yellow leaf blob pattern on it, I bought it for our new house. I was rather lucky to meet a man from Kenya who gave me the use of his car and driver, so was able to get about and sight-see.

On 23rd September, we caught the overnight train to start our journey to join Pat. All our hand luggage and the bicycle were stowed away in the guard's van. We had a comfortable two-berth compartment. The train crew were all local people and the drivers were Europeans. Meals were served formally in the dining room and were of a good standard. While one was away having dinner, the attendants made up the beds. The windows, which pulled up or down with a leather strap to fix them, had a mosquito netted outer window. These were very necessary not only because of the mosquitoes, but also because of the sparks from the steam engine that flew past the windows. These sometimes set alight to the dry bushes near to the railway line. The journey lasted over fifteen hours and was rather hard going as Timothy was a typical restless two and a half year old and wanted to lean out of the window and run about.

We reached Itigi in Western Tanganyika at 10 o'clock the following day and were met by a fellow District Officer of Pat's, Danny McKay. He drove me to their house in Singida, a couple of hours away. The countryside was very dry and sandy with mainly thorn bushes, scrub and a few trees. It fortunately was not too hot, just 70–80°F. My hostess kindly gave a dinner party in my honour the next night and I was able to meet everyone on the station. This British administration base was a typical collection of offices and homes for about ten people in all, including the Veterinary Officer and District Commissioner. For a few months before I arrived, Pat had originally been posted here as it was the headquarters for the administrative district. He was then posted to onto Kisiriri, which is further into the bush. He had collected my dog Judy on her arrival at the rail head there. Dogs had to travel in a box hanging underneath the train and it must have been terrifying for them. Quite a few people lost their dogs as they escaped.

On the 25th Pat arrived unexpectedly in time for breakfast; Timothy just held out his arms and cried out a delighted *'Dadda!'* I think he really must have thought his father had gone for ever. We left for Kisiriri that evening. The village was just a tiny group of local huts with no shops. There was a prison and the inmates grew a few vegetables such as tomatoes and spinach which they distributed to the local inhabitants from time to time. Otherwise, everything was tinned or dried goods. The meat was locally slaughtered beef. Usually this was very old livestock and was unfortunately very tough, so could be used only for stewing or mincing. Most people went hunting for the plentiful buck whenever they could to supplement their meat stocks. We saw some giraffes on the side of the road as we left Singida. Unfortunately our baggage, consigned earlier by sea, had been offloaded in error in Mombassa, Kenya. Pat was making great efforts to get it re-routed to us. It turned up over twelve months later by train coming across country from Kenya. When we opened it, we found everything that could be smashed had been and some of the boxes had obviously been dropped from a great height which was very upsetting. I was very aggrieved about the baggage not being there to meet me.

The house was quite interesting corrugated cottage style (see Fig. 6.1), but rather oddly constructed. It had a lovely large sitting room, tiny dining room and a small kitchenette referred to by the locals as the *Memsahib's* Kitchen. This was where one could do a little fancy cookery on the small paraffin stove and a refrigerator, as there was no electrical supply to the house. The stove was actually more like a primus stove with a metal box around it and was highly dangerous; when the oven was hot it was almost impossible to open the latch on the door. After a few attempts at trying to make a cake and some biscuits, I gave up. One morning I tried to make my own homemade spaghetti, as there were no packets of dried spaghetti in those days. I then hung the strips of pasta on a string line to dry. When I returned half an hour later, there were hundreds of ants climbing up the wall, along the string and carrying away quite big pieces of my spaghetti. Every single piece was festooned with ants. In despair, I tore it all down, put it outside and left them to it – vowing never to try that again. The main kitchen, located some 25 yards from the house, was black with smoke from the wood burning stove. It was for some reason built without windows and appeared to be seething with cockroaches. It had a big black leaded Dover Stove which was designed for cold European climates, as it raised the temperature in the kitchen to about 100°F at times and smoked badly. As a result, the poor cook got pneumonia and had to be rushed to hospital. We arranged for a window to be made in the kitchen building and the houseboy filled in for him for a few weeks. Fortunately, the cook made a full recovery. He made excellent bread, although he had a rather limited repertoire of main dishes.

The bedrooms were rather curiously situated about 20ft away from the main building, across the garden. There was no bathroom and we were issued with chamber pots, an enamel jug filled with water and washbasin. Curiously, they all had the name East African Railways stamped on them. The WC was a good 50 yards further down a path into the bush, and consisted a small hut with a thunder-box; a wooden bench seat with hole in middle, below it was a bucket which was emptied by prisoners twice daily. Our guest wing for visiting officials was another single room which stood alone near the kitchen. The first time I went into it to see what sort of condition it was in and left closing the door firmly behind me, it caused the entire ceiling to collapse as the roofing supports had been eaten away by termites. Eventually, we managed to get the P.W.D. to repair it. Initially therefore anyone who stayed with us had to stay in a put-up bed in the sitting room or use a tent outside – the latter not too advisable as it was lion country.

The house had previously been only used for bachelor officers, who had to spend all their time out visiting their district on safari and had no spare time to do up the house. So when I arrived I noticed that the house urgently needed some repairs done on it. It was also quite dusty and dirty and needed a good supervised clean up. Pat had taken on a houseboy-cook who was quite good, but clearly needed instruction on basic hygiene around the kitchen. The laundry room was also located in a separate building about 25 yards from the house, from which the laundry line was strung between poles. Taking down the laundry from the line last thing at dusk was quite an adventure and Pat and I always went together. We always carried a torch and a large tin tea tray. While I was putting the dry laundry inside the laundry room, Pat stood outside flashing the torch into the scrub like undergrowth in our unfenced so called garden, with

Fig 6.1 *Kisiriri House 1953: This was rather oddly constructed with bedrooms 20 metres away.*

just a few Bougainvillea shrubs growing up against the buildings. Any noise being emitted from the surrounding scrub was greeted with a bash and a crash on the tin tea tray. Then we would both run back to the house giggling. It was quite funny at the time, but I wonder what would have happened to Timothy had we both been eaten by something.

We tried to light the fire in the attractive fire place, but unfortunately it smoked like anything and we had to leave the main door open. We felt most uneasy about doing this as there all sorts of nocturnal noises in the bush around the house, including lions roaring. So we gave up trying to warm the room up in the evenings in the end. The cook served our evening dinner, course by course, from the outside kitchen and we always hoped he would not encounter a lion, leopard or hyena in the process. There was a story doing the rounds about a similar household in another part of the country, where the cook was actually snatched by a lion as he brought the soup through to the dining table. Whether this was one of those colonial myths that frequently circulated or actually true, we never did find out.

We were actually on the far side of the Serengeti, overlooking the plain at about an altitude of some 1,500ft or so. At times it felt as if we were a long way away from civilisation. The only neighbours were an Italian family who were running a small gold mine. It was lovely to chat with them in Italian, and they were most hospitable. They very kindly gave me a gift of two sweet little kittens which I named Susan and Sammy. Fortunately, Judy was used to cats and was one of those dogs who mothered anything; so for a while these poor little kittens were wet all over from being licked, sometimes quite sticky from her meal. Our other nearest neighbours were at a Leprosarium about 20 miles away, which was a specialist hospital for the treatment of Leprosy, which was endemic in this region. We occasionally went to lunch with the European staff at the Leprosarium, which had some of the non-infectious patients working in the kitchens and serving at table. In those days there seemed to one reasonably effective treatment, Chaulmoogra Oil. There was a community of European doctors and their families. The European nurses came from a nearby Lutheran Mission and we only really saw them if we passed that way on safari. Apart from a few locals down in the village below, there were no other Europeans in the area – just Pat, Timothy and me. There was also a nearby Catholic Mission in the district of Umkalama, which we visited from time to time.

Pat was in the office in Kisiriri for part of the week and the other days he toured the district, as there was some unrest in the area. I always went with him, taking Timothy. We returned home by nightfall. The bush was always quiet and appeared deserted during the day, apart from Giraffes and some game birds like Guinea Fowl, Bustards and Ground Hornbills. Most other creatures spent their time lying up in the shade, carefully hidden and you needed to be very vigilant if you wanted to spot them. There were always some interesting and beautiful birds, and I was sorry not to have had with us a specialist bird book for the region. Apart from all this travelling around, we enjoyed spending our evenings reading and playing Canasta together. We also took long walks together in the cool evenings, Pat with his gun ready in case something sprang out of the bush. Mail only arrived when someone came our way, so the arrival of letters was a great excitement. My parents kindly sent out newspapers regularly too. Otherwise we had to rely on our radio, which we had to run off a car battery. Transistor radios were not yet readily available to buy in our area of Africa and were expensive. This meant no music unless one had an old fashioned wind-up gramophone. As there was no electricity, we lit the house in the evening by oil lamps. I never really did enjoy the crushing heat of Africa, it was just too exhausting, but I put up with it because there was so much enjoyment to be had elsewhere – the wide open spaces, wonderful wildlife and game, and full and happy life. I kept busy sewing clothing for Timothy and myself, making curtains and other household items. I also wrote regular letters home, to our friends in Eritrea and to my ATS friends.

We had a big Government Issue car which, on the bumpy dirt roads, had the rather disconcerting habit of shaking the bonnet clasp lock loose. This meant it would fly up at regular intervals completely cutting off our total view of the oncoming road. Fortunately the roads were not busy at all, but it made it difficult to avoid the large potholes and any game wandering across the roads. In October, Pat went off on a week's safari alone, staying in various official rest houses (see Fig. 6.2). I stayed at the house, but had my and Timothy's bed brought into the dining room (together with the chamber pots and wash basins). There was no way I was going out into the bush on my own to go to bed or anything else. At the end of the day the servants went home to their village below about two miles away, and left us all alone in the little house on top of the ridge. The windows were similar to the Edwardian types, with small panes of glass in them. Unfortunately, there was very little glass left in the windows. On the second night it was quite windy and my dog Judy was very uneasy and clearly disturbed. She kept looking anxiously at the windows and growling. I worried in case we might have a native intruder peering in, so I draped a bedspread over them and jammed them shut. I could hear nothing over the wind. The next morning the houseboy arrived in an excited state to say that a pride of four lions had attacked a herd of cows nearby, killed and feasted on two of them. The pride had clearly circled the house, as their pug marks could clearly be seen in the flower beds underneath the windows. Apparently, they had visited us first. No wonder the dog was so upset. We often heard lions roaring at night, but very rarely ever saw them. I was very pleased to welcome Pat back from his safari at the end of that week. He was urgently called out later that same night to the village to try and free a leopard which had become trapped in a hut when it had entered to get a goat. When he arrived he realised there was a small child trapped (under the bed) in the hut with the leopard. In order to get the child to safety, he reluctantly had to destroy it. The leopard was skinned and its pelt was sent to the government offices at Dar-es-Salaam, as the trade in leopard pelts was illegal.

We had plenty of official visitors, all glad of a place to stay, a welcoming cup of tea and meal, on their long journeys through the district. These included game wardens, veterinary and agricultural officers. It made a nice change and gave us a chance to catch up on the news and gossip and some brought post with them too. Luckily Pat and I always enjoyed each other's company and so we were never bored.

We heard in early November that we were to move to Dodoma, the provincial headquarters. In a way we were rather sorry not to be staying in Kisiriri, but the promise of a better house was something to look forward to. The Kisiriri district was being upgraded and they wanted a more senior officer to take it over at this stage. The District Officer and his pregnant wife arrived and were clearly quite shocked at what they found by way of accommodation. After a time I understand quite a lot of work was done to make the place more habitable, with indoor sanitation and a proper adjoined bedroom wing to the main house. To begin with, they must have found it all very hard too. I did wonder what his wife made of the rather strange accommodation set up. Sadly, later on she and the children were to lose their lives at sea going out to join him on a subsequently posting to the Solomon Islands. I started to pack up once more, we celebrated our eighth wedding anniversary and life continued much the same with a few safaris.

We also went to Singida, the district headquarters, for a long weekend and enjoyed the change of scene. We stayed with a fellow officer and his wife whom we knew quite well. When it came to bath time our hostess explained that, because of the severe drought affecting the area, water was rationed. Therefore, we would all have to share the same bath water. As I was the lady visitor, I was first in. The water ran out of the taps quite brown and became more and more like liquid mud as the bath filled, all 6 inches of it, but in that heat anything was refreshing. After I had bathed, the hostess took her bath, followed by her husband and then poor Pat. Back in Kisiriri we had at least been able to enjoy a decent wash-in bowl, or a bucket of reasonably clean water brought from a nearby well. It was carried on the heads of two prisoners, who repeatedly walked the 150 yards or so most of the day to refill the tank which held our small water supply. The tap was outside, and we took our water directly from it, topping it up with hot water from the main kitchen. In between trips to the well, they took regular naps. I suppose it must have been better than being locked up in a stuffy old jail.

We somehow had managed to acquire quite a lot of luggage to move down to Dodoma. It was, rather unusually, pouring with rain when we left Kisiriri and arrived in Dodoma some ten hours later, having broken down en route. We stayed with Pat's boss, the District Commissioner Leonard Heaney and his wife. They had a large sundowner (cocktail) party that night which we thought was to celebrate our arrival, but it transpired that this was a regular event. It was helpful, as we met quite a lot of people and fellow colleagues of Pat. The next day, we inspected our new home, which was a modern bungalow, with all its mod cons. As it had not rained in months, the reservoir was almost empty and water was rationed much as it was in Singida. It was turned on at the main pumping station for just one hour daily, so we frantically filled up the bath and all available containers when it was running. The trouble was that this was exactly what everyone else was doing; so the water pressure was extremely low and came out rather brown and sludgy, similar to that we had experienced in Singida. We tried to keep all the washing up water to flush the WC once a day. After we had bathed, we then washed our clothes in the same water. A certain amount of water was also set aside for kitchen purposes which needed boiling and filtering for drinking. Our house was very dusty and grubby and I set about cleaning it up and engaged a servant called Hali Mojo, who unfortunately turned out to be rather useless. He could always think of a good reason for not doing something. He had a strange laugh, something like a hyena, which could be heard several houses away but at least he was cheerful.

Pat started work, very disappointed at having to share the district with another District Officer Cadet. It must have been quite frustrating for him after all his previous sole postings in Eritrea with so much more autonomous responsibility for quite large regions of the country. Typically, he threw himself wholeheartedly into the job. I should explain that although Pat was at this time initially appointed as a relatively junior District Officer Cadet when he joined the District Administrative Service, it was the most prestigious service to be in. However, because of his Military service record in Eritrea doing a very similar job but at a much more senior level, he was remunerated on a much higher scale than the usual cadets who were generally postgraduates. Unusually, because of his high level administrative experience in Eritrea and excellent references from Senior Colonial Service Officers with whom he had worked, Pat was the first of the Colonial Service Office appointees admitted who had not attended university because of the outbreak of WWII. He did though attend the usual Devonshire University of Oxford Colonial Service training course. It made for an awkward situation because he had so much relevant experience; he was sometimes resented in certain circles by perhaps less able, but more senior officers. I too felt very resentful, on his behalf, because in effect it was rather like being demoted and it made life quite hard for both of us.

It was a very expensive time for us. We were expected to provide all our own household equipment such as refrigerators – something which I understand did not happen in any of the other British overseas territories. We had to also provide our own vehicle to use for administering the territory through safari, although a small mileage allowance was payable to us. To finance the car, primarily used in Pat's work, we had to take out a Government loan which we paid back over the three or four year tour of duty. By that time, after bouncing around on dirt roads, the vehicle was only fit for scrap and spare parts. So at the beginning of the following tour of duty we had to take out yet another Government loan. This meant that we never were ever quite out of debt. We were also not guaranteed accommodation either at any of our postings, but fortunately we always managed to be allocated one.

Quite a large sum of money was also deducted from Pat's salary at source towards a Widows and Orphans Fund, and we were liable to taxation. With all this on our shoulders, we found ourselves in dire financial straits. Coupled with this, we were expected to keep up appearances according to your rank. In reality this meant having at least two or more servants and one was expected to entertain in a proper fashion. All this was patterned on the old days of the Colonial Service, when most of the officers serving in it were from the upper echelons of society and had their own private incomes. The new breed of Colonial Service officers, to which we belonged, had no private incomes and came mostly from the post war armed forces or were graduates. Many also had their wives and children to support in very trying conditions. Previously, Colonial Service officers could not marry without permission from their Senior Officers. The only good thing about all this was that at last he was in a pensionable service, or at least he would be, once he had passed his two year probationary period. To this end, he was he was busy studying Colonial Law and Swahili, with a view to taking the required examinations. Without the language he would not be able to progress within the service. We did receive free medical and dental treatment and the government paid his passage back to the UK at the end of the three or four year tour. He was entitled to fourteen days of local leave each year. He was allocated £30 towards a uniform outfitting for the job, which barely covered the basics for the required ceremonious, office and safari uniforms, plus formal evening wear.

We found that the staff seemed to be quite different from those we had worked with in Eritrea. They seemed a lot less accommodating and generally unpleasant to deal with. There seemed to be some sort of job demarcation. This meant we therefore needed several servants with each doing only a few hours of work on specific jobs. Most houses had a gardener, laundry boys, houseboys, cook's-boy to cut wood and put it into the stove and so on. Very few women worked in the European houses with the exception of nursemaids. Rates of pay were very low and staff tended to help themselves to kitchen store cupboard food to off-set this. They were pitifully poor and you could not really blame them for wanting to improve their lot. I do not know how the poor things survived on their very limited diet of porridge

Fig 6.2 *Central Province 1953: One of the better official Rest Houses with vehicle and office staff.*

and little else. We took on a cook-safari boy and a *dhobi* (wash-boy for clothes). There was no need for a gardener, as outside the house it was a barren acre of land. Someone had put stones in circles around the driveway and a few drought resistant shrubs struggled to survive. I used to water them from time to time when we could spare the water from bathing. Unfortunately, we discovered that the staff had a weakness for alcohol and for the first time we had to lock away the liquor and start counting the cutlery too. Most of the items taken were sold on to Arab or Indian traders and people lost valuable rings, ornaments and other personal items.

Because of the serious drought conditions, a famine situation was threatening to overtake the region. The District Officers had to tour their districts for up to a minimum of twenty days a month. This meant that at this time I hardly saw Pat. Sometimes he just came home to sleep and collect a change of clothing, before he set off again for several more days away. I busied myself with sewing curtains and making chair covers. I also ordered a carpet from Dar-es-Salaam to help make the place look more homely.

We had two bedrooms, a sitting room with a fireplace, a dining room, kitchen and store room, bathroom and WC. The building walls were grey cement, as was the floor which crumbled into a fine dust which had to be swept out each morning. Some people were able to paint the floor and polish it, but this was too expensive for us to attempt. We did later move to houses where this had been done, and the floors would have a nice cardinal red polished hue which looked lovely, especially in the sitting and dining rooms. The Public Works Department had issued us with twin beds, a dressing table, four hard framed sitting room chairs with biscuit like cushions which needed covering. There was a dining room table, six chairs and a sideboard. No furniture was issued for a child, so we had to buy a native string bed and Timothy slept on that for two years. We were either issued with a desk or a bookcase, but not both. Usually, we opted for the desk. We could get wooden boxes in those days and most of us put frilly covers on them and used them in the bedrooms. I believe we did have one bedside table issued, eventually. Planks of wood, resting on bricks or wood blocks, made very good shelves for books and book cases. With a few lamps made up from bottles and a picture or two, we all made our homes as comfortable as possible. When our baggage eventually pitched up, we had a few small mats and ornaments. The Public Works Department was responsible for the upkeep of the house. They had two colours options for the walls – beige or white, depending on which was available at the time. All our woodwork was unpainted and stained brown. It was very depressing.

Wherever possible, wives got jobs to help supplement their husband's salary. These were few and far between. If you were a nurse or shorthand typist, you stood a better chance. Some people were very crafty and had everything lined up before they actually arrived. Jobs went from person to person in a sort of undercover black-market. A newcomer to a station would be safely installed in a job before we knew it was even available. I was not terribly interested in permanent work and with a three year old child it would have been difficult. I did offer my services as a relief worker. When it became known that I could take over a job for a few weeks while someone was on leave and then happily step down again, I found myself quite in demand. So, during the two and a half years that we were in Dodoma, I was able to make a little pocket money but pay was very low. Once I worked as a typist at the Law Courts, typing out a terrible backlog of court cases. The magistrate's handwriting was undecipherable and the native clerk just could not read it. Since Pat's handwriting was equally difficult to read, they thought maybe I could help type them out. So for a month I took Timothy to the Court offices and, happily seated under the desk with his Dinky Cars, I typed all afternoon. I also worked for the Chief Education Officer when his secretary when on local leave and other similar jobs.

At least there was no rabies in Tanganyika then, so the dogs were not muzzled. Judy had a bad reputation for biting people and I seemed always to be paying out 5/- to people who claimed their trousers had been ripped. Until one day I caught a man teasing her through the fence to make her jump at it and bite him. It was a good hand-out and the local people had cottoned onto the idea quite early on. The servants also seemed to know what was going on and were conniving with the villagers. So, poor Judy had to be tied up to stop this happening. This was typical behaviour of the Wagogo tribe, who we found a difficult people to work with.

My neighbour hired and fired her servants pretty much weekly. I think she tried everyone who came to the door, but they either drank, pilfered or both. I decided to work with Hali Moja, difficult though he was, on the basis that the devil you know was better than the one you did not. Another had an excellent cook who could make wonderful cakes, scones and who made peanut butter for the children. He was one of the old school of servants trained by some long gone *Memsahib*. While we were on leave, she sacked him because he refused to clean the kitchen windows. I told her if it had been me, I would have done them myself rather than lose such a gem. I was quite surprised at how some people treated the local peoples working for them. Unfortunately, by the time we got back he had departed for his own tribal area. Each servant was supposed to have a reference, which they usually presented to you at the back door for inspection. Some of them were quite amusing. One I read said: 'This boy has been with me for a year; he works well but has serious trouble with the weight of his fingers'. Another said: 'This man is a good houseboy, with very taking ways'. Very likely the references did not even belong to them at all, as they traded and swopped them. Appointing staff therefore was very pot-luck. I spotted this in the letters section of *The Telegraph* newspaper some years later:

'With reference…

SIR – Mr B Chappell (March 23) may appreciate the ambiguous reference occasionally supplied in Tanganyika: 'This man has

served me to his entire satisfaction. If he asks for a berth, give him a wide one.' T.J. TAWNEY'
The Telegraph (1987)

During our stay in Dodoma we lost several small items, one being the silver medallion presented to Timothy at his Christening and which I hung over his bed. He also lost his Swiss Army Knife, which had been my father's. Although it was too big for such a small boy, it was one of his most prized possessions. Money vanished from my handbag, so I had to take it with me everywhere, even to the bathroom. Drink was another target and we locked it up, but ever resourceful they always had a few keys hidden away and found their way into the cupboard. However, this all stopped after someone drank half a bottle of Syrup of Figs which had been locked in there too to keep it away from Timothy.

During one period when *dhobis* were being dismissed (and hired), I took on a wonderful cook from Kenya. He was from the Luo tribe and was excellent. He also did the laundry work. Hali Moja tried to get rid of him by telling me he had hashish in his quarters and smoked it, but as most locals did the tactic did not work with me. Unfortunately not long after we had hired him, the Government decided that all Kenyans would have their permits cancelled forthwith and be deported, because of the fear of spreading of Mau-Mau unrest and violence into neighbouring Tanganyika. So, I sadly lost a very good cook. I hoped he was safe when he returned to his home village, as there was quite a lot of inter-tribal fighting there too at this time.

Pat wore crisp white shirts and knee high socks, which he changed every day, so there was always a lot of laundry. Because of the heat we both had a change of underwear at least once daily; there were my dresses and Timothy's clothes, beside table linen. Everything was starched, except underwear, and beautifully done. I must give credit to the *dhobis* who were excellent. They had to iron with a charcoal iron or a flat iron. We did have electricity but none of the *dhobis* were used to electric irons, or come to that any electrical items. We had to boil and filter our water daily, and this was closely supervised by me. I always watched hygiene very carefully, so I was quite upset to discover that Hali Moja was using our toothbrushes to clean his teeth too. I wondered why he shut the door of the bathroom when he cleaned, but innocently thought he was washing the floors behind the door. Sometime later, Pat complained that his razor had been blunted and Hali Moja was again the culprit. This made Pat furious and he yelled at him very loudly, earning the nickname *Bwana Piri-Piri* (Mr Hot Pepper), by which he was known throughout his whole career in Tanganyika.

The District Officer's role was more of an elder or patriarchal figure, rather than a ruler. As before, Pat's days were taken up with visiting tribes and working with the Tribal Elders to resolve problems such as assaults, thieving, along with the general administration of the territory. By now we were both in our early thirties and had seen a lot of life. Our social life was still pretty full, with official dinner parties to give and attend, with cocktail parties being given for VIPs. We got together with friends and went on picnics into the bush from time to time.

It was so hot and dusty and there was very little game near Dodoma, so we did almost no shooting for the pot. Our main meat supply came from locally slaughtered cattle, which were underfed and tough to eat. There were no vegetables, except the occasional tomato and we lived on tinned peas. There was no tropical fruit either. However, we sometimes received bananas or oranges kindly brought by someone visiting from the more fertile Tanganyika highlands, but this was rare. The small *duka* (shops) were owned by Indians, trying to scrape a living out of the even poorer Africans and the odd European. They sold basics such as rice, curry powder, dried beans and bolts of white cloth which were made into shorts for Government staff, sometimes cotton dress material and saris. Many of them had sewing machines and could be seen pedalling away at the front of the store, making khaki uniforms for policemen or white ones for District Administration. At nights all the goods were packed into the back of the store and the family slept on the floor and on beds in the rafters. It was the custom at Christmas time for the Indian Traders to bring gifts to their customers and we were given special permission to accept these. Usually it was whisky and chocolate, which was nice. Anything else offered outside of the festive season was considered to be a bribe and could not be accepted.

Unlike Eritrea, there was a strict colour bar in Tanganyika which we found most unpleasant. No African or Indian could belong to the European Clubs and none could go to the local European school. Too close friendships between ranks were discouraged and to make the point, one senior officer justified this to me by saying: 'A man on good terms with his underlings cannot be a good general'. There was a definite hierarchy within the service. First came the Provincial Commissioner (with his wife) who had probably been in the Colonial Service for years, having worked his way up through the Service from his initial posting as District Officer. Next came the District Commissioner, usually another long service administration officer (with his wife) and then followed the District Officers (and their wives). Each one knew their place in the scale of things and defended it.

In our case, there were two other District Officers and we were third in rank, so I had four wives senior to me and on whose toes I could not tread. There was always some dispute as to whether the Senior Medical Officer, Chief Agricultural Officer, Chief Veterinary Officer or Chief Magistrate (and wives) ranked above or below the District Officers. It was very tedious and so awkward at times. It really caused a lot of unnecessary and ridiculous in-fighting between the services, who after all were out there trying to do a good job. Any officer's wife, whose behaviour caused any comment, would result in her husband being sent for by a Senior Officer and 'carpeted' (admonished). The Administration Service had to be above reproach. We were given to understand that stockings, hats and gloves must be worn at all official functions. In that sort of heat it was purgatory. Tights had not been invented, so we all had to wear some sort of corset or something to hold up the stockings. Struggling into a roll-on-girdle belt in that climate was not easy.

I found all this nonsense very hard to take, being a rebel at heart. Tanganyika, especially Dodoma, was an unhappy place for me. I tried to make the best of it and did some voluntary work for the RSPCA. One of my jobs was to go to the railway station and watch the cattle being loaded onto the train. The Government had started moving cows out of the area to pastures better able to feed them. Cattle mean a great deal more to an African than just his bank balance; they indicate his status within his tribe and are used as gifts in marriage and so on. He will therefore keep them until they drop dead rather than sell them. Although little rain had fallen on Dodoma all season, it was not enough to avert a full scale famine. The RSPCA was worried that the trucks were overloaded, but the vet who always came too said they had to be packed in to prevent them from falling over on the very long journey. I duly reported this to the Dar-es-Salaam Head Quarters of RSPCA. I had as an assistant an African who was very supportive of the work the RSPCA did and animal welfare. He used to tour the district and bring me his report. One of his reports amusingly stated: 'This man has been overloading his arses.' When I showed it to the vet, he quipped that I should perhaps contact the Medical Officer. There was always a laugh somewhere to lighten the day. Another of my voluntary jobs was to take on sewing classes. Given my sewing skills this was a bit like the blind leading the blind. However, as a District Officer's wife it was expected of me and I was happy to help out where I could. I walked or sometimes drove to a room in the town where the African Women's Club assembled. I noticed that if I invited other officer's wives to help out, they usually were not keen to take on much voluntary work. I did sometimes co-opt my friends to bring fresh ideas to the work.

An amusing moment came when I had a coffee party for several friends and Hali Moja wheeled in the newly acquired tea trolley. He was wearing a recently discarded pair of my diaphanous silk pyjamas and an old straw hat. There was a polite stunned silence while he poured out the tea and then went out of earshot, we all had the giggles. He did some quite odd things and I did once spot him crawling through the serving hatch between the kitchen and dining room, to lay the table, presumably to save time.

I took up golf in Dodoma and played most early evenings. I had the use of the car when Pat was at home, but when he was not I had to walk to the course which was some distance in the heat. When I started not going because the golf clubs were so heavy in the heat, my caddy came to find me. After that, he very kindly came to the house to fetch the golf clubs and walk with me to the course. He was only a young boy barely more than ten years old and I could not bear to see him carrying all the club selection, so I just took a putter and iron to play with which did not do a lot for my golf score. Compared to household staff, caddies were better paid and earned 2/6- per night, so it was probably worth his bother to collect me.

There were about a hundred European families distributed amongst all departments and East African Railway. The railway passed through the town, being the central line from Dar-es-Salaam to Kigoma and beyond. We were all housed in modern bungalows, some better than others. Some people were permanently stationed there and over the years had cornered the better houses. There was the ridiculous situation whereby each time someone left, there was a hasty reshuffling of houses. You had to apply to move and if granted permission, move swiftly. This meant that all the worst housing was left to the transiting people like the District Officers. Some housing was specifically allocated to certain officers such as Medical Officers or Senior Staff quarters. Our house had a short cut through the garden when we first moved in. Everyone walked through the garden and even drove through it, just to cut off 100 yards. The driveway was open ended, from the back to the front of the plot, and people used to come right by the veranda. Apart from being dangerous for Timothy, it made the dust swirl into the house and it was something of an invasion of privacy. I decided to close off the garden and hedged it with Euphorbia, which I collected up from all over the place and stuck the various 2ft high saplings into the ground. Unsurprisingly, I did have complaints about closing up a right of way, but I stuck to my guns. In the end it grew to a great height and made a good private area.

It was very hot and sticky most of the year, although the temperature cooled slightly at night and for part of the year by a few degrees. We had no ceiling fans, but as electricity was expensive this was no great loss. We also had to pay for water supplies too. The white ants were not quite so bad here, but there were scorpions, spiders, ants, centipedes. One harmless species of quite big slow moving millipede was called a *Songalolo* by the locals. Given its meandering pace, it was nicknamed 'Tanganyika Train' by the European children. There was a very large type of venomous scorpion in Dodoma, which swarmed out if there was any rain. People used to go out into their gardens killing them with golf clubs as they emerged from the sand, to prevent them from entering their homes in large numbers.

I had to make my own clothes and Timothy's, and also cut my own hair – which was not easy. Pat used to have the Indian barber cut his hair, but because of the high incidence of scabies, ringworm and head lice, provided his own sterilised comb and scissors for the task.

The weather got considerably hotter towards the middle of 1954 with dust devils becoming a regular feature. The local people became desperate for food and we had to help people begging at the door. The Government fortunately started a feeding programme and one of the international aid agencies sent food. Every available officer was drafted into teams that were sent around the countryside handing out the *posho* (grain meal) and other items for the starving local communities. During this terrible time, I rarely saw Pat as he was away from Dodoma for weeks at a time. This extract from a newspaper of the time, gives an accurate picture of the serious nature of the dreadful situation:

'IRINGA AFRICANS TOOK IN TRIBE'S HUNGRY CHILDREN'
The proceeds of the Southern Highlands Province Help for Ugogo Appeal were delivered at Chipogoro last week in the presence of a

large crowd of Wagogo, whose Senior Chief, Mtemi Mazego, made a speech of thanks on behalf of all his people.

The District Commissioner Mpwapwa, Mr F.J. Riddell and District Officer Dodoma, Mr P.W. Reardon, were also present to receive the consignment of four lorry loads of assorted foodstuffs sent from Iringa and Mbeya.

A gift of several hundred shillings collected in Iringa District was also handed over to the senior Ugogo Chief by Chief Adam Sapi, Chief of Uhehe, who went to Chipogoro together with a District Officer from Iringa.

Starving Children

The results of Mr Oldaker's appeal to help the drought-stricken neighbouring area have been generous contributions from members of all races, European, Asians, Africans in Southern Highlands Province, and an unprecedented spirit of good-will has been evinced from Africans in comparatively easy circumstances towards members of another tribe who this year are facing famine in Ugogo.

This good-will is indicated by the offer of over 60 Iringa African residents to care for starving Wagogo children until the end of the famine.

Co-operation

It is to be hoped that long after the famine is forgotten, the Wagogo will remember with gratitude the help received from their neighbours of all races and that the Help for Ugogo Appeal has established the precedent that men of all tribes and races in Tanganyika will co-operate and help each other, not only in times of trouble, but also in times of prosperity.'

Extract from a newspaper Article: Standard Correspondent (source unknown)

I went about my daily rounds much as usual, organising the household, handing out the bar of soap for the laundry, sending for the groceries and doing voluntary work. I still managed to find some time to play golf and get to coffee parties. At nights I locked myself in and did not go far. We were in wild game country and were reminded every afternoon of this, as the hyena came down from the rocks around 5 o'clock. You could hear them with their distinctive laughing call. We made sure all the children were safely in doors well before that time. Someone spotted a lion one night in their car headlights in the town centre around 10 o'clock. It all came to a head, when the Indian lawyer and his family had their little dog snatched by a leopard from under their feet early one evening. Fortunately, in all the commotion, it dropped the little dog, which somehow survived its ordeal. Local Africans returning home from their jobs were also having some serious problems, so the decision was made to put poison bait down at the back of the hotel in the centre of the town, near the dustbins. On the first night over 30 animals were killed including lions, hyenas, leopards and other smaller creatures. It seemed rather a shame to kill these beautiful creatures, but they needed to make the town safe for its inhabitants.

Timothy started at nursery school for a morning and later attended full time primary school in Dodoma. Pat was in the throes of studying for further qualifications for the Colonial Service and was finding it very difficult to do so with his heavy work load. So, we took a two week local leave break and went to Mombassa in Kenya, staying in Likoni. It was wonderful to get away from Dodoma, see more of each other and have time with Timothy by the sea. We also enjoyed being able to have a more varied diet again, with fresh fruit and vegetables. Pat managed to get his studies done and it did us all a power of good. I had not been feeling very well for quite a long while; slightly under par always, which was later diagnosed as low fever malaria. It was caused by the preventative measures, in this case Paludrine, allowing the breakthrough of the parasite. Years later, I was told I should have taken a much higher dose, but at that time one tablet was considered sufficient. Pat changed to the new drug Daraprim and promptly went down with a full blown case of malaria in the middle of a dinner party. He was quite ill and he returned to taking Paludrine daily after that.

About this time, we dismissed Hali Mojo after a series of incidents and took on a cook called Isadore and a *dhobi* called Rajab. Not long after that there was a fracas in the kitchen; Isadore accused Rajob of putting a spell on me in order to get her dismissed. The pair of them always were bickering and telling tales, so after a few months I got rid of them both and took Hali Moja back. He was delighted to be back and seemed to be a slightly reformed character. His wife was pleased too, as she had been Timothy's babysitter in the evenings and enjoyed earning a few shillings for herself.

By this time, I was quite fed up of Dodoma, as was Pat. He passed his Swahili and further Law exams and was confirmed in his appointment as a pensionable officer, which was a great relief all round. We had been three years in Dodoma, and it had been a miserable time. Despite that fact we had made many friends, most of whom I kept in contact with for many years afterwards. We were dreadfully short of money, often parted from each other and living in very trying conditions. To me the future looked dreary and never ending. The poor native peoples were poverty stricken and during droughts we could only help in a small way with famine relief programmes and support. They suffered from the usual illnesses such as TB, VD, ringworm, scabies and Leprosy. After a while, you began to accept that this is how things are in this part of Africa and tried to close your mind down to the more distressing aspects of it. We decided to take some home leave and packed up our boxes, by now thirteen tea chests, put them in store and went down on the train to Dar-es-Salaam. Judy our Alsatian and her companion, Jinny the black Beagle bitch, came too. They kindly were boarded for me by the RSPCA for the duration of our leave home. So, on 10th January, we left from Mombasa on board the SS Uganda, and had a pleasant if rough trip home to Britain.

7

KILOSA

We spent about five months in England staying with relatives and on 15th June 1956 we returned to East Africa on MU Uganda, a small 12,000 ton passenger ship from the P&O line. It was a bit of an old tub, but comfortable with a friendly crew and an excellent nursery and facilities for children of all ages. We called at Marseilles, Genoa and Port Said and travelled along the Suez Canal. It was very hot, with temperatures of 100°F and the engine room apparently recorded a temperature of 123°F. There was no air conditioning in those days. We stopped at Aden and just afterwards we left ran into a storm which made everyone very ill, but fortunately I did not seem to suffer from seasickness. On this trip we met a lot of other people, almost all civil servants from the Colonies, all of us short of money as usual. We made new friends and our Christmas card list grew quite long. Pat had decided to bring a new car back from the UK and had chosen a Vauxhall Velox. Every time we came into port, it had to be removed from the hold so that the rest of the cargo could be unloaded. Pat spent many an anxious hour watching his precious car swinging around on end of a hawser.

In Mombassa, Pat received an urgent message to take the first plane to Dar-es-Salaam, as he was to be posted up-country again. We thought it must be very important, so he cut his leave short. I saw him off on the plane and returned to the ship to keep an eye on the car, baggage and Timothy until the ship arrived in Dar-es-

Salaam. On the way we visited two fascinating places, the Germanic port of Tanga and the Arabic spice island of Zanzibar. I was met in Dar-es-Salaam by two officials and was taken to the New Africa Hotel. A letter awaited me from Pat, in which he was clearly upset about the house he had been allocated. He had also discovered that there had been absolutely no urgency at all for him to have taken up duty early, as the previous officer was still in post. Fortunately Pat's cousin, who was working for a civilian firm, was now based in Dar-es-Salaam with his new bride. They collected me the next day and I had lunch with them before catching the evening 8 o'clock train. I had nineteen pieces of baggage, one of which was a Singer Sewing Machine Co dress-making dummy, two dogs and a child. Pat's cousin never forgot the sight of me going up the platform with a string of porters, the dummy, a small child and two dogs, one of which was trying to bite anyone who came near us.

Pat met us when we arrived in Kilosa at 8 o'clock the following morning after a relatively relaxed overnight journey in our compartment, into which I had secreted the dogs this time in. We had been allocated an old German house, which had been built when it was a German colony sometime pre 1918. It was in a dreadful state and the building had actually been condemned. Nevertheless, it was all that was available for us to live in. It was located on a rocky patch of ground at the edge of a hill slope, near all the other houses. It was the usual case of last in gets the worst again. Fortunately we already knew quite a few of the other twelve families on the station, so we were a jolly crowd. Surrounding Kilosa was a very large sisal growing area. This meant that there was one or two oasis of gracious living to visit on the plantations. One plantation manager had a lovely house with a swimming pool, which they used to invite us all to use in turn. In this respect, the colonial officers and families, were all a bit like poor relations waiting for the kind handout. Apart from the tiny railway station, there was a one-room shop owned by an elderly Greek gentleman. We had to go some miles away to Morogoro for any key supplies.

The house (see Fig. 7.1) seemed likely to have started life as a store room, with bits added over time at intervals. It had one tiny bedroom, a kitchen with a Dover Wood Stove and a table with a chair. There was a bathroom which actually had running water and there was plenty of it too, which was a great luxury. The water for the house was heated by the use of a Dutch style Tanganyika boiler. This was a 40 gallon petrol drum placed on its side, in a concrete base and plumbed in. A space was left underneath for the fire. It had to be stoked constantly and lasted a year or two before it needed replacing. Then one bathed in water heavily tainted with petrol or paraffin for weeks after that until it cleared. To clean the actual drum in the first place it was fired inside, a highly dangerous practice given its contents. The house structure and fixtures were badly damaged by white termite ants, which had got into everything and continued to attack any wood they could find. The ceiling boards did not quite reach across the ceiling, leaving gaps through which the baby bats fell down into the sitting room at intervals. They flew madly about and I made a butterfly net to catch them in and

Fig 7.1   *Kilosa March 1957: Pre 1918 German house structurally condemned.*

was able to safely put them outside without touching them (as some carry rabies). It was just as well I was not the hysterical type, but I doubt I would have got much sympathy from Pat who believed strongly in the British stiff upper lip attitude to the difficult situations we encountered. We were so overwhelmed by the smell of bat dung in the roof, that Pat arranged for the Public Works Department to come and clean it out and repair the rafters. They got over half a ton of bat dirt out of the roof, which was on the verge of collapsing as a result of the weight and termite damage. The Public Works Department Engineer took pity on me in these reduced living conditions, and built on an extra veranda to add a little to our living space. Up to that point Timothy had had to sleep on his native string bed in the sitting room, as there was nowhere else he could sleep where there was any ventilation. We had the usual motley mix of government furniture supplied, none if it matching; even our twin beds were different heights. There was no electricity, so once more we were back to lighting pressure oil lamps each night. I bought myself a new paraffin stove with a nice oven.

I do not know why more was not done to make life more bearable for us all. Most of the time things were done the hard way. This was simply because the more senior old timers insisted that it had always been done that way. I heard about an administration station in Rhodesia where proper baths had been ordered and plans were in progress for the plumbing to be modernised. However, when the new baths arrived at the office for onward delivery, the District Commissioner who was one of the old guard, sent them back saying that the existing tin hip baths were quite adequate and no one would need such modern things as new baths. There was nothing anyone could do, as his word was effectively law.

All drinking water had again to be boiled and filtered, supervised by me. Despite the temperatures of over 80°F, I did the cooking myself on the wood burning stove. Our baggage did not arrive until a month later, which gave me time to have a good clean up. There were no glass windows as such, but only heavy wooden shutters. We held them open with bits of wood and we slept under mosquito nets, as we had in Dodoma. In Kilosa there was a particularly nasty type of mosquito which causes cerebral malaria, which had a high mortality rate. Sadly, the local cemetery was full of the graves of priests and earlier colonial servants, their wives and children. In those days Quinine was the only malaria preventative available and it was not effective against this type of malaria. The coming of the modern drugs changed that, but nonetheless it gave one a bit of turn to know that the danger still existed. We took the greatest possible care to keep all our skin covered as much as possible after dusk, because they were night-biters. It was the custom in the earlier days to wear special long mosquito boots, but if we were sitting outside we used a pillow case to put our feet in.

Our social life was as ever busy, everyone giving coffee and dinner parties, or those lovely East African curry lunches which are legendary even today. I had the house repainted, polished the floors with red polish and got it ready before baggage eventually arrived. Despite my efforts, the garden remained a dry and dusty mess and few plants grew. I took on a gardening boy to sweep and to chop wood. We had to fence in part of the garden to stop the dogs from chasing the locals who came along the nearby road. This was a different tribe of people and they were very much nicer to deal with. Each tribe has very different characteristics in temperament, customs, hair and facial markings, which made it very easy to tell them apart. The official language was Swahili, although each tribe had their own dialect and particular way of speaking Swahili. Pat had been taught pure Swahili, which he was required to use for official duties. The rest of us, including locals, spoke a rather less accurate form of the language, Ki-Swahili. On one instance this lead to the bizarre situation of having to interpret for Pat while on safari business, because the Swahili he was using was not wholly understood by those he was trying to work with which was most frustrating for him. Another time, after Pat had given our houseboy Hali Moji some instructions, he then turned to me and asked: '*Memsahib*, what the *Bwana* says?'

Nonetheless, Pat was still required to take the Higher Swahili Exam and in order that he could study without interruption, we once again went over the border to Kenya for a short local leave at Christmas 1956. We stayed for two nights at the Tsavo National Park in the huts on the reserve. To get there in those days you had to drive through heavily infested Tsetse fly areas. There were big 'DO NOT LEAVE YOUR CAR' notices at the start of the controlled area and one then drove with all the windows shut until we reached the Tsetse Fly Control gated area on the other side. The car was then sprayed all over the outside with DDT insecticide before being allowed to drive on. I drove most of the way and found the steering wheel was very wobbly and difficult to control, but put it down to the badly corrugated dirt road we were travelling on. Fortunately, we made it to the outskirts of Mombassa before the screw in the steering column eventually fell out and we had to get the garage to come out and repair it. At Tsavo National Park we parked the car outside the hut which had comfortable beds and a bathroom ensuite. At reception, one of the staff said: 'Do not be late for dinner please, the rhino run up and down between the huts after dusk.' Needless to say, we ate an early dinner and retired to bed and to lie there listening to them thundering past at intervals. Pat and I stayed again at Likoni to relax at the beach and enjoy the refreshing sea breezes. We stayed ten days while Pat studied intensively before making our way back to Kilosa in the repaired car. On the journey home we saw some buck and giraffe on the road, but everything else was lying up in the heat of the day.

Back in Kilosa everything went on as usual. We temporarily acquired a small monkey called Bruce from someone going on leave. I did not really agree with having such creatures as pets and I managed to find someone else to look after him where he could be kept in more suitable surroundings. We did not have a particularly safe place for him to be let out of the cage, because of Timothy and our dogs. It was quite an amusing creature at times, but because he had no fear of humans he would get into everything, running off with things and destroying them.

When we made trips into the bush or when Pat went on safari, the local people had a custom of giving gifts, such as eggs. These poor people had so little to spare, but it was part of their hospitality custom. There were usually about six eggs, tied up in a scrap of old rag. Frequently they had been under a broody hen, until the call had gone out to produce some for the visiting District Officer. Thus, on more than one occasion, I went home with an egg which was chirping and hatched it out on the warm part of the stove. If it were a hen, we would keep it to produce more eggs. The cockerels generally were fattened up for the pot. Local women used to bring us regular supplies of eggs to the back door and I always felt very sad when I had to reject any of the eggs as they were clearly in need of the money for them. We used to test eggs by floating them in water. If they floated they would be bad, if they stood on end at the bottom of the bowl, there were not newly laid. Those that remained flat on the bottom were fresh and good to eat. Sometimes we arranged for dried onions and mushrooms sent in from Nairobi, but otherwise our diet was very bland.

I did not do any social voluntary work in Kilosa, as Timothy occupied most of my time during the day. We had our books from England each month to read and had quite a busy schedule of official entertaining. Pat played tennis and there was a pool at the club, but the water tended to get very green with algae as there was no filter or chemicals. Timothy started pre-school when he was five years old. There were quite a few other children of similar age, so one of the wives was a teacher and decided to open a little school for the ten children. Up until that point I taught Timothy, through a correspondence course. It proved quite difficult to get him to co-operate with the tasks set, as he was a typical little boy who would much rather be out and about playing. He and his friends attended school from 8 to 12 o'clock and they appeared to be learning quite a lot from these sessions. The school house was with all the other houses which were 1,000ft up on a hillside overlooking the Kilosa plain. I used to drive him up in the Velox which was quite a large car. The road was only wide enough to take one car, with the odd passing place along the way, and a sheer drop on one side. The thing one dreaded was meeting a lorry coming

Fig 7.2 *Kilosa 1957: Princess Tai-Lu balancing on PWD issue furniture in poor repair.*

down the opposite way, which they often did at quite a speed. At the top of the hill, in the narrow school drive, I then had to turn the car around and drive back down. Looking back now having recently seen a 1956 model of the car in a motor museum, I wonder how on earth I regularly drove that large unwieldy car on this taxing journey. I did have moment with it one day though and demolished our wooden garage by accident.

After about four months in Kilosa, it was discovered that the other District Officers had several months more service than Pat. Initially, it had been assumed that Pat was the more senior. We then went through the idiotic process of being moved down a rung in the ladder of seniority, which was maddening. Fortunately, there were only three District Administration Officers, a District Commissioner, and two District Officers – so it was fairly amicable. One of the office staff told us of a delightful story about a tipsy villager who was staggering home through a cemetery, when he fell into a grave which had been dug for the next day. He made great efforts to get out, without success. Later on, he heard someone coming through the cemetery and called out

'Help me get out of this grave!' The other man fled with a scream as he thought it was the devil.

In October, HRH Princess Margaret came to Dar-es-Salaam to officially open a hospital. I and several other wives drove down together to see the ceremony. I took Timothy with me and we stayed with Pat's cousin and his wife again, who were about to transfer to Kenya. I watched the Royal Yacht Britannia come into the harbour and the next day was invited to a big *baraza* (native gathering) which HRH Princess Margaret was attending. She wore some lovely outfits on this visit and I was lucky enough to get a good view of her on several occasions. I got back to Kilosa in time for our eleventh wedding anniversary. Pat gave me a box of Black Magic chocolates and Timothy rather charmingly gave me a toothbrush. We were given a Siamese kitten as a present too, called Princess Tai-Lu (see Fig. 7.2), who eventually lived out her life at the Catholic Mission in Bagamoyo when we left the territory.

The rest of 1956 was much as before. The kitchen swarmed with cockroaches as usual. We were plagued by small sugar ants which got onto every surface and into the food. We had to put the legs of the kitchen table into empty fruit tins, filled with paraffin to stop them getting onto that surface at least. I started making our own bread from a recipe in a Good Housekeeping book. A very good cook, Mohammed, came to work for us and later he brought his son Sardi to work as a houseboy. It made life a lot easier for me and I taught Sardi to cook and make bread, so this meant he could go on safari with Pat. Generally, native cooks would not teach others to cook, in case they stole their jobs. There were plenty of creepy crawlies and partly because of these, and the very active big wild cats, we did not sleep out on our verandas in Tanganyika. We regularly used to hear the leopard call like a coughing sound at nights around the house, but we did not hear many hyenas there. We were surrounded by very tall elephant grass, so they may well have been there along with lions and various other creatures we could hear. We did not see many snakes, but they probably were there too lying low in the heat of the day. I was bitten on my finger by a scorpion which was in the pocket of a dress I was wearing. It was terribly painful for twenty-four hours as the venom spread all the way up my arm. Because of the bad mosquito problem our houses, walls and curtains, were regularly sprayed with DDT. It made a terrible cloud of spray which settled everywhere and was not safe to breathe in. So, before they came, I used to send Timothy to a friend's house and removed the cat and the dogs, only allowing them back in when the DDT dust had been swept out. The spray used to make one's eyes sore. Later on they used Dieldrin, both of which are now on the prohibited list of insecticides. It never seemed to keep the insect populations down for very long or seemed to have an effect on the bats which roosted in the roof space. The government spraying staff had backpacks and did not wear protective mask, goodness knows what it did to them in the long term.

In March 1957 I went back to Dodoma to stay with a friend, a nursing sister. I felt rather poorly and needed a change of air. I did not realise at this stage that I was expecting a baby, so it was actually morning sickness I was suffering from. It was all very exciting, as by then I had given up all hope of having another child. When I got back to Kilosa we were allocated a new house which was one of four bungalows built in a clearing on another hillside. I liked the new house as it was modern, quite attractive and had mosquito netted windows, but we still slept under mosquito nets for added protection. Snakes could still get into the house and had been known to settle under pillows for warmth. One always kept the nets down at all times to prevent this. This way, one also kept scorpions, spiders and centipedes and other creepy crawlies at bay.

One night Mohammed was leaving to go home to the village after cooking dinner when he arrived back, waving his lamp, and shouting *Simba* (lions). He had been crossing the small bridge over a nearby dried up stream and suddenly caught four pairs of eyes glinting. Strangely enough, the day before when I had walked over this same bridge with the dogs, I thought I saw something lying underneath it and there were areas of flattened grass nearby; clearly the usual haunt of this pride of lions. We were a lot more careful after that. I regretted very much that we just did not have any money to buy specialist books about the fauna and flora, as they were just too expensive. At that time the Resident Magistrate, who was an enthusiastic collector of butterflies, encouraged me to take up the hobby. We used to rush around the bush nearby with our nets. He had an antique book with beautiful plates, and we used to consult it if we found a new type. As was the vogue in those days, I began a butterfly collection and as a gift, Pat gave me a beautiful cabinet to display them in.

Not a lot changes in Africa especially in the bush, and the veneer of civilisation is very thin even in towns. I wonder if a lot of differences would be found from the time we spent there compared with today. For example, despite modern medicines, much was still done the tribal way. We did not try to push our own modern or European ideas onto them, nor violate their customs or taboos if we could help it. The women were more likely to ask for knowledge or assistance than the men. There were good schools, although they were not always well equipped or had enough places for all the children. Boys became herders, looking after the tribal, village and family livestock, from a very young age and were only released to attend school when the next youngest was old enough to be a herder. This meant that in a primary school, children were between seven and fifteen years of age in one class. Out in the villages and bush, there was no risk of burglars. But, there were the usual thieving issues in bigger towns and cities, entering a house silently, opening locks and appearing by people's bedsides and taking watches, cash, and jewellery – sometimes without them even waking up. In Dodoma, the poor parson had his robes stolen this way, which was most embarrassing for him. They would try and dope or poison any dogs, so I taught both our dogs never to accept food from anyone except ourselves. The burglars would also pole fish items through open windows, so you had to be quite careful not to leave things on top of the sideboard and tables near windows. To stop you from grabbing the pole, they affixed razorblades to the ends.

In September, Pat was told he was in line for a promotion, which was long overdue. We hoped it might be as District Commissioner in charge of Bagamoyo, on the coast. So, despite now being around seven and a half months pregnant, I once more carefully packed up everything we owned. I was the one who always packed things up and Pat unpacked them at the next house. As I was always a bit dispirited on arrival at quite often a shabby and dirty house, he managed to be enthusiastic and was keen to get things shipshape quickly. This system worked out quite well.

On the day of departure, we had all the heavy boxes loaded onto a lorry which set off ahead of us, just in case it broke down. The family, and animals, were all packed into the Vauxhall Velox. On the back shelf I put my butterfly collection. Timothy was on the back seat with our beagle Jinny and some baggage, along with the Siamese cat with her two kittens who were in a wire box. Judy was on the floor by my feet, and I had a cushion at my back to help me keep comfortable in my heavily pregnant state during the long journey. Pat had packed the roof rack with suitcases. At the last moment, Pat took up the name plate by our driveway and added it to the load on top. It was the custom, as we did not have numbers to the houses, so we simply put our name plate onto a wooden post, at the end of our driveway.

It was dreadfully hot and the 150 mile journey took us over miles of countryside, along dirt roads which were bumpy and dusty. Having the windows open made little difference as the incoming air was so warm. About 30 miles away from Bagamoyo the roof rack fell off the car and the screws were lost in the sand somewhere, so we then had to find room for all the cases and luggage inside the car. The boot was packed full of official papers and other things such as a spare wheel and tool kit. In the melee, the two kittens escaped from the wire cage and got loose in the car and their mother, Tai-Lu, frantically clawed her way out of the box. The dogs went berserk. Eventually, we got everything back under control, but not before my butterfly collection had been overturned and spoilt. The cat had to be put inside a cushion cover with her kittens, as the wire box had been damaged beyond repair and we left it beside the roadside. In desperation, Pat hurled our name plate into the very long grass to get rid of it. Timothy then had to lie flat on top of the piles of cases on the back seat, and the window had to be closed as the two kittens kept escaping and climbing all over the place. We continued the journey with the mother cat howling loudly in her cushion cover, in the stifling heat. The thing that struck me most about that incident was how dreadfully hot the sand was even through our shoes, as we laboured to move everything around. Once we got to Bagamoyo we had a good laugh about it all. Pat used to get quite overwhelmed by me and my eccentric animal collection, but he generally took it all in his stride. He once asked me why all our animals were such characters. He was right, they always were. Many months later one of our official guests, a game ranger, appeared with our name plate which he had found in the course of his travels.

When we arrived in Bagamoyo later that day, exhausted and dusty, we discovered that the officer Pat was supposed to relieve was not actually going for two months, as his wife was ill in hospital with TB. So Pat was to be District Officer for the time being again. We stayed with the District Commissioner for a few nights and then were rehoused.

8

BAGAMOYO

Bagamoyo was once a terminal for the slave trade caravans from the interior. Slaves were put into *dhows*, shipped to Zanzibar and sold to Arab buyers. Arab traders settled the area in the fourteenth century. It was also the last resting-place of David Livingstone's body after it was brought back from Ujiji. We moved into an apartment in an old Arab house, built of mud and lathes, with wooden shutters on every window. The netted windows were damaged and clearly had been patched time and time again, so were not effective as an insect screen. The mosquitoes were the cerebral malaria type mostly, so we covered up after dark and slept under nets. Unfortunately it was very difficult to get funds for repairs and one Public Works Department employee told me that they had some ridiculous sum like 5/- allocated towards the upkeep of a house per annum. The old house was very quaint, with beautiful Moorish architecture (see Fig. 8.1) and would have been lovely had it been in good repair. As it was over ninety years old by the time we moved in, it was showing signs of imminent collapse. The floor of Timothy's bedroom had sunk down in the middle. It had to be shored up within a week or so of our arrival, as we were quite concerned that it may collapse and injure him. We decided that the smallest bedroom would do nicely for the new baby and slept in another small room ourselves. The sitting/dining room was quite large, and we had some bookcase dividers made to give the room some character. These remained in the apartment when we left, as it was pre-allocated to another serving officer and his family. It was very hot on the coast, about 90°F, night and day throughout the year. Although there was a slight breeze on the beach, there was not much in the apartment.

The house had an interesting history. It had been occupied for a while by the famous Mehmed Emin Pasha and he had apparently fallen out of one of the windows and cracked his skull. Sadly, some Arabs in Tanganyika eventually murdered him. We had the house redecorated and it was quite cosy. Mohammed and Sardi, being coastal Arabs, came with us and so the household ran quite smoothly. We engaged a woman called Cecilia as a housemaid/nursemaid for Timothy. She was unusual in that not only was she working, but she was doing so in order to educate her children. She was a very superior character and I liked and respected her a great deal. She was good at her job and very intelligent to talk to. I hope that her plans for her family turned out well. We had no electricity, so it was oil lamps as usual, but the water came from a tap and was clean. The kitchen was the usual cockroach infested room with a Dover wood burning stove. There was no garden, but as the beach was only about 150 yards away, we had a wonderful view of the sea from our upstairs apartment. The servants' quarters were on the floor below and underneath the house, there was also a garage space. The first night we arrived the servants moved into their quarters, which opened onto a pretty courtyard. The following morning they complained that every movement we made on the floor above caused plaster and mud to crack and fall on them as they slept. We quickly found somewhere else more suitable for them and their families to stay.

As I was heavily pregnant, I did very little except sew, read and entertain Timothy. Pat worked alongside the man he was to relieve and it was fortunate that he had stayed on, as he was able to do most of the safari work while Pat stayed with me in Bagamoyo. I was a bit worried that I might have to be rushed to hospital early, so was very reassured by his presence. We had a tiny local hospital which was quite basic, under the command of an Indian doctor, who was generally away

Fig 8.1 *Bagamoyo 1957: Boma. Upstairs Apartment in Arab House with grand facade but interior was showing signs of imminent collapse.*

visiting patients for five days a week. There were two Indian shops and a few Arab ones selling mostly provisions such as rice, beans, onions, a few tomatoes and some cloth. We also could get a few oranges, bananas and plenty of mangoes. The way the mango trees had apparently arrived there was quite interesting. When Bagamoyo was a slavery port, the story was that the slaves were fed mangoes on their forced march across Tanganyika and as they went, they threw away the mango stones, resulting in a clear band of trees that stretched right across the area. You could still see the jetty and slave stockades at the port. Pat and I noticed this on our way across the plain. The trees were quite alien to the type of terrain and were very large and old.

Although we were only about 20 miles from Dar-es-Salaam which had one of the few hospital maternity wards, it was only accessible via a deep sandy track that was only suitable for four-wheel drive vehicles. There were also a number of rivers to cross, which did have bridges but these were frequently swept away in the flash floods, as this extract from a local newspaper reports:

'A flash flood is a terrible thing to be caught in. One is standing in a dried-up river bed when suddenly there is a distant rumble, followed by a thunderous roar. The next minute a great cataract of water comes hurtling down the ravine, apparently from nowhere, like a tidal wave.'

Newspaper Cutting (Source unknown)

I went to Dar-es-Salaam for a visit to the doctor who was to deliver the baby. While there I stayed with a friend I had known in Dodoma. She asked me to come and stay with her for the last two weeks before the baby was due, just to be on the safe side. This I did, and moved into her spare room. It was nice being back in relative civilisation again. As the time neared for my confinement, her husband had to leave by car on a visit to West Africa for a Labour Conference. We made arrangements to call the next door neighbour for help if required, as we did not have any transport. In the event, I went in labour at 2 o'clock in the morning. As there were no telephones in private houses in those days, my friend had to run down the road in her nightie to use the telephone at the night watchman's hut at a nearby factory. The ambulance arrived and the driver idiotically insisted on reversing up the very narrow driveway to the front door, completely flattening several bushes in the garden. When the doors of the ambulance were opened, my friend's rather aggressive dog jumped in and growled at the terrified staff inside. No one could get the wretched animal out, so in the end my friend had to rouse her six-year-old son who managed to persuade the dog to follow him. I eventually got to the hospital, with about an hour to spare before I delivered my daughter, Catherine who was born just after 3 o'clock on the 20th of November 1957. We had a good laugh about all the fuss and bother, whenever we met up with her thereafter. The hospital tried to get a message to Pat to tell him about his newly delivered daughter, but the telephone lines were down after a heavy storm. Eventually, a message was passed as far as Kilosa and then someone going in the direction of Bagamoyo kindly made a detour and brought him the good news of the safe delivery of the baby girl. All the bridges had been washed away, so poor Pat had to drive a detour trip of more than 150 miles over rough tracks and muddy terrain, eventually arriving some three days later. So, Catherine was four days old by the time he saw her for the first time. She was born in the old Ocean Road hospital, which was very comfortable and the maternity ward was air-conditioned.

I returned home to the old Arab house and settled down with the two children. Unfortunately, Catherine had colic and just never stopped crying. How anything that small could scream so much was beyond us. I had to walk around everywhere carrying her all the time or she screamed. I became totally exhausted. I felt unwell and when my gums turned black it was realised that I probably had lead poisoning. No one else was affected and it seemed that the cause of the problem was the paint that had been put on the bathroom wall. It used to melt and run down the walls into the bath water, and I absorbed it through my skin. As soon as we realised what it was, all the paint was removed and I made a full recovery. I then went down with a dose of malaria, thankfully not too seriously as I was still taking the daily Paludrine tables. They tried me out on a new type of malaria drug, but unfortunately the Medical Officer misread the dose and for two days I mistakenly had triple doses of this very strong drug. It affected my eyesight and I was semi-blinded, which made me very traumatised and frightened. Thankfully, I made a full recovery when the drug dissipated from my system some weeks later. As a result of the malaria and the semi-blindness, I became very depressed and coupled with the non-stop crying baby; I was almost always in tears. Today they would perhaps call this condition post-natal depression. The doctor prescribed tablets which put me on top of the world. They were Purple Hearts, one of the new tranquillising drugs that had been developed. I only needed to take them for about a week or so, as they were pretty effective and most helpful. Timothy in the meantime was happily working on his schoolwork through a correspondence course, but was not always very motivated and I was

Fig 8.2 *Bagamoyo 1957: Boma. Miles of beautiful floor tiles all needing to be polished.*

prone to get quite stressed about the situation. So Pat took over the supervision of Timothy's schooling work while he was working in the office, which seemed to work well for them both.

In due course, the District Commissioner left and Pat took over. We then moved to a very big building that housed not only the offices, but also the District Commissioner's accommodation. We had most of the upper floor. There were wonderful wide passages and lofty rooms. The usual Public Works Department furniture supplied of four chairs and a settee, an oil lamp stand and a desk were lost in the sitting room, which was about the size of a small ballroom. The bedrooms were on the same grand scale, with two beds and a dressing table and chair. We used four of the bedrooms for ourselves and official guests. There were several others which, as we had no furniture for them, were simply closed up and not used. The kitchen was large and there were a lot of pantries and store cupboards. Water had to be boiled and filtered and the filters themselves had to be dismantled and cleaned before use, which I closely supervised on arrival at a new house. They used to get bright green with verdigris which is poisonous. Unfortunately, two babies died when their mother failed to take this simple precaution. The dining room held an enormous table that seated fifteen people. The whole thing was quite ridiculous as no one would have had the possessions and pictures to properly furnish that sort of building. The floor had splendid tiles (see Fig. 8.2), miles of them and all needed to be polished. The staff had a strange way of doing this which was remarkably effective; they put rags on their feet and then shuffled about on it. The house, with its magnificent sea views, enraptured people who came to visit.

I never liked the *Boma*, which was its local name (enclosure for livestock in Swahili). It was too big and much more fitting as a museum or public building than a house. The archivist thought so too and eventually did get permission to use it for this purpose. I began to get bites all over me and we thought it was mosquitoes, so Pat had a cage of netting made for Timothy's and the baby's rooms. When I got up in the night to feed her, if I accidentally had my arm against the net, the mosquitoes settled on it in droves. I was still getting really badly bitten on my legs and the doctor diagnosed them as flea bites. I had seen my nursemaid covering her legs with paraffin, and thought it was an anti-mosquito precaution but when I questioned her and the other servants, they said it was to prevent the fleas from biting. Initially we thought that the dogs or cats were the culprits and regularly put them in a makeshift dip. We then discovered it was sand fleas which bred under the floor tiles. They had a twenty-eight day cycle and every new crop seemed to be hungrier than the last. The Medical Department moved in and sprayed Dieldrin every month but we never really got rid of them. I had to put the baby's playpen up on a table, which I managed to acquire from the Public Works Department for this purpose. Eventually, we heard that the floor tiles had been removed and re-laid after thoroughly spraying, although long after we had moved house.

Because we were so near Dar-es-Salaam, we had a lot of official visitors. Anyone who headquarters wanted to get rid of for a day or find something to show them was sent over to us. So, we seemed to have to provide a great many official lunch and dinner parties. In theory, we had an entertainment allowance, but it was a derisory sum. I would not have minded the visitors, some of whom stayed the night, but they so rarely wrote a letter of thanks afterwards. It would have meant a lot to us, given that we largely funded this hospitality and put ourselves out quite considerably to provide decent meals given the very limited produce available.

One day we had a formal lunch party for ten people including the wife of a senior official. I had arranged a splendid meal, starting with a locally caught fish course. Saidi came out of the anteroom with the large fish platter, all beautifully laid out with lemon 'butterflies' on the top of each slice and as he approached the table, he transferred the dish from one hand to the other with a flourish and then unfortunately dropped it. There was dead silence, and a sea of faces stared at me. It was so funny, that I just had to burst out into laughter. It broke the ice and we all had a jolly meal after that, as fortunately everything else went smoothly. Saidi, completely deadpan and very professional, simply removed the platter with the fish debris from the floor and the dining plates from the table and brought in the next course. The senior official's wife said afterwards that had it been her, she would have burst into tears and that she rather admired the way I had handled the situation, which was nice of her. Another time, we had the Governor and his wife for lunch. At that time it was the practice to say to the ADC (Aide de Camp) that the lunch was ready, he then told the Governor's wife, whom then told the Governor and then we would all troop in. This time, we had gone through all this rigmarole when Saidi hissed at me from the door. Apparently, the cream had fallen out of the fridge. So we reversed the procedure, and everyone sat down in the sitting room again. After a twenty-minute wait, while the staff borrowed a tin of cream from a neighbour, we were told the meal was ready and we began the procedure of getting to the table once again. The Governor's wife then told us the tale of one of their first dinner parties, as the young wife of a District Officer. When their house boy announced that dinner was served and flung open the

Fig 8.3   *Bagamoyo 1957: Visit of Governor, Sir R Turnbull, with Patrick at Court House.*

dining room doors, their two young children were beneath the table scraping the ice cream back into the container off the floor. It was to have been the pudding, so a tin of fruit was hastily substituted.

Still not being very fit after my recent illnesses and fully occupied with a small child and new baby, I had decided not to concern myself with any voluntary work at this point. It was however always considered part of an officer's wifely duty to undertake voluntary work for the Red Cross, Girl Guides, or women's clubs. The only one of these in Bagamoyo was the Red Cross Clinic for local children and mothers. It was well attended and run by the Agricultural Officer's wife. There were only about six European families, so when she left the clinic looked as if it might close down as no one else was prepared to take it on. It was not considered a duty for anyone except the administration officers' wives – a sort of extension of their husband's work. One woman from one of the other services once told me that she thought we had all attended a special course on this sort of voluntary work. Far from it, we were all elbowed into it and did our very best just using common sense. A deputation came from Dar-es-Salaam to ask us to take it on and, since these ladies were all high ranking Red Cross personnel and were the wives of Pat's superior officers, I really did not have much option but to agree.

So, once again, I found myself in charge of a clinic, which opened once a week on the outskirts of the village. Women brought their babies for weighing and for medicines. Some of the women had walked ten or more miles from outlying areas. We only had very limited medicines, mainly for the treatment of malaria, minor burns or worms. We referred any severe cases to the doctor, but most refused to go to a doctor or hospital. After a while I was able to get some limited stocks of powdered milk from an international aid agency and used to dole this out into the tins and paper bags that they all brought with them. I also collected all the bottles I could for this purpose. I hope it helped save some of the smaller children from starving. Sometimes when Pat was working in the office I had transport to the clinic but mostly I had to walk down there in the heat. One day, a tiny baby with smallpox was brought in and we rushed it to the hospital. On another occasion, a premature baby weighing about 5lbs was brought in as it was not feeding properly. The doctor I quickly contacted said it did not stand a chance and they had no incubators or facilities for it at the hospital. So I took the mother and baby home, taught her how to make up the bottle feeds, sterilise everything and gave her the bottle to take home. Months later, she brought the baby to the clinic, weighing a healthy 8lbs and looking very bonny. We were all delighted that it had survived against the odds. I had as a helper at the clinic the wife of the African District Officer, called Rosie. It was already the policy by then to begin training up the local people, with a view to handing over the territory for self-government, and I was instructed to teach her the ropes. She was very interested in what we were doing and eventually I handed over to her just before we left Bagamoyo. We used to have forty to fifty patients visit the clinic each week, many of them women, as it was a Moslem area and the women would not attend a clinic or hospital run by a male doctor. It was not permitted for a Moslem woman to utter her husband's name, so she had to bring another woman with her to do this. This meant that there were a lot of other people underfoot and we had to keep very careful records. In places larger than Bagamoyo, there were properly run clinics with European Health nurses but, in tiny outstations such as this, the clinics were generally run in this manner.

I have not mentioned much about Bagamoyo itself, except to say it was on the beach. There was a government rest house which could be hired and people used it for local leave. There were also two or three small private beach houses. Swimming in the sea was a bit risky as it was a known shark attack area. It helped to have a few new faces and different conversation at times. I do not recall it ever raining in Bagamoyo and it was always so dusty and dry. Apart from a few hardy shrubs like Oleander or Bougainvillea, not much vegetation survived. In the village itself, the houses were all of an ancient Arabic style with heavy carved doors similar to those in Zanzibar. There was a Mosque and we could hear the call to prayer five times daily; our servants

Fig 8.4 *Bagamoyo 1957: Patrick taking the march past on HM The Queen's Birthday Parade supported by Margaret.*

took their mats and faced Mecca each time. There was also a Catholic Mission, where a very old priest kept around fifteen cats, all strays I think. He used to ring the church bell and all these cats ran to him for their food. When we left for a short leave, we gave our Siamese cat into his good care. He was so fond of her that we did not have the heart to claim her back later. The dogs seemed to thrive in Bagamoyo and both had litters of puppies for which we found good homes. We did not go out on safari to shoot for the pot anymore as there was none to be had near Bagamoyo, although deeper in the bush there was game, including lion and other big cats. We were busy with our books, and had joined a new record club in Dar-es-Salaam, getting a selection sent to us each month from which we chose one. Pat played tennis, but there was no golf course.

The local people were very superstitious and one day when a large Albatross came down on the beach. All the servants ran screaming to the beach, together with dozens of other locals, and they beat the poor thing to death – believing it to be a witch doctor in disguise. Pat and his fellow officers encountered several instances of murder and other serious crimes connected with witchcraft and this article shows how deeply ingrained these superstitions were for the local population, even in more recent times.

'Angry villagers this week castrated a traditional healer believed to have used witchcraft to kill the local chief and scores of cattle, the Tanzanian News Agency said yesterday. Villagers in Rungwe District, west of the capital, also speared the leader of a local Christian grouping, believed to have helped the witch doctor in causing the mysterious deaths. Eight villagers have been arrested.'
Newspaper cutting 1986 (Source unknown)

Pat quite enjoyed his work in this district and got on well with the local population, especially the Moslem chief, the Liwali. We used to go to his house for tea. It was one of the few real contacts we had with the local people. Everything was strictly kept to a professional level and the Colonial Service strongly discouraged close friendships. If you became too friendly with local peoples, they considered that you were not doing your job properly and it was called 'going native'. We used to have a guard on the offices below us, exactly why I am not sure as there cannot have been much to steal. He was also deployed as a guard for Pat. One night coming back from a dinner party, we found our guard fast asleep still clutching his rifle and with his hat on. Pat gently removed both the rifle and hat, without waking him. Our door downstairs was a heavy one, more like the gates of a prison, and made a terrible noise shutting, it would have wakened the dead. Next morning the guard was 'on the mat' for his sins.

By the time Timothy was seven years old, we had decided that he should go to boarding school locally rather than in the UK. He went to Mbeya, up in the highlands of Tanganyika, which was a good government run school. He did seem really too young to be sent away to school, but he had no companions to play with and was not really getting much of a proper schooling on the correspondence course. Many of the other boys at the school were the same age and he came home at the end of every term which was lovely. I just could not believe the quiet little boy who returned home that first holiday, carefully folding up his clothes and tucking his socks into his shoes, was the same little one that I had sent away a few months earlier. However, within a few days of being home, he was back to his cheerful noisy and untidy self again.

Pat was also now a qualified magistrate and took court cases regularly. He had wide sweeping powers, but could not sentence serious criminals or murderers whose cases were referred to the High Court in Dar-es-Salaam. Sometimes a visiting judge came to the district to hear the more serious cases and advise on points of law. In 1957, the Governor, Sir Richard Turnbull visited the territory and was officially welcomed (see Fig. 8.3) at the Bagamoyo Court House.

Whenever there was an important event like HM The Queen's Official Birthday Celebration (see Fig. 8.4), about a hundred people

Fig 8.5 *Bagamoyo 1957: Patrick talking with local school children as part of* HM *The Queen's Birthday Parade.*

would parade, including the local police force and school children, Boy Scouts and Girl Guides. Pat would be attired in full ceremonial colonial uniform of a white formal tight fitting suit, high at the neck, tight long trousers elasticated under the foot rather like a Jodhpur and special boots. On his head he had a *Topee* (a white pith helmet). He looked impressive and I was very proud of him. I always had to be dressed and ready to leave before him, but there was always some last minute crisis when his uniform was put on and the servants and I would be all crawling on the floor trying to push and pull him into his boots or something. I usually arrived on the parade, with gloves, stockings and a formal hat, wild-eyed and perspiring in all the heat and stress. On one occasion, when the traditional twenty-one gun salute was fired to mark the royal occasions, the school children all ran away terrified and screaming into the bush followed by several donkeys which had careered across the parade ground. We all took it very seriously, despite these humorous moments (see Fig. 8.5).

We went off on some local leave and visited friends in Iringa in the Southern Highlands for several days and while we were there we also managed to take Timothy out of his boarding school in Mbeya for the weekend. It was lovely up there, cool and verdant. Our friends were settlers and had a lovely thatched farmhouse. We sat for drinks by a big log fire in the evenings and in the morning they brought me my breakfast in bed. On the tray were flowers and heavenly fresh strawberries and cream.

Pat decided to we should move out of the *Boma* while it was in the process of being extensively redecorated and sprayed, into one of the recently built new bungalows on a small beach on the far side of town. So we moved up to join the other newly arrived families and life became so much more bearable. The bungalows were the usual style with cement flooring, but were properly mosquito netted and quite cosy. I thoroughly enjoyed my final months, apart from suddenly going down with Bornholm disease, which unfortunately was brought to the area by some visitors. Everyone went down with it, including the baby and servants. Pat was fortunately away, as he was never a good patient. I relaxed and recovered my strength and made plans for our return to the UK. Mohammed decided to retire as he was now quite old, and Saidi took over the cooking. We then took on a new houseboy-*dhobi*, who we discovered smoked hashish. He used to go to pieces whenever we had guests and lie under the car. Pat used to take him on safari with him, which seemed to keep him out of mischief. One day, he was in the kitchen when I cut my finger and sucked it. He immediately went pale and asked why I was drinking blood. They had a superstition about blood and some earlier missionaries had been murdered after being seen drinking red wine which they had previously said was the 'Blood of Christ'. We dismissed him shortly after that.

Cecelia, the children's maid, was having another baby but stayed on until the very last moment to help me out which was kind of her. At the end of July 1959, we left Bagamoyo to go on six months home leave to the UK. Judy and her puppy Jinny went to the RSPCA kennels in Dar-es-Salaam. We had taken a house in Sussex for our leave, an area not then known to any of us. This proved to be another fateful move. My parents-in-law liked the area and bought a bungalow by the coast in Lancing to retire to, which meant that we always came back to Sussex on all our subsequent visits to the UK, and eventually bought ourselves a flat in Worthing nearby.

We flew home, visiting Rome and then Pat's brother in Switzerland. The return journey was by the Lloyd Triestino ship, The Africa. We boarded the ship at Trieste after an overnight flight. It was lovely to be back amongst Italians again. I would have enjoyed the journey more if Catherine had not cried quite so much. She was very disturbed by all the upheaval and was going through that phase when they cannot let you out of their sight without getting upset. There was a well run nursery on the ship, but I had to remove her after two hours of continual crying as she set all the other children off too. The journey, slowly taking us through the Mediterranean Sea and the Suez Canal, went along the African coast. It set us up for the next tour of duty. We made new friends and had a lot of fun together. The cabins were not air conditioned in those days and were so hot. In port we got little sleep because of the noisy cranes unloading and because of the stifling heat. At sea, the port holes were kept open in fine weather, although once I found Timothy practically hanging out of one. They were closed in bad weather of course and then it was quite unbearably hot and stuffy in the cabins.

9

TABORA

We arrived back in Tanganyika mid 1959 when Catherine was nearly two years old. It was always a wrench to leave the UK with its plentiful shops, fresh vegetables and fruit. After five or six months of leave, it was like going to another planet. There was nothing in Tanganyika that made me want to go back there, ever. I even prayed that I would be taken ill and be prevented from returning, but no such luck. The house we were allocated was a modern bungalow, similar to the Dodoma one, with the same dusty cement floor and meagre furniture allowance. It was on a corner, had a sparse hedge and a couple of dried up bushes and nothing else in the garden. We kept to the nearby roads for our walks, which had some shade from trees in the late afternoon, but did not venture too far as there was big game about at times. Locally water was scarce but we able to have supplies delivered but these were expensive. The shops were the similar to those in Dodoma, with the Indian owned ones selling a few bolts of cloth, sacks of rice, beans and a few tins of everyday things like condensed and evaporated milk, tinned peas and fruit. In some of the nearby bigger towns we would find a larger store, also Indian owned, with a slightly wider range of items, and rarely alcohol. Mostly we had to buy our alcohol supplies from the Club, if there was one. Milk was always tinned, except in farming areas where fresh milk could be obtained.

There was now talk of self-government for the Colonial Territories in East Africa and elsewhere. Pat settled into his job, this time as Senior

District Officer and Timothy returned to Mbeya School. Our social life was much as usual, attending cocktail parties for this VIP or some other important official, going to official dinner parties given by the Provincial Commissioner or District Commissioner. We also had time to have a few informal parties though, for our friends and received invitation to theirs. I began again to look for decent servants to help us keep up the standards that were expected of us, but fortunately now we had all begun to cut our staff back quite drastically. The new servants did not cause any problems apart from the *ayah* (nurse maid), so I used to have the house boys babysit for us. We had a laundry-*dhobi*, who also doubled up as a cook-safari servant. I used to prepare the food and the houseboy cooked it. It was the same old tough meat, either stewed or minced. My mincer was one of the most important gadgets in the kitchen. Disaster struck sometimes when one of the cutters would be accidentally thrown away, but we all learned quite quickly to keep spares, otherwise it could be several months before you received the spare part from Dar-es-Salaam or the UK. There was always someone rushing around borrowing a mincer because theirs was out of action. I would never let mine leave my kitchen, and counted the bits afterwards to make sure all the parts were there. The servants were not above swopping the missing parts between houses to cover up losses. It all sounds rather odd after all these years, but at the time these little things made all the difference.

I did manage to do a little social work, such as sewing classes for the African women and helped to run the Co-operative which we had started up, with goods ordered from Nairobi. Twenty wives or so contributed £1 each and we were able to order our bars of laundry and washing soap, tea and coffee direct from the factories. We charged just above cost price and in time were able to extend the range of goods. This did not go down too well with the local Indian traders.

The weather was hot, averaging between 80–90°F most of the time but could be much hotter at certain times. Despite the lack of rainfall, I tried to grow a small lawn near the veranda, by putting short lengths of the runners into the ground and watering them, but the termites ate it as fast as I planted it. By East African standards, there was a nice club which belonged to East African Railways and we were all allowed to join it. They had frequent social functions, such as the monthly dance, darts nights, etc. At Christmas time, they put on some lovely parties for the children. What we all appreciated most of all was the swimming pool. Unfortunately it was on the far side of Tabora and too far to walk to in the heat. Pat generally had the car with him and he was away on safari most of the time, so I had to rely on other people for lifts. Fortunately, one of my friends had the use of a car regularly and she kindly took us for many a lovely cooling swim. She had two young children around Catherine's age, so she was never without playmates.

I was not able to do many safari trips with Pat now because of my family commitments. The few I did manage to go on, leaving Catherine behind with my friend, were not that interesting. The bush was very flat with the landscape and villages similar to those found in the Dodoma area. It was distressing to see how poor the Africans were, scratching a living out of infertile soils, with little grazing for their very thin and scrawny cattle herds. Apart from their *posho* (maize porridge) and sometimes a native vegetable like a small dandelion leaf, they rarely ate chicken or goat meat. The system of meal times in an African household was for the family to sit round on the floor with the cooking pans in the middle. The *posho*, mixed with a little water, was a staple part of their diet. It was rolled into balls for each family member, who then communally dipped them into the main dish which had meat or vegetable. The *posho* soaked up the delicious juices from the main dish. The poorer Africans ate with their hands, but the wealthier ones, including our servants, used enamel plates and spoons. In the Moslem areas, they used the same system as the Arabs; eating only with their right hands as their left being used for wiping their bottoms using a stone or leaves. This was quite a hygienic and sensible system in a land where every drop of water had to be carried for miles on someone's head. As I mentioned before, an African counted his wealth by the number of cattle in his herd and so they were seldom killed or eaten. During the lean years these poor cattle were just skin and bone, with many dying. It was an extraordinary system which allowed women and children to starve to death, while a 200 head of cattle slowly died as a result of lack of grazing or water. To a lesser extent the goats were treated the same as cattle, but were more destructive to the local countryside as they destroyed everything that grew.

Patrick, along with tribal authority representatives and other government officials and local ministers, toured the area to explain the process of Independence. Talk of *Uhuru* (Freedom) began to be heard. There were political meetings everywhere and the local people became slightly hostile towards Europeans. It was not anything much, but the servants began to get strange ideas into their heads about certain things. One told his *Memsahib* that after *Uhuru* he would be moving in the house and she would be living in the servants' quarters. When asked why she would even be remaining in Tanganyika at all, he replied that he would still need her to pay his wages. The same sort of stories went round that had circulated in Kenya during the Mau-Mau days, whether any of them were true was difficult to tell. One I remember still was that when a *Memsahib* asked her long serving and faithful houseboy if he would really do her harm, he quickly replied 'Oh no!' and then went on to say: 'We shall kill the *Memsahib* next door and her servants will kill you!' Certainly the whole atmosphere became quite explosive at times; especially after public meetings which whipped up strong feelings for some of the locals.

It all became frighteningly real when the Belgian Congo, just across the lake from Tanganyika, gained its independence. At the independence ceremony, an African leapt onto the platform and seized the sword from the Belgian King. This seemed to be the start of a great deal of trouble. Katanga Province in the Belgian Congo erupted and many Europeans were killed, including women and children. This lead to a panic stricken exodus by the hundreds of Europeans left in the province. Dozens of cars were abandoned at the lake side, as they desperately crossed it to get to safety. They came across the lake by any available means, old rotting barges being towed behind the other old barges, each one filled with terrified people. The tiny village at the head of the railway, Kigoma, could barely cope with the constant stream of refugees. So railway carriages or trucks were brought up from every railway siding, and these poor people were piled into them. The Europeans in Kigoma did what they could to help, but they were dealing with over 100 people each time. As they came into each a new station, they must have hoped for food or water.

When the first train load mostly of women and children came to Tabora, a journey of perhaps 200 miles or more taking half a day in the stifling heat, we had been assembled on the platform by our local Red Cross branch. We had collected as many bottles of fresh clean bottled water as possible, which were eagerly seized. We also supplied fruit for the children and some sandwiches for each family. As some refugees had only what they stood up in, we had donated items of our and the children's clothing. The French speaking women were asking repeatedly for *serviettes* (sanitary towels), which ironically was the one thing we had not thought of bringing for them. This oversight was quickly addressed for subsequent train loads of refugees. We learned from them that on the way down the line through Tanganyika, the train had been repeatedly stoned by local Africans and just outside Tabora, there had been a particularly nasty attack at the level crossing. It was about 9 o'clock in the evening when the train came into the darkened station. These traumatised women and their children were greeted by the sight of ten European women from the local Red Cross, dangerously isolated on the platform and surrounded by hundreds of very hostile Africans. Fortunately they were being made to keep well back by local police and some of our husbands were around to help control this inflammatory situation. It was a most frightening experience for us and must have been a terrifying spectacle for the already stressed refugees packed into the now stationary train.

When I got home that night, I packed a small suitcase containing our passports, a little money and some precious things and a few clothes, ready for a quick take off. Pat did not share my fears, as he felt that the situation would calm down. I discovered the next morning that my friend, who had been at the railway station with me, did precisely the same thing and had made plans to pick me up in the car and flee to the airport with the children. Planning on hiding under the bushes near the runway until a plan came to rescue us. The next day bravely, despite our experiences the day before, we Red Cross women once again gathered and met the second train which came through loaded with refugees. A large crowd of Africans were there again, but this time they were offering oranges and bread. They had received instructions on how to behave by their political leaders and were following it to the letter. We all breathed a sigh of relief, but we all felt that things were just never the same again after this.

The demand for self-government was strong. I remember a letter from a local African in the East African Standard which pointed out that: 'If everyone is getting *Uhuru* and won't have to work again – who is going to do the work?" Most of the government officers began to think about their future. Pat went to see his superior officer who told him that he would be needed for many years yet. We had heard it all before, in Eritrea. So he began to ask the Colonial Office for a posting to another territory. This was not looked upon with favour by the Secretariat in Dar-es-Salaam, who felt that 'rats were not supposed to leave the sinking ship'. In all this uncertainty and political unrest and, given the experience we had witnessed in neighbouring countries at such times, we made arrangements for Timothy to leave his boarding school in Mbeya and go to school in the relative safety of England. Fortunately, the Headmaster of Mbeya School had retired to the UK and opened up Buckland House, a preparatory school in Devon, taking the main School Matron with him as part of his staff. So Timothy was sent there, to a familiar set up with some staff and several ex-Mbeya pupils whom he already knew and out of harm's way. Not long after this, my neighbour's husband was stabbed to death in a native market while he was shopping for tomatoes. The man who did it was deranged, but clearly influenced by the political talk. It made us all very nervous being about 500 miles up country deep in the African bush, surrounded by several thousand local Africans who might be likely to slit one's throat was not a nice feeling. Given that there were so few cars available, most of us would have only had the option of escaping by rail on one of the infrequent trains, which was not a comforting thought.

We were both very relieved when we heard that Pat had been given a posting to a new territory, Bechuanaland. We did not know much about it, except that its Tribal Chief had married a European woman and had been exiled in England. I thought it could not be worse than Tanganyika. I said a sad goodbye to my many friends and one of them offered a good home for our Beagle, Jinny. Judy went back to the RSPCA kennels in Dar-es-Salaam until we could make arrangements to move her down to Bechuanaland. She was nearly fourteen years by then. Sadly, we were not ultimately able to move her down to us, as she then had begun to have fits and died some months later. A few days after our departure by sea in 1961, the soldiers in the Dar-es-Salaam barracks mutinied as did the ones in the Tabora barracks twelve hours later. They shut their officers up in the cells and things were pretty scary for everyone for quite a few hours. Fortunately no one came to any harm, but it made the minds up of the people who had been undecided about leaving until then. A great many families departed shortly after this incident. Quite a few of our Dodoma friends went on to settle in New Zealand.

POSTSCRIPT: COLONIAL LIFE IN TANGANYIKA

Those years in Tanganyika were very were very difficult for both Pat and myself and we both found the situation there quite depressing and frustrating at times. Although Pat's health was generally better, despite his asthma, I suffered from repeated attacks of malaria. It cannot have been easy for Pat as he had been used to a fairly free hand for so long in Eritrea in contrast to Tanganyika where everything was so very bureaucratic. He liked to escape to the bush on his safari tours as often as possible to get away from it all.

My views on Tanganyika were coloured by the places we lived in and the dreadful houses we had. I realise that had we been sent to nicer locations such as Moshi, Arusha or Iringa in the Highlands where the climate was better, I would have had a less jaundiced memory. We were instead living miles from the sea, up a long dusty and largely uninteresting railway line, with a restricted and very limited diet, and not much money. Our possessions, such as books, would go mouldy and had to be put outside in the sun to dry out from time to time. We had to save every bottle, jar or tin with a lid as these containers were essential for storing water. Despite this, we made many friends, most of whom I am still in contact with today. That was one of the plus factors of the hardships and trials of a colonial life, it bonded people together. Despite this life with its lack of cultural activities, constant upheavals and disruption in education for our young families, there was a lot of enjoyment to be had at times. It felt as if we were always saying goodbye to fellow officers and their families who had become our friends. Surprisingly, we all demanded so very little for ourselves in all of this.

Full Independence followed our departure on 9th December 1961 and Tanganyika was declared the Republic of Tanzania a year later. Julius Nyrere, whom I had known when he was a local School Master, became its first President. I once went to a political meeting at which he was a speaker, where the audience was mainly Europeans. From my vantage point on the platform just behind him, I was able to observe the audience's reactions. He was quite an orator and when he started to speak there was an air of boredom, but as he continued everyone sat up and listened, and in the end there was a rapt air. I am quite sure he was a sincere man, carried away by the ideals of socialism. My honest opinion is that the average African is at heart a capitalist, he has always seen a value in and wants to own houses, land, wives and animals. These days he also wants consumer goods and cars. They typically do not think of tomorrow – today is what counts. If they are persuaded to plant enough crops this year to allow for a surplus, they will likely plant nothing the next year if food is still left; it is their way. One can only envy such a lifestyle, which is largely stress free.

Many films and books are being produced about Africa these days. Much of the current troubles are being blamed on the colonial administration, but we must not fudge it through modern eyes as thinking was quite different then. Today, Singida and Tabora are surrounded by Game Parks and there is a good tourist trade, but the old local problems seem very much in evidence too. Most African countries talk of 'fighting for independence', but the truth was that they were handed it rather forcibly as a result of the political times in the world. The sad thing is that now many years later, Tanzania is still struggling and it continues to receive vast sums of aid from the UK and aid agencies; the result of idealism and ineptitude, corruption and poor management. The dreams of independence are fulfilled, but one wonders at what cost to those living there today. McMillan's 'Winds of Change' speech and the independence movement in 1957 lead to a very quick handover of power, as it was thought at the time this would keep those countries more pro-British and less in danger of communist influences. In retrospect, maybe there should perhaps have been a longer more supported handover period, which might have avoided some of these issues.

The Role of Wives
When we said we were going to Tanganyika in 1953, one old hand said: 'Lucky you, it is the cream of the Colonial Service!' It does not say much for the rest of the territories at that time. Being a man, he was quite wrong as no thought was given to the living conditions for the officers' families. A wife was actually considered to be an inconvenience and children even more so, as far as Tanganyika territory service was concerned. To my knowledge, no formal recognition has ever been given for the role we women were expected to play alongside our husbands in the service of the Crown.

Administration wives had no formal training, which would have been useful in preparing us, and had to learn the hard way – on the job. Apart from being expected to do social work with local branches of organisations such as the Red Cross, Girl Guides and African women's clubs, we were also expected to volunteer at clinics. We were required to be accomplished hostesses and run households on very limited budgets. Up country, we were obliged to entertain and put up a good number of official government visitors, many of whom omitted to write the customary letter of thanks on returning home. We were expected to be discreet, keep secrets and be masters of small talk. If our husbands were engaged in strife with another government department, we were also supposed to give them and their wives a cold shoulder, which was all very petty. Our behaviour was noted by our husbands' senior officers and wives who overstepped the mark were reprimanded; in some cases their husbands were called before the District Commissioner or Provincial Commissioner and instructed to control their spouses. It was all very Victorian and the wife of the Provincial Commissioner ruled the roost. On formal occasions the order would come down from her that the ladies must wear hats, gloves and stockings. No one dared to disobey. By the time I reached the top I was not disposed to behave in this highhanded manner and thankfully attitudes had changed and none of this mattered anymore.

I was quite used to discipline from my upbringing and times spent during the war in the Women's Army Territorial Service days, but all this behaviour was just very petty and pointless. This was my first real experience of how a woman loses her own identity within an organisation and simply becomes known as an extension of her husband's job even being called 'Mrs District Commissioner' and so on. We were expected to be there by our husband's sides, but not heard.

Integration with other peoples
There were some strange ideas too in Tanganyika. People in trade were considered to be hardly socially acceptable. This included Europeans

like the Bank Manager. The Indians could not join any of our Clubs, not even if they were highly educated such as lawyers. Certainly, their children could not attend the European schools. Towards the end of our time in Tanganyika, there was some self-conscious mixing of cultures, but not very much. The local Africans were never deemed socially acceptable either. All so very different from Eritrea and how Pat and I liked to operate. In subsequent postings, we did not experience this sort of attitude fortunately.

Whatever glamorous impression has been given by books or films, our lives were by no means luxurious and household servants were a mixed blessing. In our time in Tanganyika, almost all our fellow officers and families were from lower middle or working class and few had private incomes. We were expected to keep a ridiculously high 'old colonial' standard and it was extremely difficult to live in this manner on the meagre salary provided. We had the upkeep of our possessions, such as the fragile mantles for the Tilley Lamps which were expensive and easily got broken. Officers often had to provide and maintain their own vehicles for their duties, albeit with a small loan from the government. We were so poor that I had to darn most things, including my cotton dresses. Servants' wages were low but even so they represented a large part of our expenditure: Cooks 70/-, *Dhobi* 50/-, Gardener boy 30/-, *Ayah* 50/-. The servants were terrible snobs; if you did not have the right silver, you lost face in their eyes and they would not work for you.

In Tanganyika, I had no contact with local Africans other than as servant-master relationship, or with office staff as anything else was strongly discouraged. The officers themselves were allowed a limited contact with the locals, such as was required for them to do their job properly. This very odd state of affairs meant that there was no real meeting of minds. The Africans would try and tell you what they thought you would want to know and they would politely agree with you, even if they did not. They kept their talk to neutral things like cattle and crops. The women's talk tended to be about children. One cannot sustain much conversation under these circumstances. When on safari tours, the men would be more inclined to discuss local politics or tribal affairs with the British officers. We tried not to breech any tribal customs and taboos, or push modern ideas too far. While we took great care and never discussed official or private business in front of the staff.

At one stage I had been allocated as a gardener, a prisoner who was in gaol for embezzlement of government funds. He was highly educated and spoke English well and clearly enjoyed conversing with me. I lent him books, but was warned off by one of the European prison officers and they withdrew him from my service. When he had completed his term, he was allowed to give me a magnificent box which he had made for me from tree bark and leather thongs. I treasured it and kept it for years as an ornamental fire wood box. It became a little battered over time, so when we left Africa I gave it to my maid in Botswana, who repaired it and took it back to her village. We did have some amusing moments though and we learned early on that if you invited a local Asian to an official function, they came with their entire family. This was in stark contrast to the African dignitaries who invariably did not bother to turn up at all.

Marriages and Children

Our lives were what we made them, boring or busy. There was no privacy and quite a few marriages collapsed under the strain. Many women, myself included, suffered from great stress on being parted from their children at overseas boarding schools, and did not take the choice between their husbands or children well. Tours were long and lasted three years or more, with only one paid passage per tour for the children to come home, which did not help the situation at all. Generally education in England was considered more desirable, although some pretty good schools existed in Kenya. Sadly for us, it was extremely unstable in East Africa at that time and we, like a great many other couples, made the very hard decision to send their children to boarding school in the safety of the UK. Many young children, including my own son, were condemned to years away from home with only rare visits to see us. From those Tanganyika days, I found the separation from my son at such an early age very hard to bear and it still haunts me today. I used to do whatever jobs I could to raise the money to pay the second passage, by charter flight which was solely arranged by the efforts of our fellow civil servants in the territory themselves. The next long holiday at the end of a tour, we always tried to get our own leave to coincide with Timothy's school holidays. Thus over the three year tour, without government assistance, we could only afford to fly Timothy out for one of his six week holidays. We then timed our six months leave in the UK at the end of that period to coincide with his main holiday. The Comet aircraft had a series of crashes about that time, so it was all tearful farewells and the very real fear that you may never see them again. The strain of the children flying was terrible. A friend said that she held the plane up in her mind until she knew it had landed safely. In those days, on aircrafts not only was the baggage weighed, but so were the passengers. It is a disgrace the British Government treated their administration officers' families in this poor way at that time. Fortunately by the time our youngest had got to school age, the government had become slightly more helpful in this respect.

Keeping in touch with our families back home was so difficult too, as letters could take six weeks or more to reach us. We only briefly listened to the news programme each evening, as running a radio off a battery was expensive and not very practical. It meant we felt very isolated from our families and were not able to support elderly or ailing relatives as we would have wished to.

Some notes on health issues

The African servants had amazing faith in European medicine and stole it if it was not locked up, even if they had no idea what to use it for. They believed injections cured everything.

There were many parasites, including the troublesome larvae of the *Tumbu* fly (Cordylobia Anthropophaga) which got into the skin through by laying its eggs on linen or clothes drying on a line. This meant everything had to be ironed, especially nappies, because on contact with skin they hatched out and buried themselves into the baby. They could be winkled out and carefully rolled round a matchstick until fully released. Jiggers (Tunga Penetrans) were also an issue as they used to get in through the skin if one went bare footed and were quite a problem for the locals who rarely wore shoes. They used to protrude slightly at the end of a toe and could be hooked out with a pin. The servants were good at getting them out. Ticks were also plentiful in the scrub and grasslands, which gave animals and humans fevers from their bites. We occasionally also encountered dangerous swarms of African honey bees. The servants quarters would regularly be infested by bed bugs, brought in by clothing, matting or bedding items from their homes. These had to be regularly sprayed to keep this at bay.

However, I was always vigilant and none of the family and staff ever suffered from any of these, nor from upset tummies or malaria, with the exception of the latter which both Pat and I contracted. Malaria was always quite a big issue in this region and continues to kill many more people today. Today they have more than one type of drug to use as a preventative, with each area having its own resistant strain of parasite, whereas we just had a couple of main drugs. They sprayed daily with Flit insecticide pumps in an attempt to reduce the mosquitoes. There was no rabies then, although unfortunately it was moving up from Northern Rhodesia before we left in 1962.

Some useful facts about costs and remuneration
Tours of duty were a minimum of two years, but generally were thirty months. The Government paid for a return passage to the UK at either end of the tour. There was a local leave allowance of about ten to fourteen days per tour. Housing was not guaranteed, but it was usually provided, with a very basic furniture allowance. We generally had to fund and provide our own transport. We received £90 per annum towards

boarding schools fees. Some medical care was provided free, except for operations, maternity confinements and hospital stays. Dental care was provided for the officers, but not their families. Other bills included poll tax £5 per head and income tax 1/6 per £1 up to £400.

PART 3

The Final
African Posting

BECHUANALAND

1961–1972

COLONIAL SERVICE

10

THE JOURNEY AND EARLY DAYS

Thankfully we all left Dar-es-Salaam on 17th February 1961, the day after my birthday, on board the 'Rhodesia Castle' bound for Lourenço Marques in Mozambique. I was very sad at leaving my dear old Alsatian bitch Judy behind in the RSPCA kennels, but I knew she was too old and ill to do the next journey and she was going to be very well cared for there by people who knew her well. Our heavy baggage, now consisting of a dozen large crates, was in the ship's hold. The car had been sold, so at least we did not have that to worry about too. It was quite an exhausting few weeks before we left; packing up and organising the despatch of crates and doing the rounds of farewell parties. The sea journey took only a few days, which allowed us to relax and wonder what we had let ourselves in for now.

We left the ship at Lourenço Marques, but our baggage rather oddly stayed on board to be offloaded at Cape Town. Boarding the train, we travelled to the South African border post of Komatipoort where the South African border guards came to the compartment to check our papers. The fact that my husband had been born in India caused some comment and they explained that, under the apartheid system, Indians were not allowed to travel in compartments designated for Europeans. However, having satisfied themselves that he was not actually an Indian as such, everything was stamped and we were allowed to remain on the train as it proceeded on its way to Johannesburg.

Fig 10.1 *Mafeking House 1961: A nice bungalow with a lovely garden and a green lawn.*

The countryside through which we travelled was for the main part dusty and dry, similar to the areas in Tanganyika which we had been in. This did nothing to cheer us up, but when we began to climb up the plateau towards Johannesburg, the scenery changed as it became less arid and cooler. There clearly was no shortage of water as there were grass lawns, lovely trees and shrubs in the parks, and the gardens we saw were full of wonderful flowering plants and flowers. At the station in Johannesburg we took a taxi to the Hotel Victoria, where the Bechuanaland Administration had arranged for us to stay. We were often to return to this lovely hotel on many occasions after that. What a treat it was to be in this huge city with its shops and restaurant, theatres, picture galleries and culture. We spent a few days there kitting ourselves and the children out with new clothes.

We left on the train for Mafeking in the Transvaal which is located close to South Africa's border with Botswana and as we neared our destination, the familiar countryside was again dusty and dry. Only a few years earlier South Africa had also been a British Colony, so the administrative headquarters of the British Bechuanaland Protectorate was therefore still located in Mafeking. We were posted there initially as this arrangement did not change for several years. The headquarters consisted of a dozen or so houses near the main office buildings. The whole area was within a heavily wired enclave, with the Union Jack flying and an armed sentry on the gate. As someone explained to us, 'It was a bit of old England in a foreign field!' It was quite a large area and most of the senior officers lived on the designated British soil, except the Governor who had a beautiful large house on the outskirts of Mafeking. The lower ranking staff was drawn from mostly local people, all of whom lived in their own houses in the town. Pat was to be one of a new breed of officer now being sent to the territory, with a view to giving it a more international perspective, developing its self-sufficiency and ultimately to bring it up to Independence. He was the first of these newcomers and we found ourselves amongst old-style colonial officers who had served mainly in Basutoland, Swaziland and Bechuanaland. This made us feel very much outsiders having come from Eritrea and East Africa.

On arrival in Mafeking we were taken to Crewe's hotel for the night and the next day someone arrived with the keys to our new home and drove us there. There being no house for us in the enclave, we were housed in town. This meant I was isolated from other British wives and families, but such was my delight in my new house that I barely noticed. It was a nice modern bungalow (see Fig. 10.1) with a lovely mature garden and a green lawn. The floors throughout were beautiful highly polished parquet flooring and for the first time ever, the furniture we had was generous and it even matched. We had soft club armchairs and a fireplace that worked. There was electricity throughout the house, a modern kitchen, an electric stove and water heater – all mod cons. There was just one snag; we had no baggage other than a trunk full of our basic requirements which included a set of sheets for each bed, a few pots and pans and our clothes. It was not a huge problem as, for the first time in our lives there were some reasonable shops nearby.

Our heavy baggage was due to arrive quite soon, although in reality it actually took several months before it caught us up.

Catherine, who was three and a half years old, found a small boy in the house next door to play with. This same Afrikaans family were very kind to me, lending me rugs, curtains and quite a few other essential items until the luggage arrived. They had a Siamese cat which Catherine kept bringing back to our home, until they presented her with a tabby kitten of her own. I had said quite categorically that we would not be collecting any pets but Moggy, as we called him, was such a pretty little kitten that I weakened as usual.

A few days after we had settled in, the man from the Government furniture store came to check everything was alright and asked me if I was satisfied with my furniture. I could not believe my ears as no-one had ever asked that before. I told him that we had never had such a lovely house and such nice furniture, to which he replied that I had made his day as people complained constantly. These people had clearly not been in the places that we had been living in. The next day the Governor's wife, Isabel Fawcus, came to personally welcome me and brought a beautiful bouquet of flowers – another first.

Pat started work and seemed quite happy, although he was not a headquarters secretariat type, preferring to work directly with the local tribes and peoples in the bush. I started to explore the area and to enjoy the shops. The market was full of wonderful fresh produce and we were close enough to the town to walk there, so I bought a small pushchair for Catherine and enjoyed my new-found freedom. The climate was quite hot about 80°F in the summer, but much colder in the winter. I got to know a lot of local families and was invited to coffee parties. In a way it was a good thing that I had not gone to live in the enclosure, otherwise I would have spent too much time in a small group of people and not had the opportunity to meet the friendly local community. After about six weeks, my neighbour across the road asked me if I had realised that there was an English family, newly arrived and living down the road. I had not and went immediately to call upon them. I found a rather miserable family of five, having come straight out from the UK, in a nearly empty house with just four armchairs and no baggage. They cheered up enormously when I explained that we all were in the same boat and later we became very close friends. When we entertained, we all used to visit each other taking our own cutlery, china and chairs. In the end, we all bought garden chairs which were easier to carry about.

I was taken on a tour of the famous Boer War battlefield outside this small town, which was the sight of a famous siege. It was a good hunting ground for souvenirs as it had old bottles and the like. I was also introduced to two old ladies whose brother had been one of the original Mafeking Scouts, who were the inspiration behind the Scout movement. They showed me many fascinating photos and documents from the period

Pat, now thirty-nine years old, entered the Bechuanaland Service at a salary of £1,328 per annum. He was eligible to receive a special allowance of £60 as he was married. For some reason this did not apply to officers stationed in Mafeking. From his salary, he paid contributions to the Widow and Orphans Fund, income and poll tax. Medical treatment was free, other than specialist treatment. Dental treatment had to be paid by ourselves and most officers, wives and families made sure they visited their dentists in the UK. Officers were required to pass a local African language examination, but this was not strictly enforced. Pat began lessons in Tswana and learned enough to converse reasonably confidently in. However, he found out quite quickly what everyone else had probably discovered, namely that the local peoples in Bechuanaland spoke excellent English.

He was appointed initially as an Administrative Officer, on the bottom rung as before. This did not matter that much here, because everything was so much less formal and there were only about twenty people in the Secretariat anyway. After a short period of probation in Mafeking, Pat was offered promotion as the District Officer based in Serowe, which is the main town for the Bamangwato people and the birthplace of many of Botswana's Presidents. The population of Serowe was mainly African with a few Indian traders and around two thousand Europeans, many of whom were farmers. The local Africans known locally as Tswana were from a variety of tribes; including the ruling Bamangwato. The Paramount and Tribal Chief of the Bamangwato was Seretse Khama, who had been educated in England and studied Law at Oxford where he met and married his British wife, Ruth. Because of tribal strife, he had been exiled to the UK and had only just been allowed to return to Bechuanaland a few months before we arrived in Serowe. We got to know them quite well and Catherine played with their twins, who were about her age. Sometime later, Timothy was at the same boarding school with their eldest son, Ian, in Swaziland.

Pat was of course delighted, but I was less so given that we would be losing the nice house and we did not know what sort of house we would be allocated in Serowe. I was also sorry to be leaving the shops and various new friends we had made. It also meant that there would be no possibility that Catherine could attend the nursery school in Mafeking. However it was not up to me, so I packed our few possessions up again and we travelled up to Palapye by train, where a car met us and then drove us on to Serowe. For a few days we stayed with the District Commissioner and his wife, after which we then moved into a bungalow. Fortunately it had a pretty garden, decent furniture and a highly polished floor. We still only had our few bits of cutlery and china in our trunk, as the main luggage had still not caught up with us. It was quite cold in the winter months of July and August and we had to buy some local blankets. Once we got settled, Pat went off on a few days of safari tour of the region with the District Commissioner.

There was not a lot to do there, so I read, gardened, relaxed and generally began to feel a lot better physically. Although there were areas where there was Malaria, fortunately the region we were in was free from it. This was something we had not experienced for quite some time. There was clean running water out of the taps, which did not have to be filtered – another first. However, we still boiled it for drinking purposes and stored it in Gordon's Gin bottles in the refrigerator. A few children were probably accidentally fed neat gin on occasion in error. There was no electricity, so we were back to oil lamps. Because the climate was so bearable, I decided to do without a servant and do my own cooking initially. A woman came to do all the laundry several times a week. It was such a pleasure to have the house to ourselves. Pat bought me a bottle gas stove, which was wonderful. I enjoyed sitting by the fire and listening to our first modern radio set, which we had bought in Mafeking. For the first time in our lives, we were actually issued with Government refrigerators. No one would believe that we had to supply our own in Tanganyika. The bathroom was indoors and modern, but the water heater outside was the usual old-fashioned Dutch boiler system. There was no shortage of piped water, but we were metered and paid monthly for it.

There were a couple of small trading stores in Serowe, but I quickly learned to have my groceries sent directly from Johannesburg from a marvellously old-fashioned shop which used to pack every item so carefully. When I visited the shop on local leave, I was fascinated to see that the floor of the shop was covered in sawdust and all the elderly gentlemen who served in the shop wore long white aprons. Shopping there was like being in another era. Sadly, it eventually moved with the times and became a supermarket.

I did not keep an overly detailed diary during this period of my life. I was always careful not to include any political matters, in case they fell into the wrong hands. I kept quite a few relevant newspaper cuttings and notes but I am sad that Pat is not here now to write his side of the story too.

After several months in Serowe, Pat was again promoted and had his own station (administrative region) again. Although it had been pleasant enough in Serowe, we were both very keen now to become more permanently settled. Our baggage from the ship had been in storage in Mafeking for quite some time. We were driven to the railhead and got on the Rhodesian Railways train, which chugged its way gently across the arid bush to Mahalapye. We were met there and driven to our house; an old colonial style one with verandas all the way around it. It backed onto the railway but that was not a problem as there were so few trains. I was not too keen on the house as it had very large rooms and concrete floors again, which meant it would get quite dusty and need a lot of daily cleaning. There was also a very dusty and dry garden which consisted mainly of large rocks. These had been laid out along the driveway and arranged around what must have been flowerbeds at some time. It must have been a long time since anything had grown there though, as there was nothing much left apart from the odd hardy shrub or two battling to survive in these hostile conditions. It was all rather depressingly familiar.

We unpacked and settled in. Pat went to his temporary office, which was a room in a nearby building. Later he had a small office built a distance from the town, with two rooms and a flag pole from which the Union Jack flew each day. This was taken down each night in true colonial style. The area around the building was kept swept clean and marked out with the usual white painted rocks. Until we arrived there had only been a district officer based there from time to time. The headquarters of the government agricultural department was in Mahalapye a few hours drive away, so there were quite a few agricultural officers working in the area. Before our arrival, anything that happened in the area was reported to the Director of Agriculture who took the appropriate action. Initially this continued to happen, with Pat only hearing about things second hand, which was annoying and frustrating for him to say the least. However, things changed after a short while and Pat assumed the appropriate responsibility.

By now more people were arriving from other British Territories, many of which had now become independent, to fill the expanding departments and we felt less isolated. There were also a number of officers who were part of the British High Commission and who seemed to have quite different attitude from the rest us. There was some historic rivalry between the two services. We thought of them rather as stick-in-the-muds and in time, they nicknamed us the 'when we' service, after

Fig 10.2 *Shoshong 1961: Church Mission Society Centenary and Pageant re-enacting bloodthirsty attacks.*

our much repeated phrased 'When we were in … territory such and such happened!'

Some new and more modern bungalows were being built on the far side of town, up a little country road not far from the new office which was being built at the same time. We opted to move into the first one completed, leaving our rambling place to a newly arrived bachelor. Once we were settled in, I started to make a garden and had some hardy grass runners to grow the new lawn sent down from Bulawayo. Very soon there was a lovely lawn which needed watering every day. I also made a rockery and planted bushes and plants. We used bath water to do this, as the water was charged at around £20 a month which was quite a lot of money in those days. The house had wooden parquet flooring and a nice new kitchen. The furniture was the usual basic issue. There were one or two small rather basic stores in the village which were used mainly by the local Africans, so I continued to have much of the special delicatessen type food sent in from Johannesburg by road. There was a small club, with quite a large swimming pool. Our social life was quite busy by the time we had been there three or four months. The other houses were occupied and several private families had decided to build in the same area. A friend who was a keen horsewoman bought two horses and corralled them at the back of the houses. We bought a pony called Golly for Timothy and Catherine and added him to the string of horses being kept there.

While we were there, the Church Mission Society had its centenary and a pageant (see Fig.10.2) was put on at nearby Shoshong. Guests of honour, the Paramount Chief of the Bamangwato and President Elect, Seretse and Ruth Khama and their children attended the pageant, which re-enacted the fighting between the Bamangwato and Matabele and was greatly enjoyed by those actually taking part and it certainly looked very real. Later on in Gaberones, we nearly had the real thing in the town centre when some of the labourers from Rhodesia, who were Matabele tribesmen, fought the locals one night and the police had to intervene.

The early missionaries had set up the mission in 1862 at Pitsane and Mashona (in Rhodesia) on the land of the Bamangwato tribe. The mission was then moved to Shoshong where it remained until 1889. Due to a lack of water supply and the bloodthirsty attacks by Matabele tribesmen from Rhodesia, they had to leave the area and move to Palapye. Eventually the mission closed down, and the area quickly reverted to bush again. After the borders of Rhodesia and Bechuanaland were defined, the warring tribes were separated. For the centenary celebrations, the site was cleared and we were able to see the foundations of the houses, which were of simple native construction, and have a guided tour. Later I bought the journal of Elizabeth Lees Price (see Bibliography), an early missionary's wife. It was a fascinating book and included the remarkable story of how she and her children hid when the battles were going on. I revisited the site again sometime later and saw it all with different eyes.

One Christmas we were kindly invited to a midday Christmas dinner, in temperatures of around 100°F, at the house of one of the settlers on their farm about ten miles outside of Mahalapye. Around fifteen people went and the hostess had laid the long table ready on the veranda, which was enclosed by high railings. Ten children, among them Catherine, were also invited and had their meal in a separate room attended by a nursemaid. I shall never forget that day. To start with, the sight of the table groaning with food made us feel quite overwhelmed in the heat. There was turkey and all the trimmings including roast potatoes and Brussels sprouts. It had all been provided at great expense and effort but unfortunately it had been cooked much earlier, so in the heat there were genuine fears that the turkey was not safe to eat, so it was removed. Few of the guests could cope with eating much of what remained of the heavy English-style food in the heat. The children did not fare much better and had eaten little of their food, but were out playing on the lawn and eating ice creams.

Just over the veranda, unbeknownst to us, was a cardboard box filled with fireworks and next to it a small drum of petrol. Someone flicked a cigarette butt out over the veranda where it fell into the fireworks box. Suddenly the fireworks began to explode, sounding something like a wartime bombardment, with rockets flying about at various low levels. Everyone reacted differently. I shouted to Catherine to 'Run for the bush!' and being an obedient sort of child, she did just that. Then, because there was no outside access from the veranda, I ran through the kitchen to get outside to collect up the other children who were standing transfixed and get them to safety. Several servants ran with me, while some of the guests and staff took shelter behind furniture and under tables. One woman likened the whole event to something in the Blitz. The Czech doctor vaulted over the railing like an Olympic runner to reach his little girl and kept on running with her until he was out of sight. Another man jumped the railing and picked up the drum of petrol and disappeared into the distance with that too. Pat tried to climb over the railings and slipped, fireworks exploding around him. Apparently their two dogs took off into the bush and only returned home some forty-eight hours later. I will always remember the children only feet away from the box when it first started to explode, mesmerised by the first few fireworks exploding; fortunately, no one was injured and we were all able to have a laugh about it later. Unsurprisingly, Catherine disliked firework displays thereafter though.

So far we only had employed temporary wash-girls and I started looking for someone permanent. One day a young African woman came to the back door and asked for work. She had a tiny wizened baby on her back, not really the ideal servant given she had a tiny baby with her. At first I said there was no work, but something made me call her back and she moved into our servant's quarters at the back of the house that night. She had been out of work for quite a long while and I discovered rather shockingly that the tiny baby was in fact a terribly undernourished twelve-month old baby. I set about helping her to nourish the baby properly and it put on weight and flourished. Eventually, her family were able to look after it while she worked for us. Esther was an excellent house servant and was very grateful for the opportunity for work she had been given. She was neat, willing and very cheerful. She did the housework and laundry, while I continued to cook. If we had a dinner party, she arranged for her friends and family to help with the washing up and other chores, for which they were reimbursed. She was able to lay tables and serve the food. It was a system that worked well on many levels. I was so happy and so was she.

It was not generally the custom in Bechuanaland for men to work in the house; they worked as gardeners only. We had decided to offer the opportunity for work to (non-violent) prisoners from the jail to do our gardening. Over the months there were several who came to work for us. In later years, they came up to me in other towns or villages, once even in Johannesburg, and reminded me that they had been our gardener in Mahalapye. This opportunity for work meant they received a good reference from us, and this helped them find work elsewhere when they were released.

Life went very smoothly, we were very happy and began to have a large circle of friends. At this stage, I did not do any voluntary work as I was busy with Catherine and a steady stream of official visitors. In any case, the local women seemed to sew better than I could and did beautiful traditional craft work. There were adequate clinics which were properly staffed and a small hospital. Everyone seemed to speak excellent English and there were no terrible diseases. At that time there was also no rabies. The local Africans were very pleasant and there were no tribal wars or political issues. Pat played tennis and I swam at the club. We read a lot and listened to the South African and Mozambique radio stations, and so kept up with world news.

There were of course a few snags in this paradise. There were the usual insects such as cockroaches, but as it was a new house it was not too badly infested. There were ants of several kinds, but not soldier ants which would eat anything in their way as they marched through your house, including a chained-up dog and the baby if you were unlucky. Bats flew around after dark and scorpions and centipedes kept to the dark corners, so one was always careful to tap out one's shoes before putting them on and never walked barefooted. There were quite a few snakes including the deadly puff adder, but somehow we managed to avoid them. Snakes generally tried to get away from us, and it was only when cornered or accidentally trodden on that they became a danger.

Because of the two cats I lost to leopards in Tanganyika, I was trying to get Moggy our young cat to come in at dusk one evening when Pat was away. He was sitting stubbornly by the rockery. So I ran down the path, only to be stopped in my tracks as he was facing up to a Cobra. It was the first time I had ever seen one with its hood spread, ready to strike. It remained quite still perhaps confused by my sudden appearance while Moggy, who was then only twelve months old, and I fled up the garden path into the house. I was always very careful after that to take a torch and long stick with me if I was ever in the garden after dark.

Although there was no fear of personal violence in Bechuanaland, I always locked myself in and let the servants off early if Pat was away. Old habits die hard. The local Africans were a pleasant lot in Mahalapye and

I do not recall any incidents of house break-ins or other unpleasantness towards the Europeans. However, there were various misdemeanours being committed against each other which went on as usual in the villages, some of which Pat would have to sort out as part of his job. It was quite possible to have an intelligent conversation with the maids and that way one was able to have a fair idea of what went on. In fact, sometimes I was able to tell Pat small bits of information usually about the goings on of the local people, which he found valuable on occasions.

When newcomers arrived at the administration station, one tried to see them settled in by giving them a meal, or practical help like the loan of china and cutlery. We also used to show them the shops, tell them where to get items and give them any help possible. Newcomers from the UK complained a lot about the conditions, the lack of this and that, and the standards at the local hospital. What they had expected, I just do not know. People coming from other British Territories mostly took it in their stride. There were no jobs for wives, so we were all in the same boat. A lot of us had young families, which kept us busy. There was fortunately very little nonsense about the pecking order in Bechuanaland and we certainly were not going to inflict it on those below our rank. The most senior people were stationed in Mafeking and rarely seen except those that came on tour once in a while. Neither were there any terrible secrets that had to be kept nor political nonsense going within the service. It had not always been like that though from what I was told, and there were stories about a District Commissioner's wife years before who had run everyone ragged.

Because of the unusual situation of there being a British enclave in the Republic of South Africa, we had to be issued with identity cards for travel into the area. We had to enter Bechuanaland as 'immigrants' which was a most unusual procedure for British administration officers. At the time there were no border gates between the two countries, just a small hut on the side of the road where a perfunctory check was made. There was a great deal of traffic between the two countries. Many of the 150 or so European staff had houses in the Republic and at weekends would leave Bechuanaland to return home. Coupled with the fact that a lot of expatriates also went to Johannesburg for the weekend, to the theatre and shopping, it meant that there was a bit exodus of personnel on a Friday night. Pat and I used to joke about being in sole charge of the territory over the weekends. In due course, we used to get permission to visit Johannesburg for the odd weekend every two months or so as it really seemed to refresh the mind and spirit.

I found South Africa quite different to the way it had been portrayed in the British newspapers and books. I had expected the African people to be forbidden to use the pavements or shops, but I found that this was not so. They would be shopping alongside us in the big stores quite normally. I remember the surprise of finding myself sitting alongside a smart African woman who was also trying on shoes, served by the same white assistant. In the city, the only difference seemed to be that they could not use the bars or restaurants. There were other restrictions of course such as separate entrances for the post office and railway station which were ridiculous. Having experienced living in multi-racial societies in both Botswana and Eritrea, we found it all very awkward. We did not condone apartheid and very few did, apart from the most conservative Afrikaners.

I have not spoken as yet about Bechuanaland itself, which was a British protectorate rather than a colony. There were clearly defined tribal areas under their traditional hereditary chiefs. In the main, the Africans were pleasant and likeable. We did not go on any long safaris such as those that were undertaken in Eritrea. I made some day trips with Pat on occasion. Pat did some safaris which entailed staying away a day or two, but the distances involved were not too great. In this particular territory, it did not seem the custom for District Officers to tour the districts for lengthy periods, although agricultural and public works officers did so when required. In the cooler weather, we used to go on big picnics with several friends into the bush. The roads off the beaten track were dusty and corrugated. The main road to the South African border was very bad and it was always an enormous relief, after several hours of this bone-shaking journey to reach the outskirts of Johannesburg and get onto the tarmac. It used to do the cars no good at all. We had decided by then to buy a Peugeot 404, which stood us in good stead for the rest of the time we were in the territory. We had earlier tried a VW Hatchback, which was a bit of a rogue car and everything that could have gone wrong did, so we sold it and cut our losses.

While we were in Mahalapye, although she was only four-and-a-half years old, Catherine went to a small private school, known locally as '*Ma* Skonkins'. She did well and learnt to read quickly and had a lot of friends at the school, both English and Afrikaans. Timothy flew out to join us for his long summer holidays. By then, the British Government was being more generous with children's passages. He had also joined us during a previous holiday while we were still in Mafeking.

At the end of 1962, we went on long leave to the UK again, sailing home via the Suez Canal on the 'Boschfontein'. We rented a house in Shoreham-by-Sea for six months. This meant that Catherine was able to have two terms of primary schooling locally, which set her up well for the future. Pat flew back after four months to his next appointment in the Territory.

11

MOCHUDI

Early in 1962 we sailed back on an enjoyable trip to Durban with Catherine who was then five-and-a-half years old. We took the train to Johannesburg, staying the night there before catching the South African-Rhodesian Railways train onto Gaberones in Bechuanaland. The train always left at night and we had a sleeper. There was a restaurant car which served very nice meals on the train. This meant it was a very comfortable journey. The attendant always came round selling small hand towels and soaps in plastic packs for a few pence. While one was at dinner, the bunks were made up for the night and we had someone babysit Catherine. Sometimes during the night the guard banged on the door and demanded to see the tickets. This could happen twice, as the train 'became' Rhodesian Railways when it travelled over the Bechuanaland border. It arrived early in the morning at Gaberones, which was then still a small wayside station.

Pat met us at Gaberones and we drove to Mochudi, which was one of the bigger villages in the Bakgatla tribal region about 37km northeast of Gaberones. The road was just sand, very corrugated and the dust streaked away covering anyone travelling behind us. One always kept a good distance away from another car travelling in the same direction, to allow the dust to settle or blow away. It helped to cover one's hair and keep the windows almost fully closed, but in that heat (80–100°F) it was too hot to have them completely shut. It was very dry and arid everywhere. There was a very low rainfall in this region, which bordered on the Kalahari Desert and from time to time we came across nomadic Bushmen, who visited in order to get supplies and water, which they carried with them in emptied ostrich eggs.

Our house was large; an old colonial type with big rooms and a veranda around three sides, which had been modernised over the years and was divided up here and there in order to incorporate the veranda into the house. At one time the garden had clearly been lovely (see Fig. 11.1). It was terraced and full of orange, lemon and grapefruit fruit trees. Two prisoners from the local gaol tended it all. They were usually in for petty things such as drunken brawls or assaults. Someone had set up a system of small concrete furrows which watered all the trees, using water which came from the bath and wash basins. By operating small barriers, the water could be stored or diverted. I do not know who enjoyed playing with it more, the prisoners or Catherine as it was rather like having a watery train set.

We planted some more shrubs which we got sent down from Bulawayo and there were some tired roses in one flowerbed, which started to grow and bloom again after a little water and some care. At some time there had been a vegetable garden, neatly enclosed by a wire fence. A mango tree was struggling for survival, but this was not really the best area for them to grow as it was too arid and it never did very well. There was also a collapsed chicken run, which I re-erected. We got a few chickens from the Agricultural Department, a cock and four hens. Sadly they did not last very long as one night the polecats got in, killed and ate them. After that we contented ourselves with a small pen of Muscovy Ducks, which we provided a small pond for. They survived the polecats, but we never got any eggs either. The Agricultural Department said they must be breeding or at least laying eggs by the time I complained. We had the ducks killed and ate them, to a chorus of protests, so someone had clearly done well out of the eggs. Sometime later I began to collect up some scrawny indigenous hens, hoping to get at least a new laid egg for Catherine every day, not much came of that with these either. One morning just as Henny Penny, one of the long legged local hens was

Fig 11.1 *Mochudi 1962: At one time the garden had clearly been lovely.*

about to hatch out her eggs, a 12 foot python swallowed her and all the eggs. Catherine, who was awaiting the happy event with excitement, had got up early to go to the chicken run to see if any had hatched overnight. She came face to face with the python which was fortunately stuck half inside and half outside the wire enclosure; having swallowed the chicken whole it could no longer get its body back through the hole it had come in. She came screaming back into the house shouting "Big snake, big snake!" and everyone within earshot came to her aid. Later the prisoners killed and ate it, having carefully prepared the skin for sale. I also had a small chicken as a pet. It was from one of the eggs which Pat had bought in one of the villages. When he got it back home, I heard it cheeping and hatched it out on the stove. It was imprinted on me, and would run to me and sit on my foot and I had to show it how to perch at night. Unfortunately, it was amongst the hens killed in another polecat attack. We gave up trying to keep hens after that.

Mochudi camp was a tiny place which consisted of three houses besides our own, in the Government zone. There was the District

Fig 11.2 *Mochudi 1962: The 50ft* Kopje *gave good views of surrounding plains and the village.*

Commissioner's Office and a little further down the road, there was the prison and the police lines which consisted of a small village of purely native huts housing the local police personnel. The main local village of Mochudi was a one mile or so away and was quite large and this was where the Tribal Chief had his home. On the far side of the village there was a Lutheran Mission with a very basic small hospital which they ran with about twelve workers and a German Doctor. During the time we stayed there in Mochudi, I was never invited to visit the Mission. The staunch Afrikaners spoke very little English and deplored the use of lipstick and rouge. One of the African women told me that they considered me something of a scarlet woman because I wore make up, and we were both quite amused by it. However, they always turned up at any official party we gave. We used the hospital whenever necessary and the elderly German Doctor and his wife were very pleasant. After we had been there about six months, a young Afrikaans nurse arrived to work there and she had a little girl of Catherine's age. The doctor arranged for us to meet and the little girl came to play with Catherine every week. Neither could speak the other's language, but they obviously enjoyed having company. Sometimes the mother came too, and I found her pleasant to talk to as she had worked in Johannesburg and was a bit more worldly. She was the only female visitor there for months.

I began to make the house more homely with cushions, mats, pictures and books. We had two bedrooms with a bathroom for ourselves. The first visit of the Governor and his wife resulted in a special guest room with an ensuite bathroom being built, after they had to squeeze in with us for a week. They were a wonderful couple and realised that we were getting a lot of official visitors and being greatly inconvenienced by the lack of suitable guest quarters. There was a never-ending stream of official visitors. During the very hot season around Christmas time we never saw a soul but as the weather cooled down, the Heads of Department and others from Mafeking began their rounds. We noticed that the cooler it got, so the number of visitors increased. Then came the VIPs from England, who were always sent up to us or Serowe to get a feel of the real African bush. They were usually all men and I rather missed female company.

We had brought Esther with us and we had another girl to do the laundry. One day poor Esther went very peculiar, she began shouting and throwing things. By nightfall she was so bad that we had to fetch the doctor who took her away in an ambulance. The other maid quit her job instantly and never returned as she said the evil eye was everywhere. We did not know what had happened to Esther or why and neither did the doctor. Her family came to take her home and later we learned that she had been given the native treatment for driving out the devil – hot needles in the skin. Had we realised this, we would have encouraged her to stay in the hospital. After that, I had terrible trouble finding and keeping a servant. The house was believed to be bewitched. Some maids came for interviews, but did not come back. Others simply would not come at all. I wondered what I could possibly do. At this time we had a prisoner called Wright, a gentle elderly man who was in gaol for hitting and hurting someone who had stolen his bicycle. He used to do the gardening, but stepped in and helped sweep and wash up, light the fire and carry the wood. One day, after a month of this, a woman arrived at the door asking for work. I asked her if she knew about the bother we had had and she said she had. She was tall and a very no-nonsense type. She said she needed work and her name was Ellen. I took her on and she was excellent. She stayed with us until we left the country many years later. A week or so later, she produced another women called Violet who was a cook, and I took her on. Both these local women had worked together in Johannesburg for years. They took over the work and ran the household like clockwork. Violet undertook to see Catherine into her bath at nights, feed her and put her to bed if I had visitors. A great comradeship developed between the two maids and Catherine.

While we were in Mahalapye, we were given a Pekinese puppy which we collected when we returned from our leave. Someone brought it to us in Mochudi. It was called Pepsi as that was Catherine's favourite beverage at the time. It was quite a fierce little thing and terrorised the household. Catherine used to ride around with the puppy in her bike basket. The cat had a tough time too, being put to bed like a baby in the dolls' cot. They were all the poor child had to play with, apart from the odd games with me.

Gradually, the houses near us were filled up; one of them by an African Education Officer and her family. She had a large family and two of her girls came to play with Catherine, who used to organise them into parts for plays. At about this time one of our visitors brought her a baby rabbit, which was kind of him. It was a Hampshire Brown, which we called Susan Bun after a character in one of her books. She stayed in a cage in the garden during the daytime and slept indoors at night. I did not realise that rabbits burrowed underneath wire and the wretched thing was always escaping into the bush. Until we dug down several feet, and put wire under the cage, it was a daily event for everyone to be rushing around the area calling her name. She was never far away, luckily. Later on, she was joined by a white rabbit. They were either two mild tempered bucks or both female, luckily for us as they did not breed. We accidentally killed them off by feeding some tomatoes to them with the household scraps, which we learned later were poisonous to rabbits. Our next pets were two guinea pigs called Squeaky and Fatty; a male and female, which bred prolifically and ran loose around the place. We managed to find good homes for their plentiful offspring.

We had decided that I should teach Catherine through the Rhodesian Education Department's Correspondence Course from Bulawayo. Our plan was that she should go to a private boarding school in Rhodesia and not go to the UK. I just could not face up to another series of long term partings like the ones we had with Timothy when he was ten years old, plus the worry of another child flying back and forth. Pat agreed with me on this. So Catherine was enrolled and we received a weekly packet of papers, full of instructions, arithmetic tests, drawings to be done and painted, and spelling lists to be mastered. I had to make the equipment from household product containers, such as VIM tins, which were numbered and used for mental maths. You would use a ball and knock them down like skittles. I also had to make other equipment, project charts and so on. It was quite fun. She started to work at 9 o'clock and each subject lasted around twenty minutes with breaks in between. She had learnt to read in Mahalapye and in the UK, but now her reading became better by the day, as did her spelling and arithmetic. I found her an eager pupil. We kept to strict term times. Each week the written work, essays and paintings went to Bulawayo for marking and assessment, and were returned to us to revise if need be.

It was quite a tranquil time, though I was busy all the time with visitors and the schoolwork. I had also been roped in to help at the newly created community centre. I decided to teach patchwork, which I was quite good at and the Africans were interested in as they loved all the pretty brightly coloured material scraps. Because the villagers were so poor and would not have been able to buy the variety of fabrics required, I wrote a letter to the Editor of the Johannesburg Star newspaper asking for people to send materials for the project. To my surprise, I had a dozen large parcels from some very kind people

Fig 11.3   *Mochudi 1963: The government oxen used to pull the 'scotch-cart'.*

containing embroidery silk, crochet cotton, templates and suitable material remnants. I wrote and thanked each sender personally and put a note in the newspaper. So, my class got off to a fine start and we made a lovely quilt which was then raffled for funds. I was very embarrassed when I won it, probably because I had bought a book of tickets, but they insisted I kept it. I was very angry and upset when it was stolen some many years later in Johannesburg.

Pat was very busy in his district and magisterial work. He toured the area frequently but was not away for more than one night at a time. We used to drive to Gaberones each Friday night to go to the cinema show at the Club. At first we took a picnic supper then, when we got to know some people there, we would be invited to supper at their house. In the end, we were invited to stay overnight too. It made a lovely break for us all. We were able to return the kindness by inviting them to stay with us. Even though we were not that far away from Gaberones, Mochudi was a traditional tribal area and this was very interesting for people with no experience of life in such areas.

In places like Gaberones, there was quite a mixed population made up of the various different tribes, with very little individual tribal culture as a result. The European type culture tended to dominate therefore. In the tribal areas, the Chief was important, and ruled in the old way. Our local tribe was the Bakgatla, they spoke Sekgatla. The Paramount Chief was Kgosikgolo Lentshwe; a young man with a lot of responsibility. He had been educated in England, where he had met the author and wife of a Labour MP, Lady Naomi Mitchison. She had appointed herself as his surrogate mother in the UK, and then kept appearing for visits to his house in Mochudi. She was a bit of a thorn in the side of the administration in Mafeking, although she got on well with Pat and spoke well of him in her books. I even got a mention something along the lines that I was the only white woman whom she had seen sit at an African's table, or some such statement. I am sure she was sincere in what she did, but she did some rather silly things prompted by her left wing ideals; such as taking Lentshwe to Mafeking and insisting on having a picnic in the main square, obviously intent on sparking an anti-apartheid incident. Local people came to warn them that the police were on their way. Lentshwe told me how scared he was. Lady Mitchison arrived regularly for visits and she gave Catherine a signed children's book which she had written, *Little Boxes*. Some time later she told me that her granddaughter wanted to come out as a voluntary service officer but that she would not allow it saying: "How can I allow her to come here?" which I thought was very telling. One of the interesting things about my life has been the opportunity to meet with the famous and controversial individuals in some of these territories. I wish I had taken more detailed notes at the time.

I had very little cause to go to Mochudi village except for official functions or visits to the community centre. This was run by a young man sent from the UK by some organisation or other and who in the manner of the 1960s came down to African level or so he thought by wearing ragged shoes and simple clothes. My contacts within that community whose opinions I valued were quite mystified by this behaviour. To their way of thinking, if you can afford decent clothes, why not wear them. It was only the very poor that dressed like that. These more educated Africans we met did not approve and said so. One of the things that upset the female tribal members was the back to nature ideas being peddled, such as making clay pots for cooking in the old tribal way. One local lady said that when they could buy such nice saucepans in the local store, why on earth would they want to make their own.

Pat could now have given me a great deal more information of what went on in the area, but alas he is no longer here to do so. I would have liked to ask him more about the back door escape route from South Africa, which was operating via the boarder about fifteen miles away into the Transvaal, which meant meeting with officials from both sides. This had evolved because the tribal lands of the Bakgatla were cut in two by the division of Bechuanaland and South Africa. Half the tribe lived in one country and the rest over the border. There were about 20,000 or more on their tribal lands in our district area which covered approximately 3,000 sq miles.

At the back of our house was a large rocky 50ft kopje (hill), which we loved to climb. Although it must have been a favourite place for snakes, we did not see any on our scrambles up there. We had a wonderful view from the top of the surrounding plains and the huts of the village in the far distance (see Fig. 11.2). Very large monitor lizards several feet long lived in the crevices and were often spotted sunbathed on the rocks. My other memory of Mochudi were the pretty yellow weaver birds, building their communal nests in the big tree near the back door, the small doves cooing, the sounds of the cicadas at night. It was so wonderfully peaceful. We did have one constant noise though and that was because we were on a party line, shared by half the village. Each person had a special ring code, which one became attuned to and the operator was kept very busy. After a while it drove us mad because the policeman on duty used to phone their girlfriends who were working at the hospitals, who would then phone them back for a chat. The constant rings during the night woke us up, so after a lot of persuading the engineers installed a separate line. It should have been done in the first place as it was most inappropriate for the District Administration to conduct its business with half the village listening.

Prior to our arrival there had not been a District Officer in Mochudi for a year or so, but due to the increasing political activity one was now needed there. It had not been a very happy place for the last two District Officers, one of whom had accidentally shot and killed his wife while cleaning his gun and then hung himself. By this time were both in our early forties and Timothy and Catherine were growing up quickly. It was a lovely life for the children. Timothy flew out for his holidays twice a year now. We also managed to visit Johannesburg regularly for weekends, shopping and to the theatre or just to dine out somewhere nice. We had a swimming pool in the garden, about 15ft by 18ft, built by a former resident, but it had no filter or means of emptying it. The prisoners used to bail it out with buckets, which they rather enjoyed as they got a bit of a dip in the cool water as a result. When it was refilled, for a few days it was wonderful but gradually it would go green with algae and became rather uninviting. Had we known more about it, we could have used chlorine to keep the algae at bay.

Our cooking stove was fired with logs brought in on a scotch-cart by the prisoners. This strange vehicle was a type of sledge which was dragged along the ground by two huge oxen, leaving behind rutted tracks and an impassable track which became water courses during the heavy rains. They went miles with it collecting wood. I could not understand why it could not be put on wheels, even on a car chassis instead of churning up the roads. The government oxen grazed just outside the grounds of the house near the road, where there was a cattle grid to keep them out. At the end of our correspondence course lessons, I regularly walked down with Catherine to see them as they were quite placid despite their fearsome horns (see Fig. 11.3). Our hot water boiler, known as a Dutch boiler, was the same type that we had in Tanganyika. The 40 gallon drum imbedded in concrete and supported over a fire, always outside just by the back door, with the pipe leading into the house. Once again there was plenty of water, but we paid for every drop we used. We used to have two storage rain butts at the corner of the house.

It was becoming obvious that we had to do something about Catherine's schooling. Although she was quite happy and could amuse herself for hours, she clearly needed more companionship and schooling than she was getting. She was doing well on the correspondence course and it was when she began to read the instructions each time and criticise my interpretation of it all that I realised the time had come for her to go to boarding school. We had been thinking of Rhodesia because the curriculum was similar to that of UK schools. We heard that other children of the same age in Mahalapye and Gaberones were all preparing to go there too. Before we could get together on the details, instructions were issued from headquarters in Mafeking that children living above a certain designated line on the map could go to school in Rhodesia; those below had to go to South Africa. In order to qualify for the education and school fees grant, we had to comply with these instructions. As we could not afford to pay the fees without this assistance, we had to accept this ruling which was most disappointing. So, together with six other children, when she was seven years old, Catherine went to boarding school in Pretoria. I have no idea why such a strange ruling was made. It could have made no difference whatsoever to the cost to the British Government. South African history was heavily anti-British, despite the fact that the school was a private Anglican convent run by the Wantage order of English nuns in charge. It was compulsory to learn Afrikaans and have some lessons in it. I felt that although Catherine lost a lot of ground at first, nevertheless she was very happy there and was well cared for. The pupils were from local well-off homes or farms, embassy and other international business families. Unusually for South African European Schools, there were also some mixed race children from the diplomatic corps.

The weather was varied throughout the year. Over the summer around Christmas the temperatures could be 120°F indoors which was unbearable. Yet, in the winter months of July and August, it was so cold that we had a fire in the sitting room and wore winter woollies. All the rooms were large, and the draught that whistled in from the passage froze us initially as there was no sitting room door, so we had one put in which helped a little. We used wood and coal in our sitting room fire. The coal was brought up from South Africa on the railways. Collection of firewood locally was quite an issue for many reasons. Continual cutting down of trees by the local population was causing some erosion issues, especially where the population in a village was growing. We had the usual insects in Mochudi, such as scorpions, centipedes, ants, ticks and plenty of cockroaches. There was little game to be seen, and those there kept well away from inhabited areas.

The servants had private quarters at the back of the house about 25 yards across the garden with their own bathroom and toilet. Each maid had a room with a bed, table and chair. They provided their own bedding. They had a rather strange practice of raising their beds upon bricks to height of 15 inches. Apparently, if this was not done, a creature call a *Tokolosh* would come and get them. This was a little man wearing a fez, which could perhaps be the description of an Arab slave trader.

We were expected to pay and feed them on a ration using the South African scale, as laid down by the regulations. While this made it easier for employers, as everyone knew approximately what to pay them, we liked to supplement this. So both maids had a daily 2½lb meat daily ration and a monthly ration of 25lb bag of sugar and 25lb bag of mealie flour. They were able to take as much tea as they required. All the food and accommodation were part of their wages. I also provided salt and spices, onions and coffee. Heating, light and hot water was also provided. This meant that they were able to save quite a lot of their money. They spent it just before a visit to their own outlying villages. Ellen used to leave with a string of people behind her carrying sacks of food and tins all destined for her family. She had several children and during the time she worked for me she had two more. They also grew a small patch of crops.

On 5th February 1965 Pat received a memorandum from head-quarters in Mafeking informing him that the Secretary of State in London had approved the creation of six posts as Permanent Secretary, and that he was going to be promoted to the very important position of Permanent Secretary, Ministry of Commerce and Industry (Mines) and Water Affairs, starting on 28th February 1965. This was very exciting news, but there was talk of setting up self-government again and that meant that independence loomed yet again. He was working himself out of a job for the third time. The new job meant a move to Gaberones. The headquarters in Mafeking was to be closed and re-opened in Gaberones, for which a big modern air-conditioned office block was being constructed, along with a very nice Government House. There was a big building programme in progress. Costains Ltd were building most of the houses and roads and there was also a large dam which was being constructed to supply the new capital of Bechuanaland. A few months prior to departure, we had unexpectedly acquired a honey coloured Labrador/Rhodesian Ridgeback cross called Jess. She had belonged to a family we knew in Mafeking who were returning to the UK and felt they could not afford all the quarantine fees; she faced destruction if they could not find a suitable home for her. So, of course, we offered her a home. The first thing that Moggy the cat did when she arrived was to box her ears soundly, but after he had established who was the boss they all settled down as good friends.

We packed our boxes up gradually. I started to collect up beer tins with a view to planning seeds for hedge plants and other cuttings such as Bougainvillea into larger containers. We knew that the house we were to be allocated would be standing in a cleared and fenced place without a single feature, except maybe a mature tree if we were lucky. So I added a few more tins to the pile and planted some tree seedlings, plus some mulberry cuttings, and so on adding more and more as the days went by. No house had been allocated yet, so we could only wander around the building site looking at them whenever we visited Gaberones. We knew we would have a Supergrade level house, but we were not sure which one.

12

GABERONES AND INDEPENDENCE

We moved over to Gaberones with two trucks, one of which contained our crates of personal household belongings, servants and the dogs. The other truck contained all my plants, about 300 tiny hedge plants in beer tins, growing quickly as plants did in Bechuanaland, together with small shrubs and other items for the garden, which took up most of the back of the truck. We had been told the number of our house plot, but had to get someone to meet us and direct us to it. The town was laid out on a grid system and the houses were built on a building line, with dirt access roads. Trees had been bulldozed out of the way of the building work and only a few were left standing here and there. It looked a bit like a zoo, with each house surrounded by a 3ft wire fence. Having found our house we unloaded the plants, placing them under a shady bush that had been left standing smack outside our garage door, so that we could not use it. Just behind that was a stunted tree. There was nothing else left standing on what was left of the building site. Luckily both water and electricity was connected.

The servants moved into their smart new spacious private quarters. We were delighted that Ellen Mpeti (see Fig. 12.1) and Violet, along with Wright Selinbogwe our ex-prisoner gardener had decided to come with us to the new capital. In no time we all got to work, everything was swept or dusted and we began to unpack sufficient things to tide us over for the night. I was most grateful for their help. Friends in the old Gaberones village, where the club was located, invited us over for supper which was kind of them.

Our house had a dining-sitting room in an L-shape, with folding doors. The dining room was quite small, had double glass doors onto what was to become the garden patio. The kitchen was quite modern, with running water and electric stove and water heater. There were three bedrooms arranged around a closed courtyard which lead to the guest room with its own bathroom. We had our own bathroom in the bedroom wing. The floors were all nice parquet blocks, with Marley tiles in the bedrooms and bathrooms. I was very pleased with it and Ellen set about polishing them all until they shone. Violet organised the kitchen side of things. We had the usual Public Works Department supply of furniture; some rather heavy wooden arm chairs and a settee, a table and six chairs, sideboard, serving table, desk, beds, dressing table and a fully furnished guest room. We made table lamps from bottles with bought lamp shades and I got a nice red square carpet and made some cheerful cushion covers. These, plus our own ornaments and pictures meant that it was very comfortable. I went to Johannesburg with a friend to do the necessary shopping. It was quite a long journey by car, over bone-shaking corrugated roads that continued each side of the border for many miles. It took over four to five hours and was very hot and dusty. Going to Johannesburg there was always the excitement to look forward to and the shops, etc., but coming back it was a different story. We used to dread the long dusty road home.

Wright and I began on the garden which was very hard work. We prepared the area inside the wire fence for the hedge. I used to go round in the cool of the evening collecting abandoned and broken bricks from all the nearby sites and managed to find enough to build a path from the gate to the front door. I did it entirely by myself and when it was finished it looked wonderful and later when the grass grew between the bricks, very rustic. The servants thought I was very strange to bring back my finds after my evening browse. They considered that it was not really what someone in my position should do.

All the hedge plants had to be watered daily, after the sun went down. As they became established, the gardener and I started on the lawn. We scrounged grass runners from people in the village. The patch to be planted was dug over and in the evening I would plant 3 inch sections of the grass runners in rows ready for next day when they were watered in. During that period we planted a lawn about 50ft x 25ft x 30ft. It grew well and soon looked quite green. I restricted the amount of lawn, as it all needed watering daily and we had to pay for every drop as it was metered. Our monthly bill was often £20 or more. I filled the rest of the garden with bushes and trees. By the driveway leading to the back of the garden, I had a small strawberry bed under a small Acacia thorn tree. At the back of the garden I planted several Mulberry trees and later fig, guava, lychee, orange, lemon and grapefruit trees. Along the roadside, near our house, I planted pretty purple blossomed Syringa Trees which grew well. Unfortunately, they produced poisonous yellow berries, which I regularly scooped up in case the passing local children accidentally ate them.

All attempts at growing vegetables seemed to fail for some reason. Part of the reason for this might have been that conditions were too hot or the armyworm ate them. The staff did sometimes manage to grow a few lines of not very healthy maize though by their quarters. Insects were quite a blight for the locals and our staff often complained of bed bugs in the clothes and bedding. We used to use DDT smoke bombs to clear the hut of infestations, and treat the clothing and bedding. In the cool season, I had flower beds full of dahlias, daffodils, sweet pea, tulip, etc. I did all the planting out myself and Wright did the digging and watering. I asked him to build me some garden arches, but the poor man clearly had no idea what he was doing, so we ended up with what friends teasingly called my 'Heath Robinson' structures. They were soon covered in Coral and Morning Glory creepers and looked lovely. I was as brown as a berry, from having worked outside for most of the time. Pat did not do any of the gardening, but gave me lots of support and applauded my efforts.

Pat was very busy setting up his Ministry in a brand new air-conditioned office. His new Minister was Amos Dambe, who was such a nice man and we got to know him and his wife very well. All the new Ministers were local Tswana people. The main Administration Secretariat people were still to come from Mafeking in one big organised move, so various other people arrived before them. Most had never been out of South Africa and suffered something of an instant

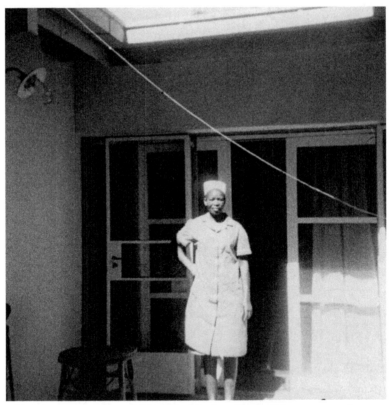

Fig 12.1 *Gaberones House 1965: Ellen Mpeti outside the dining room, one of our two wonderful maids.*

cultural shock. Several resigned and so recruitment had to take place in the UK. We used to see someone and their baggage arrive at one of the nearby houses and could almost feel their bewilderment as they faced the empty, arid garden and concentration camp like wire fencing compound around the newly built bungalow. One day a couple arrived at a house a few doors down, while we were sitting on our rapidly growing lawn enjoying a late cup of tea. I could hear the woman shouting that there was no way she was staying there. Alas, as they stood there quarrelling, the bulldozer dug the ditch behind them and they were marooned on the plot. So Pat went over and brought them back for tea, to cheer them up. I think the sight of our rapidly growing lawn and the garden taking shape, together with our calm and settled appearance, must have helped because later we helped them unpack their car and stay that first night.

The big move up from Mafeking and closure of that Head Quarters was quite an event. Plenty of parties and official farewells took place. It was after all the end of a long historical period of occupation by the British. It was all organised much as a military operation. Pantechnicons brought up the furniture as all the old houses were to be sold. A reception office was opened in Gaberones to deal with problems any newcomers had. The vans made several trips during that day and the next, until finally everyone including the Governor was installed in their new homes. In all fifty to sixty families moved up, including the lower grades of staff. Many of the people had not been in the bush so far from civilisation and certainly never so far from decent shops. In the end, everyone became resigned to the situation and began to establish gardens and a new way of lifestyle. The social round began and before we knew it, we were as busy as ever. During the day in the heat, I usually wore sleeveless cotton dress and sandals. We attended many official events and on these occasions we were expected to wear stockings and shoes, sometimes with hats and gloves; even if this meant we were standing at midday in the heat on the airport runway (see Fig. 12.2), as part of an official welcoming party for the President on his return to the country. During the weekdays Pat wore white regulation shorts at the office during the hot season and long trousers and shirt and tie for meetings. He wore a suit or official uniform for special parades. For evening functions, I had more glamorous clothes usually in washable fabrics and dark colours and evening shoes. Pat wore long trousers every night, either in white if staying at home, or black for functions when he wore black cummerbund around his waist.

The headmaster of the secondary school approached our Women's Institute for help with lessons about European social customs, and the laying of tables, use of cutlery, especially useful for Sixth Formers who would very likely need these skills if they were to become diplomats or wives of high ranking officials. I offered to be one of the team and, as usual, enjoyed myself. We used to take linen, china and glasses down to the Domestic Science rooms and set up a beautiful table, usually much admired by the students. The Mining Company, RST, provided food for a feeding programme in the village area. I joined the team of six volunteers which was formed to go each day and mix up this special feeding powder in buckets with water, until it could be formed into balls about the size of a tennis ball size and these were then given to the one hundred or so children who sat in rows on the sandy ground. A film of this was made by the company. This special nourishing food was gratefully received by the undernourished youngsters suffering from malnutrition and kwashiorkor. As usual, there was much initial enthusiasm for the work to start with, but helpers quickly fell away and the old stalwarts like me were left to keep the programme running in the long term.

Gradually the Secretariat began to function as before and more building work was begun. High Commissioners from various countries came, including from the UK. Interesting houses were planned. The roads in the capital were tarmacadam. The Town Hall was now built and ready for use. A resourceful Indian brought in film equipment and gave a cinema show there two or three times a week. In the winter, July and August, it was so cold that I wore my English fur lined boots and my heavy coat. The water in the bird bath froze overnight too. We used to have a lovely log fire lit in the afternoon and it was lovely to sit in front of it with all the animals asleep around my feet in the warmth. Those were very happy days.

Catherine, who was at school at St Mary's Diocesan School for Girls in Pretoria, came home at half term and so was not away for overly long periods. We used to organise a single vehicle pick up of all the children at the school and in that way only one of the parents would have to make the double journey once in a while. Sometimes several children stayed overnight, awaiting the arrival of their parents from further up country. When it was our turn to the do the journey, we took two days leave and stayed in Johannesburg a little longer.

Because we were becoming so comfortable in Gaberones and felt that we had a true home at last, Pat decided that instead of taking the long leaves of three months or so to the UK, we would fly over for brief holidays from then on. In that way, we would not disturb our lives too much and could retain the house while we were away. Sometimes, when people went on long leave, their house was re-allocated as there was a shortage of accommodation. So during early 1966, we took a few weeks leave, staying with Pat's brother in Switzerland, continuing on to Portugal for a week, and then onto the UK to see the rest of the family. We stayed briefly with our parents, in turn. We left Catherine at school and in the charge of a close friend, should there be an emergency. When we got back to Gaberones, we found everything in order at the house. The garden had been well cared for by Wright. Ellen had been in charge of the animals and they were all fat and healthy. We gave her a few weeks holiday with pay when Violet returned from her own holiday in Mochudi. They quickly gave us all the news about what had been happening while we were away; somehow they always seemed good at finding things out.

Pat went back to his office and later came back with the news of the date of Independence, which was to be 30th September 1966. There was not much time and we wondered what would happen to his job. Lists were made of visitors who would need to be invited, ambassadors and other VIPs. There was a terrible shortage of suitable official accommodation. Hastily, a hotel was designed and after much discussion it was located in the town square which was a decision made by the President to be, Seretse Khama. It was to be named President Hotel in his honour. I thought that it might have been nicer to have had it set in some pretty grounds, but then the decision was not mine to make. However, Pat gave me the plans and said that a company from Johannesburg was to be doing the interior decoration. He asked me to choose the china, cutlery and other items required such as designs and curtains. I travelled up to Johannesburg, conferred with the company and was full of admiration at the way they made up the curtains from measurements on the plans. Fortunately, when the time came they all fitted. The hotel was finished and furnished with days to spare.

A manager was appointed, which was quite difficult as not many people were keen to take up a post like this in an African company just about to be independent. A chef also arrived, a German, who was in charge of teaching the local cooks who were to take over from him after a while. The Government had insisted that only local Tswana were employed, so initially there was a great deal of training to do as almost all the staff were new to their roles. The President and Lady Khama were among distinguished guests who attended the official opening of the hotel. Mr Jimmy Haskins the Minister of Commerce, Industry and Water Affairs, opened the hotel and in addition to thanking the contractors and various other institutions, kindly acknowledged my hard work and effort in selecting the materials and fittings appropriate to the particular public rooms and bedrooms.

I was also given the job of finding out how many people, local and European would be able to accommodate the many VIPs who were expected to come to the days of celebration. The hotel could only take thirty, so everyone else had to make their guest rooms available for this purpose. I borrowed a bicycle and went around with a clip-board and managed to get offers of suitable accommodation from both Europeans

Fig 12.2 *Gaberones Airport 1966: Margaret greeting Sir Seretse Khama on his arrival.*

and Africans. In time, we got everyone comfortably settled. All senior
ambassadors were put into either the houses of the very senior officers
(i.e. Chief Secretary, Attorney General, etc.) or into the houses of the
Permanent Secretaries and Ministers. As we all had private guestrooms
with bathrooms, this arrangement worked quite well. I had no hand in
deciding who went where, as this was done at a higher level. We were
asked to have the Swiss Ambassador (Hunziges) as our guest for the
two to three day celebration. He was a charming and easy person to
entertain and so we got on well. Apart from breakfast, which Violet
took care off, most of the meals were taken at the various banquets
or functions. It was all very exciting and we all bought new evening
dresses for the occasion.

One of the receptions was held in the large conference room at the
new hotel. I had suggested the name of 'September Room' in honour
of the Independence Day. This was approved by the President. I also
suggested that the long bar be called the 'Copper Bar' because it was

being mined and would be one of the main exports from the new Botswana initially. This too was adopted and lovely copper surface was laid along the whole bar, with matching lights. The manager was instructed to set in place a dress code and to admit no one to the hotel without a tie and jacket, which kept the place smart.

On the big day, 30th September 1966 after the formal dinner we and other invited guests and VIPs drove to the stadium which had been erected on the far side of town. We had to be in our seats about forty minutes before the start of the ceremony and before the arrival of Sir Seretse Khama and the Queen's representative, HRH Princess Marina (see Fig. 12.3). The day had been a warm one, but there was a slight breeze which was freshening. It did not seem cool enough to warrant warm clothing, or so we thought. As we sat there awaiting the arrival of the President-elect and his party, the wind became stronger by the minute and as the start time for the ceremony drew near the temperature started to drop quite noticeably. We all started to shiver in our sleeveless, thin cotton dresses; someone in the seats behind us had brought a hip flask and offered nips to all of us of brandy which helped a bit. I fortunately had a thin silk stole which I wrapped myself up in. When the President's party arrived, the road which had been closed for half an hour for them was open to traffic again, but by then it was too late to rush home for shawls and cardigans as the ceremony had already begun. The wind suddenly grew much stronger. The red sand flew in gusts all over us and we froze. We were sitting just above the Royal Box and noted that the Government House car rushed off to fetch the President's *Kaross* cloak, made of civet skin, for HRH Princess Marina, which she seemed very thankful for.

Speeches were made and the marching and tribal dancing began. Then dramatically the lights were lowered and only one focussed on the British Union Jack Flag as it was ceremoniously hauled down, the Botswana national flag started to go up amid cheers. Then it stuck and no amount of tugging would move it. So someone hauled it down, unravelled it and the flag went back on up into place. We all sighed with relief and hoped that no one considered it a bad omen. The wind by now had become something of a gale which really was not typical at all of this area or season. The fireworks were then lit and whizzed about dangerously in the wind in all directions. Rockets shot across the arena towards the stands instead of going straight up, which was terrifying. Some were going through the stands just a few feet above our heads. Just as the British Ambassador gave the urgent instruction to get HRH Princess Marina away, so she could be protected from injury, the firework display ended. When the lights went on again, we noticed that in the general public arena which previously had been filled with expatriates and locals had been complete deserted during the firework display. Everyone began to laugh, as it was all very amusing. We drove home thankfully, covered in red sand from head to foot. When we looked at our faces, we had hysterics as half the face was normal and the other side was thick with red sand, we looked rather clown-like. The next day the gift presentations took place as all the VIPs started to leave. Our guest gave the new Government a beautiful Swiss clock for State House.

Life settled back to normal and one of our senior African staff said to me: 'Thank goodness that's over and we can all get back to work now!' It was a very different attitude to that which we had met in our previous territory of Tanganyika. I think we all waited for some change in the people's attitude, but it fortunately did not happen and everyone continued much as before. A lot of building work was going on in the Capital. A shopping mall was built with a chemist and hairdresser, as well as a bank and off-licence. A vegetable shop and several dress shops and a shoe shop were opened in the mall. Then the United Stations Embassy opened in the town centre. A Government printing department was built nearby, which produced all the official stationery and a daily news sheet which was eagerly awaited. It gave news of all the local events, including official visitors to the capital. Several countries sent consuls or ambassadors and houses popped up all over the place. More new staff arrived from England, and more local staff was engaged.

They all had to be housed and Constains Ltd had work for several years in Gaberones in these early days.

The only grocery shop was still a very small one in the old Gaberones village, so it was decided that a Co-operative store should be started. The idea was initially muted by the Vicar and taken up by the Government Training Officer and several other Government officials. They hired a small room from Barclays Bank, and people were invited to pay £1 to join and the money was used to set it up. To start with volunteers ran it for the first few months. When it became a much bigger affair and the wall was knocked down to incorporate a store room, an African manager was appointed. As he had little experience, the decision was made to engage someone to help oversee things initially. Pat had rather a habit of volunteering my services (hence the hotel decoration and accommodation for VIPs), saying I enjoyed doing these things and perhaps he was right. So it was not surprising that I received a telephone call from the African Minister whose role it was to look into these things, asking me if I was willing to help set up a Co-operative Store. He had apparently heard that I had experience of doing just this in Tanganyika. In the end three European women shared the role, so that no one did it full time. The rates of pay were not that good, but we enjoyed helping for several hours a day with ordering the stock, training cashiers, etc. This worked quite well until one of them was taken ill with Hepatitis and unable to work for quite a few months and the other was involved in a serious car accident. At this time, it had been decided to enlarge the shop once more and purchase some large freezers. I was to remain on as the under manager (at a token salary of £30 a month), which I agreed to do. I oversaw the ordering and general hygiene and cleaning. I usually worked half a day, which fitted around some of my social and formal engagements.

The international community was growing quite fast and we had many nationalities at our formal parties, and in turn we were invited to their houses and embassies. This meant that we were able to enjoy some wonderful different cuisines – Indian, Chinese or Arabic food, or maybe a Thanksgiving Dinner at the American Embassy or Independence Day celebration at another Embassy. The British High Commission was housed in a magnificent building, air-conditioned and fully furnished down to the last spoon. It always seemed very unfair that we should be treated so very differently when we all were working for the British Government and expected to do official entertaining and hospitality for visiting VIPs.

Catherine was happy at school and by then Timothy had joined us out in Africa too. He had finished his 'O' Levels in the UK, but was not wanting to stay on there for 'A' Levels. Lady Ruth Khama, the President's wife, suggested the newly opened Swaziland Waterford School, as Ian their son who was the same age as Tim was studying there. The school was founded by a small number of teachers who were opposed to apartheid in South Africa, with a British Headmaster Michael Stern.

I managed to get a lift to Johannesburg with Tim and we took the bus from there to Mbabane. It was a very long hot journey, taking a whole day. We stayed at the local hotel and the next day the Headmaster, who after interviewing Tim, accepted him. We returned to Gaberones to discuss it all. Finally Tim decided to go and we arranged for a friend living in Johannesburg to help him get his uniform for him, which was a rather old fashioned grey flannel type. For a while I really did think he was going to rebel, however he went off quite cheerfully and studied for several 'A' Levels. Each boy had a study-bedroom and was required to work by himself, with tutorials every so often. It was quite a successful system and he passed. Then he came back to Gaberones, where I got him a job working for the Co-op as a clerk in the newly set up office. The Co-op had by now set up proper headquarters and were planning to open other branches throughout the country. Working like that at the office gave Timothy something to do and prepared him for getting down to the serious idea of a career. After about twelve months of parties, and relaxing at home, we decided that he should take a Hotel Management Course. He started work at the prestigious Best Western Hotel Group in

Johannesburg and after successfully completing his training he was moved to one of their hotels in Cape Town.

Just after Independence, Pat bought me a five-year-old second-hand VW Beetle car. I had learned to drive in Eritrea, so it was just a matter of getting used to driving again. I loved my car with its two wings, which had been replaced at some time in its life, in slightly varying shades of red. Timothy added further to its charm, by redesigning one of the wings while learning to drive, which meant that yet another shade of red was added to it. I drove everywhere after that and took it to Mafeking for a regular service. When reversing out of our garage, I had to learn to go around the tree which had been left just outside of it. Fortunately, my car was small and easy to manoeuvre. At some point, Pat decided that the tree needed to be cut down, but unfortunately Wright left a quite large stump, which I could not see when reversing. As a result, I regularly hit it on the way out, further denting the car.

Another of our adventures at this time was while I was teaching Tim to drive. The very heavy rains had caused enormous ridges and cart-ruts in the mud and one day while driving carefully down one of these tricky roads, he slipped off the top of rut and the car was stuck sideways on the central ridge. Being on one of the very quiet back roads outside Gaberones, we thought we would be there for ever. Luckily a huge lorry, which had been bringing beer from South Africa, came along and kindly pulled us out. There were a lot of funny moments and it was a very good time in our lives for the family. In the middle contract terms, we used to go on a local leave and visit Durban and Cape Town with the children. It was lovely seeing the sea again. The South African beaches were wonderful with miles of unbroken sand but, because of the risk of shark attacks, not that great for proper swimming except in netted areas. We also went back to Mahalapye to visit friends. Sadly, both our fathers died in 1966 within a few months of each other and I was fortunate to be able to fly home to my father's funeral, but Pat was unable to do so for either.

One of the new pets we acquired at this time was a budgie given to us by a friend. I tried to teach him to say 'Hello Peter' without much success. After each lesson I used to sit and talk to the cat saying 'good boy' to Moggy, who throughout the bird lessons sat fascinated on the armchair just below the cage. So imagine my surprise, when the budgie suddenly said 'good boy' one day. From then on, he learned very quickly, and was very tame. When we left Botswana, I gave him to a lady newly arrived from the UK. She had suffered from a stroke and was largely housebound and had left her own budgie in the UK and missed him. So it seemed a perfect match. Catherine brought home a white mouse and several small brightly coloured laboratory rats from school in Pretoria once, but these were returned with her when she went back.

I thought it might be quite nice to breed budgies, which were a popular pet with everyone in those days. I had bought a pair in Johannesburg, little knowing how successfully they would breed and that we would be quite overrun with baby birds by the following year. I had built at the back of house a good sized aviary with nesting boxes. Fortunately I had plenty of takers and I quite enjoyed trying to breed

Fig 12.3 *Gaberones 1966: Independence Day celebrations with HRH Princess Marina (central) having some fun with the official photographers. President Sir Seretse Khama (2nd left) and Lady Ruth Khama (right).*

some unusually marked or coloured birds. Every hatchling was reserved weeks before it was ready to leave. Unfortunately, quite a few birds escaped when people cleaned their cages or allowed them to fly free in their houses. I often wondered if there were any colonies established in the wild, but as the winters were quite cold this may not have happened.

Pepsi our Pekinese had a mutual love affair with the dog owned by the African Minister who lived opposite us. It was a black and white lanky mongrel with the strange name of Needle. They did look rather odd together. We had tried unsuccessfully to mate her with another Pekinese which had come out with a family from the UK. Unfortunately, this poor little dog was subsequently lost up near the dam one Sunday afternoon and may have been caught in a trap or by killed by a wild cat or something. While we were away briefly, Needle covered Pepsi at a crucial moment and she had a large puppy. It caused terrible problems as it was too big for her and she needed a caesarean and ultimately lost the puppy. Unbelievably, they did it again some months later and we ended up spaying her to solve the problem. The two dogs remained good friends despite this set back.

The building of Gaberones Dam was very interesting and we watched it being created. Initially a large area was bulldozed and the earth piled up high to form the high banks. An area was left as a spillway. In the centre of the dam a watch tower type of building was built. The area was very large and the tops of the banks were flattened to allow plants and bushes to be planted on them, and it was possible to walk along them. It was a very pleasant area, and much used as a Sunday walk and picnic area by all those living nearby. It was hoped that the dam would supply all our water and would fill naturally over three years or so. Instead, we had heavy rainfall the first season and it filled completely to the top, water came over the spillway to the dry riverbed and it was a magnificent sight. Everyone went up there to look at it several times a week. In an area bordering the Kalahari Desert, water lying in a mass like that was unheard of and it was a great morale booster. People bought boats and some swam there.

Unfortunately Bilharzia soon established itself there and made it off-limits for most water sports.

Every eighteen months or so, we went on leave paying brief visits to see our parents. Flying there and back, sometimes staying briefly in Italy or a night or two in Switzerland, Vienna, Venice.

I was getting busier in my job in the Co-op store, which was being enlarged yet again. We now had three cash-out tills. I was responsible for the freezers and overseeing the delivery of frozen goods from the enormous van which Pat's department had organised to come up from South Africa with goods. If they were not supervised, it was found that the staff sat outside on the path unloading the chickens, meat and cheeses, pricing each one while they defrosted. I had to teach them to store everything as quickly as possible and have a price list displayed instead of individually pricing such items in the heat. Later in a not too busy period, they could then quickly price some chickens individually. This system worked well. Originally before the Co-op store was opened, we had to go to the old Gaberones village where under a thorn bush we queued to give our orders at the back door of the van in temperatures of 80–100°F. You then had to race home and hope that nothing had melted before you put it into your own freezer. We had only twelve pots of cream delivered from the Agricultural farm each Saturday. As we now had over a hundred families it was causing a problem. Everyone thought they should have priority, so I made a rota. It meant that the all the names on the list got some cream. I learned a lot about the less attractive side of human nature doing this job, as I was quite often accused of favouritism or even of taking some myself out of turn. The milk came from Rhodesia in plastic one pint packs and was much enjoyed as previously we all had to use powdered or tinned milk. It arrived by train in the early morning in refrigerated boxes and was collected by headquarters and delivered to the store.

We had Co-op stamps and books to stick them in, but before my time there were not a lot of profits to share out. Because I checked everything thoroughly there were no fiddles, so for about a year or so everyone drew a lot of money after the dividends were declared. When I tried to hand this aspect over to the staff, things did not go quite so well. They created a corrupt system, discovered one day by headquarters, in which the van driver drew goods from the warehouse on invoice and delivered only part of them to our store, even though the full consignment was signed for. The missing goods were then left at someone's house. At one stage I resigned and a European Manager was employed, but he too left under a cloud. So I was asked to help out again and this time had an assistant, who was an African American of Ethiopian extraction, whom I got on well with. He was with the Peace Corps, which was a volunteer programme run by the United States government. It was rumoured that he was with the CIA, but as all Americans were supposed to have some such connection in foreign countries, it probably was not really so. While I was away on leave, a whole freezer full of 'TV Dinners' was ordered and we were stuck with them for many months. Given there was no TV in Botswana, there was not unsurprisingly little demand for these. I was on call to sort out any problems as well, which could be quite disruptive to our lives as I still had a busy schedule of VIP entertaining to do.

Pat was now very busy forming the policy for tourism, water usage and for mineral and industrial development. He was Chairman of the Public Utilities Corporation and a Board Member of the National Development Bank and Corporation and set up negotiations with World Bank for the implementation of major mining project. As a Government Director of the RST (Botswana) Mining Board he was involved in the talks with De Beers (see Fig. 12.4) in respect of the proposed diamond mines. He went to London as a delegate for Trade Conferences and also to Washington, USA, for the International 'Water for Peace' Conference. He attended a great many other conferences and meetings in various countries, including South Africa, Lesotho and Swaziland. One of his more enjoyable trips was to the game parks of Uganda and Kenya to see how they were set up, with a view to setting similar parks up in Botswana. Unfortunately on this occasion, I was not able to go with him. He was accompanied by our new Minister, Jimmy Haskins and several other senior local officers.

By 1967 life continued to be very pleasant and we had settled into a routine of swimming in the pool at the newly enlarged Club and attending various functions there. Attempts were being made to invite more senior local Africans to join the Club, which they were hoping would be completely multi-racial. In reality, there seemed to be more issues with culture than colour, as sometimes the cultures seemed worlds apart. The Tswana preferred to return to their villages at weekends rather than join in the club activities. We had some limited friendships with certain of the local ministers, but that seemed to be as far as it ever went. Sometimes we invited them to a meal at our house to meet a VIP, but usually we met them at official functions really. It seemed to be a mutually awkward relationship, but all quite amicable. None of us like being patronised, and the local Tswana custom was to be extremely polite and did not openly disagree with people in social situations. They found the more trendy Europeans, who were not aware or respectful of these customs and boundaries, difficult to deal with.

Sir Seretse and Ruth Khama regularly came to our house to dinner and to our parties. Seretse used to join in and enjoy himself. We were very fond of them and the children grew up together. During this period 1967–70, there were a great many official cocktail parties sometimes there were two a night, perhaps followed by a formal dinner somewhere. A lot of businesses were sending representatives to ascertain the potential markets and more representatives from countries not already established with Embassies also visited. Sometimes when Pat was away on business, I often had to represent him. Kenneth Kaunda, President of Zambia, came for an official visit and I was seated next to his secretary who I had to ask to read the menu. It was then I realised that I would probably have to wear reading glasses. Kaunda gave an excellent, but rather long, speech at the dinner. Afterwards Seretse made an amusing reply, saying among other things: 'Give an agitator a microphone and you can't stop him!' It was applauded wildly as Sir Seretse Khama was an excellent and very humorous speaker, especially off the cuff.

Pat and I sometimes attended the new church which was a rather modern one with an altar like a carpenter's bench. As was the trend at the time, the very modern vicar encouraged jolly singing to guitars. Having been used to traditional Church of England services, I was quite shocked when I first attended. The ladies of the church organised a sewing group in part of the women's prison, where there were some long term prisoners. These were mainly old women convicted of murder, usually associated with witch doctor practices such as the ritual killing of a child or person with a view to removing certain organs used to make medicines. In the beginning there were a plenty of

Fig 12.4   *Gaberones 1966: Signing the agreement with De Beers: Patrick (standing left) with President Sir Seretse Khama (seated left) and Vice President Quett Masire (seated right) Minister Jimmy Haskins (4th left).*

names on the rota, but one or two visits to the jail were usually enough to make the excuses start coming in. Eventually, there were only two people left, the vicar's wife and me. We took it in turns to go, each week. The women were often illiterate, so we read to them or helped them with sewing or knitting projects. One woman had such trouble seeing her work, that I realised that she actually needed glasses. No optician existed, nor were there any plans to help people like her. So, I found her a pair of my old reading glasses, which we found suited her well. A friend's maid had been sent to jail for being involved in an abortion, which had resulted in the death of the young girl. She had been given eighteen months for this and was in our sewing class. Poor girl, she always cried as soon as she saw me. My friend often sent her things like soap or talc. I was approached by the male prisoners' warden on one of my visits, who asked if I could help get materials for the men to make rag rugs. I did manage to acquire some by approaching various people in the community and my friends.

Every quarter the High Commissioner's wife arranged, with the help of all the other wives from the High Commission, charity whist drives at their lovely large house in aid of the Scottish Livingstone Hospital at Molepole. There must have been twenty tables and a supper of pastries was organised, with a raffle too. They raised a considerable amount of money for the hospital, which was being run by Dr Alfred Merriweather and his wife. Their daughter, Joy was at school with Catherine, and we all became quite close friends as a result. Dr Merriweather went on to work as a close and trusted advisor with Sir Seretse Khama and served the country for over fifty-five years.

I belonged to the Women's Institute which was quite active at one time. Unfortunately as the younger women who came from the UK did not join it, it disbanded after a while. I served as Chairman for a point and tried very hard to get the local African women to join, but they were not interested as most were already members of an African women's club. I did not play tennis, but resumed playing golf and played up at the so called Golf Club. In the early days it was just a tin hut with a bar, in the middle of a rather rough golf course and the bush. It was far too hot to play in the afternoons for most of the year, so I used to drive up and do about four holes at about 4 o'clock when it was cooler and before it got dark suddenly at 6 o'clock. For the most part, the fairway was rather like playing on a ploughed field and so we were allowed to tee the ball up all the way round. The rough was mainly tall elephant grass and goodness knows what else hiding in it. There were also some huge trees in the centre of the fairway and you had to try to aim round them, otherwise the ball would end up further back than when you started if you got a direct hit. We had young local boys as caddies, who loyally waited for us at the gate and we tried to tip them well as this was valued income for them and their families. Pat bought me a lovely bag of matched ladies clubs and my caddy lugged it round. We also had to have a T shaped wooden scraper because the greens were actually 'browns', made up of sand mixed with old engine oil. After someone had played the hole, it looked as though cattle had been over it, so we had to use the scraper, which folded down, to flatten it all again. In order to make things interesting and challenging, holes were laid out over ditches and one had a tee that was up on a high rock. This was reached by several narrow steps cut into the rock. One day I went up there to tee off and came face to face with a long snake that was sunbathing on the top. We both moved out of each other's way, it slithered down the far side and I turned and fell down the stairs. The spectacle was clearly amusing and my caddy fell about laughing, as did I. The Africans always have such a good sense of humour. Annoyingly, I twisted and injured my knee in the process which took a good while to heal.

We celebrated the first Anniversary of Independence in September 1967. The country remained stable politically with no changes at all. The multi-racial relationships were as good as ever. Unfortunately, a shanty town had begun to spring up in the outskirts of Gaberones, which was a disgrace with no sanitation and very poor living conditions. These people, attracted by the possibility of having a better life and finding work, were joined by less honest types such as criminals. There was no violence towards Europeans, nor were there any burglaries taking place in European homes and doors and windows did not need to be locked. Because of the number of people crowding into the capital, local scrub and trees suffered as people cut down a great many for fuel. This unfortunately deforested the area and caused soil erosion.

Sometime in 1968–1970 the First Game Lodge opened. As Pat was involved in tourism as part of his remit, we were invited to the official opening, together with our Minister, Sir Seretse Khama and Ruth together with a number of other officials. We were flown up there by a Dakota aircraft, which narrowly missed a large tree at the end of the grass strip runway that had just been cleared for it. Before we left it had to be chopped down, as the pilot needed a longer take off strip. We spent a very pleasant night in the thatched safari hut with all mod cons. It was a lovely interlude. However, on a subsequent official visit, things did not go quite to plan, as can be seen from the following extract from the Botswana Government Press Release:

The Minister of Mines, Commerce and Industry, Mr Amos Dambe, and other occupants of a launch travelling on the Chobe River last Saturday, had a narrow escape from drowning when a hippo smashed a large hole in the boat and threw them all into the water. The party, consisting of the Minister, his Permanent Secretary, Mr Reardon, Dr Lloyd Swift of the Food and Agricultural Organisation; the Game Warden for Chobe Mr Hepburn, had left the Game Warden's camp at about 11 o'clock in the morning. They proceeded up-river in a launch owned by the Game Warden, to study flora and fauna in connection with an ecological survey.

Whilst approaching an island mid-stream in the Chobe River – which had a large number of elephant on it – the engine of the boat stalled. Then a baby hippo was seen at the nose of the launch, and when Dr Lloyd Swift made to restart the engine, the boat was suddenly shot into the air and the four occupants were thrown in the water. Apparently, the mother hippo had come to defend her baby and had erupted below the boat, smashing a large hole in the hull.

Fortunately the party were quite near to the island. They abandoned boat and clambered into a tree overhanging the river. The Minister who does not swim was helped out by Mr Hepburn. The noise of the party frightened the elephants away from the banks, enabling the party to get ashore safely. The hippo was seen with its head through the bottom of the boat. It was apparently so startled by finding its head through in a boat that it did not attack further, but made off. The party eventually managed to attract the attention of a passing motorist on the mainland, who drove to the Chobe River Hotel, whose manager rescued them in the Chobe River launch picking them up at about 1 o'clock. A spokesman of the party told the DAILY NEWS: 'We are none the worse for the incident, but we did see a little more of the fauna than we had expected.'

Undeterred, the Minister and Mr Reardon, accompanied by Dr Lloyd Swift and Mr Graham Child, the ecologist, set out by air on Sunday morning to study the northern boundary of the Game Reserve. In two hours' flying they travelled as far as the Selinda Spillway, running into the Okavango Swamps, and covered a big area of the Game Reserve and various safari company areas.'

(Botswana Government Press Release No. 1530/65)

A new type of European began to arrive in 1968. The men and their wives were products of modern university education and thinking. They had little time for anything vaguely colonial and some attempted to re-think the way in which house staff should be treated, without really having any desire to understand their culture. One couple made their staff sleep in the house and fed them at their table on tinned peaches, salad and ham. The maids complained to my friend and asked her to explain to the couple that the servants actually preferred to eat their own local food, in their own quarters because it was their custom to do so. They also wanted to eat the local maize staples, mielie-meal and *samp* and expected meat to be available daily, plus vegetables for their stews. They also did not want to sleep inside the house, as their boyfriends were unable to visit them and this was causing issues. Most staff had very high standards and a view as to whom they wanted to work for, which depended largely on their rank within society as it reflected on their own status. They seemed to prefer employers where they knew where they stood and disliked any weakness. They valued employers with a high standard of living and seniority. Those who gained a bad reputation usually found it extremely difficult to appoint and keep staff.

Pat was awarded the Order of the British Empire in June 1968 for his services to the British Crown in its overseas territories. Towards the beginning of 1970, there were a lot of changes starting to happen. Pat's Minister was changed during a cabinet reshuffle and the new Minister was quite difficult to work with and appeared rather lazy. He could seldom be found when required for document signing, meetings and when the President wanted him. For some reason, he rarely came into the office. One day when he left the office yet again mid-morning, his long serving departmental secretary asked the routine question: 'Where will you be Minister?' He turned on her and accused her of spying on him. She had only wanted to know where to reach him should he be required, so she gave in her notice the next day. He insisted they replaced her with a local girl with little or no office experience and Pat complained that unfortunately, the work was then not up to the standard required.

This episode made Pat think about his future, especially with the possibility of localisation of the entire Secretariat. There was by now a change in the attitude of the local peoples. Returning students from overseas universities in Russia and China were bringing in new ideas which did not fit well with the current administration. Politics began to become a very important issue and there was certain trouble fermented by political parties. A university was set up and before long there was a strike there. In December 1970 he asked to be relieved of his post and made enquiries about other postings. Not many other territories now remained which could offer colonial service officer jobs. Only two senior postings on the islands of Tristan da Cunha and St Helena were offered to Pat, but he had turned them down because it would have meant months of parting from the children because of travel issues. On 21st July 1971 Pat retired from the Colonial Service after seventeen years of service.

We had been very happy in Botswana and were considering remaining there, but there were several experiences which started to make us feel uneasy, and one incident tipped the balance in favour of leaving. On his way back from Johannesburg one weekend, Timothy accidentally killed a goat which ran across the road in front of his car. A police patrol arrested him and held him on the side of the road about ten miles outside the capital for around three hours. We were desperate, wondering what had happened to him as he could not get word to us. Fortunately, someone also coming from Johannesburg saw what had happened and came to tell us. We contacted the Commissioner of Police, who went to the scene and brought him home. Given that Timothy had offered to pay for the goat, which was the usual practice, the Police Patrol should have released him right away. We were so sorry that things had turned this way.

I resigned from my job with the Co-op and we had a little party. They were very sorry to see *Ma* Reardon go and the African Manager said that he would have no-one to protect him from the angry customers. He used to telephone me at home and I would drive quickly there to help him sort things out. Usually it was a European making a fuss over there being no milk or something left. They were just planning on building a double storied Co-op in the mall, selling furniture as well as groceries. I was quite glad that I was leaving, as it would not have been our cosy Co-op which we were all used to. I heard later that the Manager left because the Committee upset him by insisting that someone's sister being given my old job, who was not capable of carrying out the duties properly. Sadly, when the new store opened, it did not do very well and no dividends were paid after I had left.

In December 1971, we found good jobs for the servants, packed up and left the country. We had been there for nearly eleven happy years. It was with great sadness that we said goodbye to everyone, but we were not sorry to be going. Pat had a whole year's paid leave accrued, so we decided to move over the border to South Africa and have a long holiday before deciding on the next step. It meant not having to have the animals put down or rehomed, or cause disruption to Catherine at school and it gave us some breathing space to make decisions about what we would be doing next.

13

South African Stay and
Departure from Africa

In December 1970, we found homes for the remaining guinea pig and the breeding pairs of budgies in the outside aviary. Peter, the talking budgie had already gone to a good home. We obtained permission for Pepsi and Jess, the two dogs, along with the cat Moggy to be taken into Johannesburg. The rest of our baggage was ready and packed. Just prior to our departure, we found a house to rent in Parkmore, a suburb of Johannesburg. So, we drove up with the large lorry behind us with all our crates. In many ways I was very sorry to leave Botswana, but not as deeply upset as I might have been as I was very aware that change was in the air.

We settled comfortably into our rented house quickly. Our impeccable references had done the trick, and were able to have our pets with us. For the first month or so we simply relaxed and soaked up the civilisation all around us and enjoyed the shops, theatres and restaurants.

I knew Pat would get bored with that after a while, so was quite relieved when he was contacted by someone he knew. He was invited to do a paid consultancy for a low cost local housing project in Botswana. In the end, this particular proposal did not get the go-head, but Pat was retained to take over some part time legal work and conveyancing preparation. He was put in charge of a team of house agents selling houses all around South Africa.

We decided to buy a ranch style house in Kelvin, which was a small village style development in Johannesburg and this meant that

Catherine's school was just forty minutes away. It was quite big and consisted of three bedrooms and two bathrooms, with a hall and cloakroom, study, dining room and large sitting room. The kitchen was brand new, modern and lovely with a scullery area attached. Carpets were laid throughout the house and for the first time in my life I had the curtains professionally made with matching furnishings. In addition it had a courtyard just off the kitchen and a garage set apart. The plot was three quarters of an acre in total and had forest of Australian eucalyptus trees along one side. It was the very first house that we had ever owned and so we went quite mad and had the garden professionally landscaped and a swimming pool with underwater lighting installed. A strong wooden fence put up around the property to keep the dogs in and we had a smart main gate. The servants' quarters of two rooms also had a nice bathroom and were at the very back of the plot, in a private walled area.

When the old VW Beetle I had been driving for several years went in for a MOT test and failed, the examiner suggested that it was probably two different cars; chassis of one and body of another, not even bolted together properly. So we bought a brand new VW Beetle. I used to drive to get Catherine for her fortnightly exeat weekends and brought her and her friends back to Kelvin, where they swam all day and ate me out of house and home.

After a few weeks, I took on a maid called Margaret and she showed me her identity passbook which all non-whites had to carry by law; whites had to carry identity cards. It may not have been her actual name, as I learned afterwards that they used to lend their cards to family and friends. She seemed neat and efficient. One week when I was just about to go out shopping, I gave her pay early to her as she told me she needed to visit her mother that day. When I got back Herbert, the weekly gardener, asked me why I had sacked her. When I replied that this was not the case, he told me that she had left with all her suitcases in a van, which had arrived to collect her not long after I had gone out. I rushed into the house and found that she had stolen all my clothes including some English tweeds, which she had packed into my suitcases. She also took my hats, gloves and shoes. She was going to be very smart. I was stunned, as was Herbert, who called her a *skellum* (rascal). As I had not realised that I was required to register her as my servant, my neighbours warned me against calling the police. Everything operated so very differently in South Africa to anywhere else I had ever lived in Africa.

After this, I decided not to have any full time servants, and asked a friend to help find me a part-time one for two mornings a week. A woman arrived who at first seemed to work well, except that she kept nipping outside for a quick smoke, but all the work was being done. One day two weeks later, I returned home to find the house locked from the inside and I could not get in with the key. The gardener helped me prise open the back door and she was lying on the kitchen floor completely stoned on some narcotic. I dismissed her and for a while had no one, but then Herbert brought me a fellow Zulu woman called Emma who was excellent. She came twice weekly and on Sunday her school boy son came to clean the swimming pool. I made sure that they all had a meal as part of their wages each day.

About this time, Pat had become somewhat disillusioned by his work as it was not challenging enough. He had also been contacted by a friend of his in the British Foreign Office, who thought there were several senior postings that might suit his experience and be of interest to him. He decided to go to the UK and visit the Foreign Office and see what postings were available. Unfortunately, as I had no one I trusted to look after the dogs and the house, I decided to remain behind at the house; supported by my kind neighbours and trustworthy Zulu staff. Even though we had an alarm installed, it was not too nice being alone and I kept the dogs with me at all times. Burglars would trigger the alarms regularly, which meant that people thought they were faulty and switched them off, at which point they would then break in. Our alarm went off several times, once at 3 o'clock, but I just checked around and then reset it. Also, at this time I noticed that someone was coming in and using our servant's quarters at night and taking baths, so I had the water disconnected out there. Then someone took all our garden furniture. On the nearby estate, things had become so out of hand that they had appointed a guard. It was unpleasant to feel that you were closely being watched all the time.

Pat took Catherine with him back to England to see her grandmother, his mother, where Catherine stayed while he attended several meetings with the Foreign Office. He was immediately offered an overseas senior appointment, this time in the Pacific. He also had several meetings with contacts in Vienna and Venice on the way back, which made it a bit more of a holiday for them as they were able to visit some of the sights. He wanted to consult me first before confirming he would take the appointment. In some ways I was quite dismayed about leaving the house with all our lovely furnishings and fittings, and pretty landscaped garden. Having Catherine so close by at school was lovely, but the situation in South Africa with regard to personal safety and the apartheid politics did not really suit us at all. So I supported him, as I knew it was the type of work at which he excelled and could not let him turn the job down. Once he had formally accepted, he had his medical and flew off immediately to his new posting in 1972.

I was left to dispose of the house, furniture and cars, make arrangements for the animals. Pepsi our older bitch had died of tick-bite fever earlier in the year, so we had a sweet little Pekinese called Suzie Wong. She was sent back to the UK to be quarantined for rabies, before she was allowed to travel to the Pacific posting. Sadly, Jess was too old to travel and a friend took her on for us and she lived happily with them for another few years. Our dear old cat, Moggy had to be put down as he was quite old and I did not think he would cope well with the long journey and quarantine.

Pat had presumed that I would have had sufficient funds from the house and car sales, which would make the process of leaving South Africa and joining him a relatively simple one. Eventually after several months with no interest from prospective purchasers, we used a reliable letting agency that rented it to the English couple who eventually bought it from us. I also discovered that legally as a lessee, I had to pay the rates and utilities six months in advance, so in order to do this I had to sell my own car much earlier than I had planned. Fortunately, I had looked after it and the garage bought it for almost the same price as I had purchased it. I was very worried and running very short of money, so I had to withdraw Catherine from her last term at school thus saving funds from term fees. It was illegal to have done so, and I hoped no one would follow this up. To cap it all, Pat's Peugeot car was handed over to what seemed to be a reputable English run car dealership, only for them to abscond without paying for it. This same outfit was unsurprisingly involved in another big scandal several years later, when a lot of people lost money on another of their scams. Pat also arranged to have a small amount of money regularly transferred into our account, but tried to keep this to the minimum as there were stringent currency laws which regulated funds leaving the country. I then moved into a small block of serviced apartments with Catherine, to wait for our passage out to New Zealand the Pacific.

I also had to consider where best to educate Catherine in secondary schooling and decided upon New Zealand, as I had a network of friends and family there. It was also closer to our posting to the Gilbert & Ellice Islands and would therefore qualify for a government grant.

My expected tickets for my passage to New Zealand did not arrive. In the cables back and forth between us, Pat confirmed everything was booked and even gave me a date. Lloyd Tristino however insisted there was no booking. Our heavy baggage was now in storage. I had the bill for that to pay and the rent at the flats to find, to say nothing of funding Suzie's quarantine trip to England. I telephoned the shipping company twice a day. There was now only a few days before our ship was due to sail and it had become critical that we sailed with it, as it was the last passenger service to leave Cape Town for Australia due to the oil crisis. At this point I decided to send the baggage down to the port anyway and despatched the dog to the England by air with all the documents and inoculations in order. Things were becoming critical, but thankfully four days before the boat departed I had a telephone call from the shipping company informing me that my tickets would be waiting for me in the office at Cape Town. There was now just three days left to get everything sorted out and travel right across South Africa to Cape Town. We managed to get a sleeping compartment for the overnight train and made a booking for a hotel in Cape Town. Fortunately, I had just enough money for the bill and had a little money left over and Travellers Cheques too for the journey. The tickets were waiting at the shipping office as promised, and we checked to see if the baggage was on board, which it was.

Throughout all these stressful last few weeks, Catherine and I had regularly walked to the post office and collected our mail and read the sunny letters from Pat, who was quite oblivious of the drama going on in Johannesburg – my letters to him with all our troubles, seemed not to be reaching their destination. It was an extremely difficult time for me emotionally, not helped because so many things went wrong, and I was beginning to suffer from exhaustion. Pat was many thousands of miles away and out of communication, except by cable. In 1973 as we sailed out of Cape Town harbour, I felt a mingled sense of relief and sadness as it was likely to be my last sight of Africa ever.

POSTSCRIPT: REFLECTIONS ON LIFE IN THE COLONIAL SERVICE IN AFRICA

There was an old colonial saying: 'Officers were expected to be bachelors, if they had wives it was unfortunate – having children was considered even worse!' There seems to have been little recognition of the fact that women played any part in the Colonial era at all. Sir Rex Niven, who had served for over forty years in Northern Nigeria said at an event: 'I regard wives who supported their husbands in Africa as being as important as those they were supporting.' This was generally less of a trial in Botswana. We received a small entertainment allowance for official events, which was rarely sufficient; we had to fund most of it ourselves, which is just not right.

Botswana was one of our happier postings in Africa, and we were very sorry when we left. Although it was very hot at times in Botswana, there were cooler seasons and in postings bordering the Kalahari Desert, temperatures dropped quite considerably overnight. We were bathed in perspiration most of the time and suffered from heat oedema, with hands and feet swelling. Many also suffered from prickly heat. We were all as brown as berries through just being outside doing gardening or walking about; very few sunbathed as such. We all tried to ensure good health, by having vaccinations and boiling drinking water, checking for insects such as scorpions in shoes and clothing, etc.

Fortunately we had plenty of books, radio news and newspapers, however old or delayed, which kept us connected with the outside world. In the more remote postings visitors were very welcome and the odd social gathering was helpful to break up the isolation.

Having staff was a great bonus in hot and difficult climates. There were those Europeans (usually trendy or left wing) who chose not to have servants. In so doing, generally they were looked down on by the local Africans who considered them inferior. By employing staff in some areas, this meant that there was lighter better paid work for the women and more interesting work for men. Skills learned through this also meant that some were in a better place when independence came. The women tended to save their money and support their extended families back in their home villages. After independence, HNO people started to arrive. The maids were very selective about whom they worked for and for some reason they deemed non-Europeans to be lower down the rung...They used to give their employers nicknames, and a friend's servant was a very good mimic and was quite able to indicate who had called if they had not left their name!

There was an agreed pay structure for staff in the larger places such as Gaberones, but we did try to supplement this with additional food essentials, gifts of clothing, linen, etc. My one regret is that we were not always in a position to give them a higher remuneration; I very much valued their service. We always seemed to get on well with our staff, respecting their needs, traditions and customs. Their quarters were usually purpose built homes near the house, with a private WC and shower. They also had a small cooking area, where they could cook their own food and store things. They were basic quarters, based on their tradition homes back in their tribal homelands. If the terrain was suitable, they were able to grow some additional crops for their own use such as sweet corn and maize. In Mochudi, previously someone had planted grapefruit and lime trees, so we shared this fruit, eggs and other fresh items with our staff. In South Africa, many staff had worked for the same families for a great many years, sometimes more than twenty years. Although the pay was not high, they were fed and comfortably housed with all their living costs paid for. It also meant that they lived in much safer and better conditions than most of those in townships and could save money up to educate their children, which helped them escape township poverty.

Another one of my regrets was not having more of our own furnishings and making ourselves more comfortable in the homes. This was made more difficult as there were so many house moves; at least one a year if not more in some postings. We lived too long thinking we would have it all when we retired, which was a long way ahead of us still and of course, Pat never lived to see his retirement.

During the early days when travelling to our posts and returning on leave, we sailed to the UK and back on the following ships. First class travel was partly paid for by Pat's salary. The ships we sailed on included the P&O Strathnaver and Chusan; Lloyds Triestino's Africa, Europa and Marconi; Holland-Africa's Boshfontein and Jagersfontein. On board ship there was no mixing with the crew, with the exception of the senior officers. This applied to all the shipping lines, except on the Holland-African trips. Selected VIP passengers were always seated at officer's tables. You had to be very senior to be asked onto the

Captain's Table. We never quite made it there, because by the time we had reached such an exalted level, we were flying instead! However, I did once make it onto the Purser's Table... There were lots of ship board activities, fancy dress parties, etc. Food was usually good and beef tea (not my favourite) was served on deck at 11 o'clock in cold weather. In the early days there were canvas pools erected for swimming when the ship travelled into warmer climates. Latterly, there were permanent pools. The ships went through the Suez Canal, until the 1960s, and then afterwards we went by air to the UK.

There had been a hope that when their Colonial Service came to an end long-serving and loyal officers returning to the UK would be allowed to fit into Civil Service or Foreign Office positions at their suitably senior and pensionable level. But despite several schemes proposed by the Colonial Office no such arrangement was made by the British Government. Instead compensation schemes were introduced in most territories, and officers were permitted to commute part of their pension on leaving the Service. Most of them chose that option, fearing that the new African or other government would renege on the agreements made with the British Government whereby the pensions were to continue to be paid by the incoming government just as before Independence. Several of the new governments did renege and the British Government was slow to make provision for the pensions to be paid from UK funds, causing hardship for officers and widows affected at the time. The Overseas Service Pensioners' Association, founded in 1960, played a significant role in fighting the cause of the pensioners and successfully campaigned over a number of years to get the British Government to accept responsibility for the payment of the pensions to these loyal servants of the Crown. That this seemed to be done with some reluctance was resented by some who felt they were treated rather shabbily, after enduring considerable hardship during their work overseas and afterwards in retirement.

As I have said elsewhere, the problems in Africa seem these days to be caused by ineptitudes mainly of the newly Independent

Governments. Aid is not used for the purpose it was given, through inefficiencies or corruption. Stable governments and systems, law and order, schools, hospitals, clinics, libraries, irrigation and agricultural practices and other essential elements, were all in place when we left; unfortunately people intent on using power changed all that. Apart from Botswana, in almost all other African countries, there has been widespread corruption and unstable governments and coups d'état. Experiments with Marxism have brought countries like Tanganyika and Mozambique to near disaster. Despotic leaders such as Idi Amin and Robert Mugabe have ruined former self-supporting affluent countries like Uganda and Zimbabwe. These now have to import most of the food and where their people are starving because their economy has been ruined.

It is to be hoped that this situation will improve in time. All memory of benign colonial stewardship is being expunged from the history books in these countries. Young people in these countries have unfortunately now grown up never knowing what it was like to have this stability and real freedom; some are experiencing ethnic or religious persecution.

Our postings were at a time of great change throughout the colonies as the sun began to finally set on the once great British Empire.

PART 4

Six Years in the Pacific

Gilbert & Ellice Islands

1973–1979

Foreign and Commonwealth Office

14

THE JOURNEY THERE

Catherine and I sailed from Capetown in late 1973 on the Lloyd Tristino SS Marconi. After all our problems of the past few months it was an enormous relief to be on board, despite being allocated a much lower grade first class cabin with a shared bathroom as a result of a booking error. I had lost a lot of weight because of the terrible worry in South Africa, so it was wonderful to find the food was excellent and the relaxing life on board did me so much good. The ship was full of immigrants from Eastern Europe and Italy; there were also a handful of South African and English immigrants.

The journey to Freemantle was largely unremarkable but there were rumours circulating that the crew were about to go on strike. We docked at Freemantle for twenty-four hours, which enabled us to take a bus ride to the nearby charming city of Perth which had been built around the Swan River. It was quite beautiful and lush and was so evocative of English cities. When we set sail from Freemantle again, everyone sighed with relief and we decided that the strike talk was indeed nothing more than a rumour. A few days later we arrived in Adelaide and rumours continued to circulate about a possible impending strike, but we sailed again on time to Melbourne twenty-four hours later. I was worried about our heavy baggage and what would happen if the strike took place. Talks were taking place between the Union and the Shipping Line Representative. Apparently, the problem was that the company wanted to withdraw all the ships because of the cost, now that oil prices had risen so high. This of course meant the loss of a lot of jobs, hence the strike threat. In the end, we sailed onto Sydney, but not before we made an unscheduled stop in Tasmania and sailed into Hobart for the opening of the new casino at Wrest Point, on what was probably the last passenger ship full of customers for a long time to come. We went on a tour of the area and up to the top of Mount Wellington, where it was snowing lightly to the delight of the South Africans who had never seen any before and visited the casino. They enjoyed the evening out immensely.

On arrival in Sydney, the crew immediately went on strike and we all had to leave the boat, despite the fact that we had been booked all the way through to Auckland. Our steward assured me the boat would leave in due course, so we decided to leave our hand luggage including Catherine's guitar, my typewriter and various other things with him. The Lloyd Tristino representative came on board and gave us all £80 each for the four days which they thought it would take to resolve the strike. We were told to check with their office in Sydney on a given date. So Catherine and I had £160 between us for the four days. I managed to cable Pat about the situation and he got in touch with someone he knew in Sydney and asked them to meet us. By then some of my frantic letters had eventually arrived in the islands, recounting my traumas in South Africa and en route. A very charming middle-aged lady met us and took charge and organised a small holiday flat for us right in the middle of Sydney, which was very comfortable. She arranged tours and took us sightseeing. She also said that the account would be sent on later, so not to worry about paying there and then and that if I needed any more money she would arrange this too. So we were able to relax and enjoy what turned out to be a very busy five days. After checking with Lloyd Tristino every morning, we toured all over Sydney and even managed to visit the famous Bondi beach and Sydney Harbour Bridge. When I was a young schoolgirl, I had been taken in a school party to see a beautiful working model of the latter, displayed at the library in

Cambridge. It then being one of the wonders of the world; little did I ever imagine that I would ever actually see it for myself. We also went across the bay to the zoo to see the strange and wonderful Australian animals including the cute Koala bears. We drove to Botany Bay, which looked very exclusive and I imagine quite a bit different to when the first convicts saw it.

At last the industrial dispute was over, and the ship was able to proceed. I then discovered that our passage had only been booked in as far as Sydney, so we had some last minute stress and trauma to get this sorted out. When we arrived in Auckland our heavy baggage was put into Customs Bond, until I decided what the next step was. On arrival in New Zealand immigration, I had just £400 in cash and a note from the Governor's Office in the Gilbert & Ellice Islands which confirmed that I was a bona fide traveller and en route to the colony. My cousin met me at the dock and took us to a motel. She was the matron of the nursing home for the blind nearby and lived in a small flat attached to it. A few days later I took over a bungalow belonging to my cousin's friend who was off on a world tour. So we were very comfortable.

I set about reading up on all of the school prospectuses which my cousin had kindly collected for me. Catherine and I then went all over the place looking at possible schools, but to no avail. Most of them could not take her for at least a term or two, but I eventually tracked down a school in Hawkes Bay near Napier, called Woodford House which had a vacancy. We flew down to Napier and I was rather worried when we saw the school with its rather old fashion grey uniform. I was sure that Catherine would never accept any of it, but thank goodness she knew why it was all necessary. The headmistress met us and welcomed Catherine to the school. It was the beginning of term, so she was to start immediately. We rushed into Havelock North to buy the uniform and set about sewing on name tags which I had brought with me. We spent a sad last night together, before she was delivered to school the next day. I felt awful about it all; putting her into a school where she did not know anyone, in a strange country and then having to fly off to a remote island and not be close at hand if there were any problems.

By then my onward flight ticket to Gilbert & Ellice Islands had arrived and I flew onto Fiji, where I had to spend two nights at the airport hotel, awaiting the weekly air service to the islands. Fiji is one of my favourite places and, although the hotel was quite simple it somehow managed to be very exotic with palms and lush beautiful tropical plants. The mosquitoes were awful and in their thousands, but it was not a malarial area although they did carry dengue fever.

So about two months after arriving in in the Pacific region, I took a seat on the Air Pacific Fokker Friendship, a propeller-powered plane that would take me on the eight hour flight necessary to get to the Gilbert & Ellice Islands. We landed at Funafuti International Airport in the Ellice Islands to refuel. The airport buildings consisted of a rather damaged straw hut. The rest of the island had been laid wasted by a recent hurricane, but fortunately there was little loss of life. The airstrip looked rather like a battlefield with coconut trees flattened around it. On the flight it was fascinating to see the turquoise sea below surrounding the occasional island, sparkling in the horizon-to-horizon deep blue of the endless deep ocean. For some reason they decided to serve lunch just as we left Funafuti, during a particularly turbulent part of the journey. There was something of a battle to get the food trays out before the pilot put the seatbelt sign back on and the hostesses had to sit down again. Then you had to hang onto your tray as the aircraft lurched wildly about. It was all a bit unnerving as you tried not to get your food and hot coffee spilt all over you. Fortunately, most of those travelling saw the funny side of this.

On the approach to Tarawa airport on the island of Bonriki in the Gilbert Islands, the aircraft had to come in extremely low over the lagoon, then bank sharply to get into position to land on the very short runway, which had been placed across the width of the only piece of land deemed suitable for this purpose. The plane taxied to the straw airport hut, which had 'Bairiki International Airport' on its sign. I always thought these pilots needed medals for the skill they showed in landing the planes on these tiny islands in these old propeller aircraft with some pretty basic navigational aids. Once there was a letter in the local newspaper *Atoll Pioneer* from an American pilot who regularly used to fly small two or four seater aircraft from the factory in the USA to Australia, stopping en route to refuel at Tarawa and rest overnight. He said he was always so thankful to see the island appear below him and to hear the air traffic controller's voice. It was his first contact with the world for many hours on that lonely crossing over this almost empty area of the Pacific.

15

FIRST TOUR IN TARAWA

When I arrived, Pat was there to meet me with transport. There were few formalities, just a quick stamp in the passport and we were off home, which turned out to be a brand new prefab house right on the beach, facing onto the breezy ocean side of the island (see Fig. 15.1). It was the second house he had been allocated, the first one being in such poor repair that when the new prefab was completed he asked to be moved. We lived in Bairiki village where the Admin headquarters was located and had the same house for the whole stay, which was wonderful after the many house changes in previous postings. The spacious house was set in a quarter of an acre of white sand garden full of coconut trees, the fruit of which plummeted down regularly. The large sitting room, patio and main bedroom overlooked the reef about 100 yards away, which broke the full force of the sea on the ocean side of the island. There was always the most spectacular surf breaking and I could have watched the roll of the surf, making tunnels, forever. The other two bedrooms, the bathroom, kitchen and dining room were at the back of the house. The house was just 10ft from the high tide mark and during some of the King Tides at certain times of the year, the sea actually rolled gently to the edge of our veranda. At first the noise of the surf breaking was deafening, but after a while one got used to it and it ceased to register. Initially, I was also a bit worried about the vulnerability of being surrounded by the sea on both sides, on such a low-lying strip of land sometimes no wider than a few feet and not much higher than sea level.

Suzie, our Pekinese, was despatched by the quarantine kennels in Hampshire where she had been for six months. We had to have her spayed as part of the deal. She caused a great deal of interest in the Ellice Islands when exercised on the tarmac, but as usual she took it all in her stride and seemed none the worse for her journey, which lasted around thirty-eight hours. She recognised us immediately and settled in well to her new life. The temperature clearly suited her and she was perfectly happy. As we had no front fence to our garden which was essentially the beach, she had to be tied up on a long rope as she tended to wander off.

The islands are atolls with a ring shaped lagoon and made up largely of coral and fine white sand; the former of which had grown on top of an extinct submerged volcanic caldera. There was as a result very little natural vegetation, apart from the coconut trees and in parts of the islands there were mangrove swamps and breadfruit trees. In a few areas some straggly hardy grasses seemed to tolerate the salty conditions and there were also salt bushes which the local livestock seemed to like. All the trees belonged to and were cared for by local people who carved their names or initials into them. We put a few more into our garden to help provide shade and the staff asked us to give the trees to them, which we did and they carved their initials into them. We also gave some to the old man who came to sweep our patio and garden each week and he in turn used to bring us watermelons once in a while. We also grew some paw-paw trees from pips, which grew quickly and in eighteen months bore some lovely fruit. We gave some small plants away to friends, who also planted them successfully and the fruit was always in demand. Pat also tried to grow tomatoes, but less successfully. We were very short of water, and used to use bath water to water our plants.

We had tanks attached to the house for collecting rain, but unfortunately very little rain fell. Every day a tanker came to fill up the house tank, which was perched high up on a girder at the far end of the garden. This water was for the laundry, flushing the WC, showering and washing up. It was strictly rationed and came from the ground water table top level which was only slightly salty. The lower levels were very salty. We boiled our drinking water from the rainwater butts and used this for cooking. We decided also to use some of this water to wash in as the tanker water had an unpleasant smell. We boiled an old kettle up with the smelly water and topped it up with the other rainwater, thus diluting it. Luckily, we did not have to filter our drinking water. Our shower only had cold water and was a chilling experience, not always welcome even in the warm humid temperatures. We used a bucket and an old mug, first soaping all over and then washing off the dirt by pouring mugs of clean water all over our bodies. It was easy once you got the knack of it and we had two or three of these baths during the day. As the months went by, the showerhead became very rusted up and our official visitors battled to shower in a drizzle of water supplied by about three holes.

Pat used to swim on the ocean side of the island, but the waters around the island were quite often full of seaweed and could be quite murky. There were few sightings of sharks in the shallow waters, but it was quite possible to encounter some other rather large fish. Catherine was swimming on her own in water several metres deep on the ocean side, when she was aware of something large going along quite nearby her about the size of a coconut frond, which turned out to be a manta ray. Although they are harmless, it was very unnerving and she did not swim in this area much after that on her own.

Each evening after afternoon tea, I would put on my old tennis shoes and take the dog for a mile or so walk out to the edge of the reef on the ocean side when the tide was out. Suzie loved the water and would plough along through the rock pools, some of which were quite deep and chase about after the fish. She always headed for the big black sea cucumbers and would sink her teeth into them with disastrous results. They always put out mauve protective foam, so her face used to disappear in a cloud of froth. The first time it happened, I panicked and washed her mouth out, but subsequently discovered that the locals considered them to be a great delicacy on the islands. There were so many wonderful and interesting sea creatures and fish in the pools and shells, although the majority of them were cowries. There were some more dangerous things out there too though, including cone shells with poison darts that could kill an adult in seconds and stone fish which look much as their name, with spikes that could paralyse an adult and kill a child. I wore tennis shoes at all times, mostly though because the coral would have cut your feet to shreds. When the tide was out, it exposed a long reef which was between 200 yards and 15ft wide; some of which was above the water level while other sections remained ankle deep. The sea was a dark inky blue colour and was more than a thousand feet deep, with the surf foaming white and pounding down with a terrible roar. I had to keep a sharp watch for the tide turning as the sea ran slowly back over the reef, deepening until it reached waist high and then it continued rolling towards the beach where it was just knee deep. The surf though would then pound all over the reef where I had just been walking. On the days of the high King Tides, I used to vary my walk to the lagoon side of the island and here my time was usually taken up chatting to various people that I met on my way. Pat would sometimes get the car out and drive us up to the area behind the airport where there was an area of beautiful unspoilt beach. It was not suitable for swimming, as the surf was too close to the beach and the current was strong, but it was a good place to pick up driftwood and shells.

One of the things which I found so trying about the islands was the dense population on such a limited habitable island space. The village of Bairiki consisted of a collection of expatriate houses and local huts, stretching along both the ocean side of the island and the leeward lagoon side, with just a single width tarmac road between the two. Every inch of the island had a coconut palm or tree and a house, hut or office on it. While the Europeans were better off in some ways with larger garden areas around their properties, even so houses were close enough to hear ones neighbours talking. Given the crush of humanity on the island, any walks to the quietness of the reef or deserted beaches felt very special. I used to look back towards the islands and feel quite refreshed. The population of Bairiki was at this time about two thousand islanders and around sixty Europeans. It was unbelievably noisy as most had motorbikes. Later on when someone at the secondary school in Bikenibeu introduced pop music to the islands by starting up a band, there was a sudden outbreak of amplifiers and electric guitars, and so the noise intensified. The locals seemed not to need much sleep as the twanging of strings and blaring of music went on all night. Around this time we decided to get an air conditioner for our bedroom to help on the very humid, sticky nights, which fortunately also helped to drown out every other noise.

Pat had engaged two Ellice Islanders as staff when he first arrived. One named Apasasa and the other Noama. They were Polynesians, akin to the Maori people of New Zealand. At the time few Gilbertese worked as staff in European homes. Apasasa cleaned the house and prepared some of the food for him, but was not a cook. Noama was the laundress. There was not a great deal for them to do. He also had a Gilbertese woman who came to sweep the garden. Unusually, she was not very pleasant and quite hostile, so I was relieved when she decided to leave one day. Noama stayed with us until the separation of the Gilbert Islands from the Ellice Islands around independence. She was very fond of Catherine and showed her how they cleaned sea shells like Cowries, by putting them into the sand to get the ants to clear them out. She then helped her wash them and make them into pretty necklaces. Noama also loved to cuddle Suzie, the little Pekinese, rocking her much like a baby, singing songs to her on the sitting room floor. Their idea of housework was somewhat sketchy and I needed to regularly repeat the instructions if I wished basic routine things done such as dusting, sweeping the floors and changing the bed linen. We had no hot water system, so they washed up in cold water, despite my pleas to boil a kettle and use the hot water. We paid about £15 per month for them each, and 20p per hour for the gardener who kept it neat, but could do little else as it mostly consisted of white sand.

When we sat on our veranda at night, we could see the whales spouting water and dolphins leaping in the deep sea on the other side of the reef. We seldom saw ships or the submarines that were rumoured to be out there, but there were always a few canoes with fishermen in them. Generally the local people fished off the lagoon on the leeward side of the island, as they had to rely on the wind for their sails as few had outboard motors. Several times during our time in the Colony, fishermen were carried away by the wind and tide over long distances in the empty Pacific Ocean. In one instance three men, having gone missing on a fishing trip over a three-month period, fortunately arrived safely in Samoa some 2,378km away. Another incident was reported by *The Telegraph's* Auckland Correspondent:

'Fishermen saved – Four Kiribati fishermen, adrift in their disabled fishing boat in the Pacific Ocean for 23 days, have been rescued by an American tuna boat. They survived by eating raw fish and drinking rainwater.'

(*The Telegraph* newspaper: August 1987)

Later on, when outboard motors became more common, there were still more people drifting away as they had no sails to rely on as a backup. Another cutting from the same newspaper the following year states:

'Eight people from the South Pacific island of Kiribati survived 29 days at sea by catching sharks and turtles by hand. But two of the party, the youngest (a boy of 2) and the oldest (a woman of 67) died as the islanders drifted more than 1,000 miles from their homeland. Their ordeal began when they were hit by a storm while travelling to a nearby atoll. After lashing their two canoes together, they first survived on coconuts and rainwater, but later caught four turtles and sharks by hand, before being rescued by an American fishing boat.'

(*The Telegraph* newspaper: 1987)

We were able to buy fish if we went down to the harbour when the boats were returning. It was mainly tuna which cost only 15p/lb, and it was delicious. We found out this early on and had plenty of it. It has a firm flesh which can be cooked without disintegrating, so lends itself to being curried. Most Europeans had not cooked and eaten it, and were put off by the grey pre-cooked flesh. I did encourage newcomers to try it, and usually they were hooked. Sometimes we would have a red tide of algal blooms, which made the fish that ate it toxic, but the local people were well aware of the dangers and did not fish during this time.

By far the best thing I had ever tasted was the local dish of *Kokoda*, raw fish in coconut milk. At first we tried it with caution; it being raw fish. The islanders marinated the fish in lemon juice for twenty-four hours, then squeezed the fish out with their hands, and dressed it with coconut milk sauce. Once you had tasted it, it was always the first thing all of us went straight for at any local feast. There was also an unlimited supply of live crayfish sold door to door by the locals for 25p/lb, which Pat loved. Catherine and I cooked one once in a pot of boiling water and became traumatised by the process, so neither of us could eat it later. The women used to bring round mussels or similar shellfish, which they used to grub up from just beneath the sand at low tide. We avoided these, as we considered the beach to be quite polluted given it was used as an outside natural latrine by the locals.

Unfortunately, the sea around Bairiki on the ocean side and adjoining islands was littered with cans, plastic bags, tyres and anything that was drifting in with the tide. Some things had been thrown overboard by passing ships at sea. The coral reef around the islands was dying and we were told that pollution was one of the probable causes, although there was also a plague of crown-of-thorns star fish which destroy reefs too. For a number of weeks each year, marine algae floated about on the surface and made swimming in the sea very uninviting. Added to which, there was no sewage system as such for the local homes although the European houses had cesspits. A couple of these had also been dug in the village and toilets erected in a public block. However these were

Fig 15.1   *Bairiki 1973: Patrick and Margaret relaxing on the veranda on the ocean side.*

quite smelly, so most islanders preferred to use their time-honoured system of the *I-Nakatari*, which means 'go to the sea'. A 30 yard jetty was built out over the sea, with a hut placed at the end of it. This was divided into two sections, for men and women, and had a drop to the sea. Here, all day long, chattering people went back and forth. Those inside called to those waiting, who would sit dangling their legs over the edge of the jetty laughing and joking. It was all very friendly. When the tide was out, a lot of people preferred to use the beach and one would see squatters everywhere. Some brought a native mat with them to drape it around themselves while they did this, and occasionally a toilet roll was used. This all took place in front of our houses, just 15ft away. The *I-Nakatari* was about 100 yards away on the lagoon side of the island. The Government tried to alter the system, but failed because there was just insufficient water to use for flushing more toilets. A World Health team came and decided that, under the circumstances it was as good a system as anything else. Needless to say, we always were grateful for the high tides which cleaned the beaches and we discreetly never went down onto the beaches at low tide. Walking back later along the beach, I would occasionally encounter a lone figure inside their mat and be greeted politely.

At night the beach was alive with hundreds of huge crabs, which waved their massive front claw threateningly while they were busy digging holes. One of the biggest disappointments was that there were not many birds on the islands. We did see a number of sea birds, herons, boobies and fairy terns. I found a fairy tern nest in our pandanus tree, which was wonderful to watch. These tiny white birds are so dainty and for some reason lay their eggs in precarious spots such as on a branch. In this case sadly, the nest was destroyed when a storm blew the tree over. Occasionally, there was a heron on the beach, but very little else. I found the silence very strange after Africa and missed the chirping of the wild birds.

There were very few flowers too, except those brought in by the *I-Matangs* (Europeans). If you wanted to plant things, we followed the local practice of either using a container filled with composted leaves and debris or dug a hole in the ground and filled that with the same sort of compost. Someone gave us some Hibiscus cuttings which did quite well too. Because of the salty breezes, all plant leaves were salt burnt and some really struggled to survive. We had to put them all by the back door and erect a shelter to keep them well away from the wind and sea spray. Pat was the one who did the gardening in Bairiki and got very keen as it was a sort of challenge, which he rather liked. He planted a Bougainvillea in a large bucket, buried in the ground. One of the locals allowed me to take a cutting from the big bush by his house, and the cuttings took well after we planted it under the water tan near the cesspit. It bloomed in two colours after only a few months, half the bush was the usual mauve shade and the other half was orange. It grew well and over the years I was able to take more cuttings to give to friends to pot up and plant out. Soon, there were quite a few Bougainvillea established in Bairiki. Unfortunately, the flowers were nearly always taken by the locals as soon as they appeared. The Gilbertese women made beautiful head wreaths out of any available flowers, even the tiniest buds were used. The Agricultural Department found this out too, when they later ran rather unsuccessful trials of growing peas and beans, because every flower disappeared the moment it appeared. Someone had grown a Frangipane tree at some time in the past and cuttings had been distributed, so there were many of these lovely pungent trees. They seemed so much more pungent than the ones grown in Africa. The locals loved to tuck the flowers behind their ears or used them in celebratory *leis* (wreaths). There is a beautiful set of commemorative postage stamps illustrating these beautiful traditional floral head wreaths.

The local people dug deep pits which they filled with manure and hummus until they were in a satisfactory state for planting. Into these pits they put *Te Babai* (Taro), a plant with an edible root which forms part of their staple diet. These pits were used for years and handed down in the family and closely guarded. There were also a limited number of breadfruit trees, which grew to quite a big size and fruited for several months. When there was a surfeit, we were able to get half a breadfruit, and then we would cut it into slices and fry it the local way. It was a staple food source for the local people. Europeans were not encouraged to eat it because of this and our Governor, John Smith, told me he considered it wrong to rob the local people of their scant resources in this way. Some Europeans disregarded this and ate local food supplies. Yams were also available, but we only ate these when the supply ship failed to arrive. Coconuts however were in plentiful supply. The staff used to open them with a traditional type of machete and quite a few islanders had some serious hand injuries as a result. I was pleased to see that some were using the alternative method of opening them by hitting the eye with force against a stake driven into the ground, but then sometimes the precious milk was lost this way. The local population used coconut milk together with a sauce made from the grated flesh of the coconut to flavour most of their dishes.

The pandanus was another tree that grew and had a coarse stringy nut, which could be sucked, or made into a marvellous toffee like substance. The locals made this into a flat mat about 2ft wide, which when dry they rolled up and stored in the roof of the hut. It had traditionally been a hedge against starvation in the very early days. So the islanders had a perfect diet of taro, fish, pandanus and coconut which gave them every vitamin they needed and a pretty good balanced diet.

They made everything from the coconut palms; their huts from the wood, the roofs from the palm fronds and the mats they rolled down to make walls for shelter against rain, and they also slept on palm mats. They also made clothing, traditional dance costumes and many other items from this valuable resource. The process by which they soaked the Pandanus and palm fronds in seawater to soften them to work them, and the skill by which they wove the mats was impressive. They skilfully also worked these leaves to make a rope for tying the palm fronds onto the roof and down the sides of the huts – it just had to be seen to be believed. One was left thinking of the hundreds of years behind all this knowledge which had been handed down generation after generation. A delicacy for very special feasts on the island was palm salad which was the top growth of the palm. We were given some to try and it was a rare treat, but not one of my favourites. I loved the coconuts and always had one ready in the fridge, but they do give one dreadful gripe if too many are eaten at a time, so we were careful not to overindulge. The local people used to tap the coconut palm for *tody*, a very nutritious drink. They also left it to ferment and it turned into a fiery alcoholic beverage, which some locals used to mix with beer. Unfortunately some people drank rather too freely of both the beer and the tody, and frequent fights broke out amongst the islanders. The number of motorbike accidents was high and drunkenness was rife. It was not a good combination and collisions with coconut palms happened frequently and many people died.

The climate had few variations; it was about 80–90°F each day, with a slight drop in temperature at night. So we usually only used a light blanket if it got breezy or cool from the air conditioning. The windows were always wide open to catch any air that was to be had. There was also not much variation in the length of the day, with sunrise just after 6 o'clock and its setting again just twelve hours later. Seeing the sun slide behind the horizon over the sea very quickly was a wonderful sight and we always tried to watch the green flash that happened just at that moment. At night as we sat outside, we could watch satellites going over far above us. The skies were so clear that we could see several going in different directions each night, and plenty of shooting stars.

Mosquitoes appeared to be in greater numbers as night fell. There was no malaria, but they did carry dengue fever, for which there was no protective medicine. In most cases it was not fatal, but locally known as the break-bone fever which it apparently felt like. It took weeks to recover from it, with the palms of the hands and feet itching as it receded. I was very fortunate not to contract it, but poor Pat did. As it happened I had left the island for the UK to attend my mother's funeral, when there was an outbreak which laid the whole station low. The other plagues we were bothered with were sand flies which sometimes swarmed on the beaches at certain times of the year. They were minute and hopped onto one's legs and bit. Another problem we faced was outbreaks of Hepatitis C, which again was down to the mosquitoes. Fortunately we both escaped this, but several expatriates got it very badly and had to be flown out to hospital.

Rain was very infrequent and was usually less than 15 inches per year, with quite a few severe droughts. We were not generally in the

Pacific hurricane belt in the Gilberts, but the Ellice Islands were and had been struck by Hurricane Bebe in 1972 which caused extensive damage. Both the Gilbert and the Ellice Islands were completely flat and just a few feet above sea level. Massed with coconut palms and people, the forty-two islands were scattered over two million square miles of sea; some were only reached by a solitary ship which took about eighteen months to do the rounds of all the islands in the group. Communications were very difficult at this time and were only possibly by ship-to-shore radio. The inhabitants of these outer islands used to visit each other by canoe. Sometimes they ran out of staples such as rice or flour and an impassioned plea would come to headquarters, who communicated with the supply ship to try and get it to alter its course to visit the relevant islands and come to their rescue. Later on an air service was inaugurated in 1975 and small airfields were built on some of these islands, making life a lot easier on some of the outer islands. Sometimes, the Governor would make an official visit to the outer islands by sea in one of the boats, taking all the other officers with him and their wives. I was warned by a local officer not to go on the boats, as they were very basic in terms of accommodation and food. Pat went along once and found it very hard going. So, sadly I did not see what life was like on these outer islands. A friend of mine who did go and stayed in one of the guest houses had a traumatic time, as did their seven-year-old daughter who accompanied her. There was no lavatory at the guest house and they had to use the beach with the locals. Unfortunately, the local population seemed to find the whole process fascinating; eventually they had to take some mats with them to get some privacy as they attracted rather a lot of onlookers every time they went.

The island of Bairiki had been joined to another called Nanikai by a small causeway, with just enough room for a vehicle to drive carefully over. If one met another car coming, the custom was for one vehicle to drive to a small passing layby to wait. There were fortunately very few cars on the islands when we first arrived, but a bus service operated from Bairiki to the airport at either end of these islands. Another causeway joined the next island and a further one linked to Bikenibeu, making eighteen miles of road. This particular string of islands was called Tarawa and it was here that the Americans landed in 1943 when there was a big battle to recapture the islands from the Japanese. Total control over all the islands was not reasserted until 1945. There were still a great many rusting landing craft lying on some of the beaches and bodies of both American and Japanese soldiers continued to be found when digging drains or foundations, identified only by their dog tags. There were some *Shinto* shrines erected by the Japanese on Betio, but most the American dead were in the Pacific National Memorial Cemetery in Hawaii.

We bought a Morris Minor car and shipped it from Australia, which meant we could get about the island. Cars only lasted around two years before they rusted badly and the bottoms sometimes just fell out. When we went on leave we sold it and later on we purchased a Japanese Toyota from an enterprising Australian, who with his local wife had opened up a garage. What with the increasing number of cars and the large number of powerful motorbikes the roads became quite busy.

Pat was employed by the overseas civil service as Development Secretary and Deputy Financial Secretary on contract terms of three years with leave half way through. Two years later he was appointed as Financial Secretary, which was a responsible job. During this time he was also the Chairman of the Copra Board, a Governor of the Asian Development Bank, Board Member of Air Pacific (a subsidiary of Fiji Airways). He attended conferences worldwide representing the colony, including the Commonwealth Conferences and Trade Ministers meetings in London, and served on the Economic and Social Committee for Asia and the Pacific. He was away quite a lot, especially during the latter part of our time there.

Catherine regularly flew up for school holidays and seemed reasonably happy at the school, where she took the New Zealand School Certificate examinations and passed. All the rest of the school children arrived from the UK en masse several times a year and then there was a big bunch of teenagers about who had a wonderful time. We used to combine with other families to give parties for them.

The club used to organise suitable films and on Club Nights, the place was packed. The projector was on hire and so was the film, which was flown in from Fiji. The sound on the projector seemed always to be poor, quite often inaudible and sometimes the speaking did not match the visuals. One became quite clever at lip reading in order to get the gist of the film. Our club was a double storied high hut, the idea being that members on other islands could sail up and moor underneath it; something I only ever saw one person do in all my time there. It was very useful for having dances in, as all the sides of the bottom storey were open. We had many happy evenings up there at Christmas and New Year. Everyone brought food along and records or sometimes a local band would play so that we could dance. The children could come and join in and when tired, crawl into the car and sleep as these were all parked within sight of us. Another film show where supper was served was held at the local hotel, managed by another Australian and his Gilbertese wife. This was always eagerly attended and we got there early to book our seats. They made the most delicious fish and chips. We were all very sorry when he left to manage a hotel in Fiji and the service at the local hotel was never the same after that.

Some enthusiastic golfers had managed to lay out a course of about six holes near the club on sand and two of the holes disappeared at high tide. I did not play during the day because of the heat but some wives did. The men always wanted the course in the evening after work, so I gave up golf. There were no tennis courts at the club and none at Government House which was unusual. Pat played tennis when he could on a private court at the school, which meant for few opportunities during term time. A few people had outrigger canoes, which took some skill to sail. We bought a motorboat with two other families, which needed some extensive overhauling before we could launch it into the water. It was quite difficult to find somewhere to moor it with easy access as we did not have a RIB dinghy. Initially, we moored in the small harbour but it was constantly being sunk. Sometimes it was the small ferry which sent it to the bottom and sometimes the local children used it to dive off from, which rocked it until it turned turtle. After that we tried beaching it on the lagoon side, but it was very heavy to pull up without winches and we only managed it with the help of the fascinated and ever-helpful locals. We did use it for a few trips to visit islands in the lagoon with picnics, but after a few months of all this hassle for so little reward we decided to sell it.

There were no snakes on the islands and, although we understood that scorpions and centipedes might be present, I never saw any of these. What I did find nasty were the rats, which were quite numerous. There were large black rats, which looked very much like the common ship rat, and tiny coconut rats which were quite pretty in their own way. Suzie had one of these sweet little rats as a plaything. It used to come out at night and sneak along the skirting boards quietly and drink from her water bowl. She used to go and investigate it and it would run off, which instigated a game of chase. One night we came in late from a dinner party and I surprised it in the bathroom and yelled. Suzie rushed forward and seized it and then looked rather mystified when it did not move off again, as she had accidentally killed it.

Our social life was much in the same style as in all the other territories we lived in. We gave informal and formal dinner and supper parties, and sometimes lunch parties at our house and in return, we were invited to similar events in other houses. It was a full time business and our calendar was usually full of engagements. Sometimes the Governor gave big open-air buffets in the small grounds of Government House and Gilbertese choirs would sing their traditional songs, or a group of islanders would do their traditional chants and dances. Gilbert Island singing is fascinating, it has a wonderful sonorous sing-song tone, accompanied by feet stamping and hand clapping. Some hand movements seem very similar to those in Indonesia and it has something of a Polynesian element too. At first I thought the words might be charming traditional tales, but found that quite a few were topical and had lewd references, which the locals all chuckled at!

People arriving from the UK tended to be quite shocked during their first few months; the remoteness of the islands and the frightening feeling of being cut off completely from outside help, was quite difficult for them to adjust to if they had not been in remote territories before. In our early days, the plane came once a week only. There were no shops to speak of, no vegetables and precious few tinned goods available. This all did not help them adjust to the situation. The feeling of panic died away in time and most enjoyed the more simple and relaxed way of life there. It was certainly so in our own case. The local people were so pleasant and easy to like, the sea was all around us and there was plenty going on socially.

16

ISLAND CULTURE

When we first arrived the Gilbert & Ellice Islands were governed as one administrative British colony, although the people were largely Micronesian and Polynesian respectively and had no real traditional connection with each other. The area was over 2 million square miles of isolated and clustered coral atolls spread out along the Pacific Ocean. Europeans named the Gilbert Islands after Captain Gilbert of the Charlotte and the Ellice Islands after the Member of Parliament Edward Ellice, who had helped sponsor the voyage.

In the Gilbert Islands, where we were based, the population was in part from various different ethnic groups including Chinese and European, but the majority were Micronesians, with some Polynesians from the Ellice Islands. This had come about initially because some of the early traders, in trying to establish trading posts in the Pacific, would drop off some unfortunate employee with a limited supply of food onto an outer island and sail away leaving him to get on as best he could. Usually he would be taken in by one of the local families and marry the girl chosen for him, otherwise he would have starved to death. The ship might then come back a year or more later. Some of these individuals were successful in setting up trading posts. There had also been a Negro escaped slave who settled on one of the outer islands.

One of the new teachers at the local school started a local history society which I joined. We learned a lot from the interesting local guest speakers about their navigation by stars, local medicines from plants and sea creatures, traditional customs, and the process of weaving mats from pandanus and coconut palms. There were moves to get an official museum going. Sadly, there were so few artefacts left on the islands, as most were stored in European museums. However, given the damaging nature of the humid and salty climate, this may be helpful to preserve them for future generations. This means though that the local people do not have access to them.

At public functions, important guests, would be placed on chairs at the front in the *Maneaba* (meeting house), but as there was no crowd control, people would crush forward practically on top of them, which could be quite disconcerting. Sometimes we would have VIP visitors to the islands or an official occasion when special dance and singing programmes would be arranged in this communal building. One excellent evening occurred when Ted Rowlands the Member of Parliament for Merthyr Tydfil came on a visit. The women traditionally danced without clothing on the top half of their bodies but at most other events usually wore some sort of modest woven bodice which must have started with the missionaries perhaps. However, for this event, they reverted completely to the original traditional dress (see Fig. 16.1). They put on a spectacular display of some wonderful dances, and it ranks as one the best evenings of its kind that we attended. The men sang, drummed and performed and their costumes were magnificent. Everything was made from the traditional materials, embellished with cowries and other shells. As the years passed, these costumes were embellished with more modern materials such as Christmas decorations and crepe paper, which did add more colour, but I felt took away from rather than enhanced these lovely traditional costumes.

In general wear, the women wore one of two types of blouse and a *lava-lava* (sarong-style cloth) wrapped around their lower half. The men were bare chested and had the *lava-lava* wrapped around their lower half. As time passed though, at certain official events locals wore more European clothing, only reverting to the local style when they

Fig 16.1   *Gilbert Islands 1973: Islander in traditional dance dress.*

were in their own homes. Ironically, the Europeans enthusiastically adopted the *lava-lava* fashions in their own homes, and Pat always wore one around the house, and even to bed. The teenage girls from the UK, including Catherine, also wore them twisted around their neck into a dress or traditional style with their bikinis.

The Gilbertese Micronesian population were a strong well-built stocky race, with those of mixed blood tending to be slightly taller. It was a very multi-racial community and the mixing of races still goes on there especially with the advent of more and more Europeans on the islands and their relationships with the islanders. While we were there in Bairiki, quite a few marriages took place between Europeans and the locals, some emigrating to Australia and New Zealand with their partners and there is a growing community of Pacific Islanders in both these countries. Others came to the UK, where there are active communities which meet up regularly to keep their traditions going. What they made of the drastic changes in their lifestyle, as some had never been anywhere else before that, I just cannot imagine. One of the girls had never worn shoes, so I helped her get used to wearing them before she left for the journey abroad.

The Gilbertese had never been subjugated peoples and were therefore not servile in any way. Fortunately, these days the islanders had moved on from eating their enemies. Initially we found that they were quite reserved, but as they got to know you, their feelings changed slowly towards you until you were finally accepted. We all, especially the ex-Africa people, found this very refreshing.

Over time, various different Christian missions reached individual islands and as a result the various islands had their own brand of Christianity. In the Bairiki district, the area of Taeoraereke had quite a large stone cathedral and was the headquarters for the Roman Catholic Mission, with a Bishop and nuns who taught there. One of the oldest of these nuns had been some seventy years on the islands and was in her nineties. They all told very interesting stories of the Japanese invasion during the 1939–45 War. The islanders kindly protected them from the Japanese, by hiding them away and feeding them on the rarely visited island. The Protestants had been non-conformist in origin and an American missionary, Hiram Bingham II, had written down the Gilbertese language. Until this point, the language had not been known in a written form. The Baha'i Faith had a place of worship in Nukulaelae and there was a Protestant church further down the islands which we attended. There was also a theological college.

The local people seemed generally not very long-lived, with sixty being considered as old and so there were few elders of great age in the community. These elders could recite the family pedigree back to the eleventh century, but aside from this little was known about their origins and how they came to live on the islands. It was thought that they may have sailed great distances and probably were well travelled in this region, as were the other peoples of the Pacific. The Gilbertese creation legends are about large turtles and spirits and are described in Sir Arthur Grimble's book (see Bibliography). They had a tradition about a white skinned stranger, called the 'man from Matang', who was to appear after a promise by one of their ancestors. So, when mariners arrived two hundred years ago, they were treated like the promised stranger and became known as *I-Matang*, a name which continued to be used for all white skinned peoples. Robert Louis Stevenson also lived for a while on one of the outer islands and in a book about his wife Fanny there are some chapters about his stay on the island (see Bibliography).

The Gilbertese had a wonderful custom in that they *Bobasi* items, so if someone said: 'I would like that', it was customary to give it to them. So anyone landing on the islands was likely to have lost their personal items almost straight away, but they were shared amongst the community. This particular custom was not always welcomed by other nationalities. Several New Zealand girls married islanders and returned with them to Tarawa. One of them told me sadly that they had lost every one of their wedding presents in this manner.

The houses were simple structures of coconut palm poles open on all sides to let the breeze through, with roll down matting if the weather was very wet or windy. The flooring was covered with matting on which they sat cross-legged. Some had rolled matting pillows, but most had moved onto European style pillows and mosquito nets. They used to embroider pillowslips with mottos like: 'Two heads are better than one.'

and I had several given to me as presents over the six years we lived in Tarawa. One of our maids also made one for Catherine for Christmas one year. Sometimes, if the local islands came to the house for a buffet meal, they would sit on the chairs cross-legged. It was not the custom for the local women to make polite conversation in such situations, so it could be quite hard going at various official events.

The Gilbertese prevailing sexual attitudes were what we might describe as very liberal and there were some issues at times at European houses from the odd peeping tom. One homosexual local used to tap on the windows of lone men, including those whose wives were away, and tell them he liked them which seemed to unnerve them all. Rather a shame really for him, but the women all thought it was quite amusing. Because of the possibility of sexual attack, all European women who were alone at times had a large alarm bell fixed over the bed with an emergency cord, which rang out very loudly when pulled outside the house. On the odd occasion when the alarm bells rang, everyone ran to the house concerned. Usually it was issues with a peeping tom, but occasionally someone accidentally caught their arm in it while they were asleep. Alas, one poor young teacher at the High School was gang raped by a group of local men, which must have been dreadful for her.

17

ACTING GOVERNORSHIP AND
OVERSEAS ROLE

At the end of 1972, we returned home to the UK on leave and rented a flat in Littlehampton. Initially, Catherine remained behind in New Zealand to finish her studies and then flew out to join us several weeks later. We decided to try and buy a flat for the time that we spent in the UK. We decided on Rossyln House in Weybridge where she could study languages along with a secretarial course. She had to continue to be in some sort of higher education or she would not be eligible for assisted passages to the islands, which was part of Pat's salary package. A special allowance was now being also paid for a wife on station, but it was not a great deal. Some women chose to be based in the UK, just coming out for holidays.

After a few weeks rest, Pat returned to Bairiki and I remained to enrol Catherine into her new school and also to take possession of the new flat in Worthing. England was in the middle of a three-day week and furniture was very hard to get hold off, so I did my level best to furnish it with the bare essentials before I left to travel back to Bairiki. I was sorry to leave my new home and the shops with the fresh milk, fruit and vegetables. After my nice comfortable flat in England, the Bairiki prefab house somehow seemed so much more basic. The windows were louvered glass and as the metal fixing rusted, they had a tendency to fall out. They would be constantly covered in sea spray which made them sticky and opaque, so they needed cleaning constantly. Fortunately, the two maids seemed to quite like doing this job. The furniture was simple Public Works Department issue of four heavy wooden chairs that weighed a ton if you wanted to move them about. There was a similar dining room table and six chairs, with sideboard and settee in the 'L' shaped room which we used as a sitting-dining area. We had bought a beautiful locally woven mat from Pandanus leaves which was about 15ft square and was surprisingly heavy to move about. This was put in pride of place in the sitting area over the top of the dark Marley tiled floor. With our small tables, lamps, various ornaments and shells, together with a bookcase we had had made for our books, it made the place seem quite homely.

Not long after my return, we decided to pack up most of our more valuable and sentimental possessions, like the pictures, silver and clothes we were not wearing, to be sent back by sea to the flat in England. There was the distinctive smell of mould when I unpacked them on my next visit home. The problem of mould was a serious one, as everything exposed to the humid and salty air turned green, including leather shoes and books. We had to store things in a cupboard with a low heat light bulb on inside it all the time, to keep things dried out.

I kept my stamp collection to work on, as I had started to collect Gilbert & Ellice Island stamps just after my arrival. There were very interesting with themes about local matters such as ships, flowers, wreaths and traditional customs. I bought a couple of Chinese carved sandalwood chests to store my collection in and we put an electric flex with a 25w bulb inside and the warmth this generated kept things dry and mould free. During this period, through a Philatelic magazine I subscribed to, I was contacted by collectors worldwide asking me to exchange stamps. People wrote from Russia, Korea and other interesting places. An Australian woman and I began a correspondence which lasted well over six years. She helped me build up a lovely Australian collection and I, in exchange provided her with Gilbert & Ellice Island duplicates a-plenty to pass on to her many correspondents.

The Gilbertese and Ellice Islanders had a casual relaxed attitude to life, especially at sea. Taking the small ferry launch to Betio, the nearest main island to Tarawa, was quite nerve-wracking given the number of people with their bikes and baggage that were loaded aboard. The launch used to chug slowly along with the water lapping very close to the upper sides of the boat for forty minutes or so. It took a little longer in the rougher seas. On arrival at the jetty as everyone attempted to leave at once, the boat tended to list and one did eventually turnover. In the end I refused to travel over except on the much bigger old landing craft ferries, which took cars and lorries. Betio had a cold store, harbour, philatelic bureau and the Marine Trading School. Quite a few expatriate families lived there, so it made a good outing and gave one a different view of life for a few hours. Another outing we enjoyed was to Bikeman in the lagoon. It was a tiny atoll, about thirty minutes away by boat from Tarawa, with clean golden sand and clear unpolluted beaches and sea. It was uninhabited and frequently nearly washed over by the King Tides. Occasionally on weekends, we used to make up a party of friends, such as Corona Society members (see Fig. 17.1) from Betio and meet there in our own launches and boats for a picnic with our families. There was a rather quaint hut to house a lavatory of sorts, which had been built on the occasion of Prince Charles' visit to the islands a few years earlier for him to use. It was always a source of some fascination to the children. The sea was the centre of our activities and our lives. One morning, probably after an earthquake-type disturbance somewhere in the Pacific, the sea receded back across the reef as though sucked back and I waited in fear that it might come back in a rush, but fortunately it did not. Just as well really, as there was no high ground to take cover on.

The islanders kept pigs, old-fashioned types which may have been descendants from those put off from ships in far off days. They ate anything they could find and ran freely over the shared land of the islanders, and sometimes through your house if you left your doors open. With few natural predators, the chickens could also roam freely. Little children occasionally tied pieces of cotton to the chicks' legs to play with them, and then afterwards I found them later caught up in bushes and forgotten about. So for a while I built up quite a flock of the

Fig 17.1   *Betio 1973: Women's Corona Group (Margaret seated on right).*

rescued chicks which I fed with kitchen scraps. They were joined by an old hen whose leg was practically severed by a thin cord tied around it. I managed to free her from it and she sat on the doorstep for the rest of her life accepting titbits from the kitchen. Sometimes I found a lovely freshly laid egg in the garden. One day all the chicks suddenly vanished and I never did find out where they went.

In the late afternoon, the men would climb the coconut palms to milk their *tody* cans and collect coconuts; while up there the men sang loudly. When I asked why they did this, I was told it was to warn people of their presence. Some of the men climbed very tall palms without belts, using only their hands and feet. Some had footholds cut into them, but most did not. I did not hear of anyone falling from the trees and several of the English school children learned to climb them too.

By the time we had been there a year or so, some more expatriates our age group had started to arrive, these were largely ex-Africa. Old

Pacific hands were quite resentful of the Africa-Corp, as we were called. We came with new ideas and altered things from the way they had been done for years. This meant an increase in the social life and a lot more entertaining, which I was beginning to find rather hard-going given the culinary challenges of producing decent meals with such limited ingredients. It was also quite hot and humid during the day, which put paid to any preparation of perishable foodstuff. Pat had earned himself the reputation as a cook while I was away, having mastered the art of de-boning and stuffing a chicken, and making a superb lime cheesecake. Subsequently, everyone assumed that it was he who did all the cooking when I put on a dinner party, which I found rather trying. Also, I had two excellent cooks as friends, who used to try exotic recipes, so I felt that my kedgerees, spaghetti pie and other homely dishes were rather tame. Although I did notice that these dishes were very popular, especially my trifle and fruit whip.

The islands started to open up and new airfields were built on the outer islands. Arrangements were made for a ship to come in at about six to eight weekly intervals and the freezer store was enlarged in Betio. After that, we had a relatively plentiful supply of Australian meat and goodies. We all bought chest freezers and filled them up. It made quite a difference from corned beef and Fray Bentos tins of steak and kidney puds. Later on, fresh food items were added to our supplies and a ship would arrive laden with vegetables including staples like potatoes, apples, cabbages and celery at about two monthly intervals. Occasionally it was held up by storms and we ran very short of supplies. On a few occasions the electrical supply failed on board, so they would have to dump a freezer full of food overboard, which was heart-breaking. At other times whole consignments of potatoes would be condemned as unfit to eat or returned. This was when I learned to freeze potatoes (either mashed or par-boiled), onion rings, sliced lemon and any other vegetables as a hedge against shortages. Prior to the arrival of the meat shops, we used to send for meat from Fiji by air. Unfortunately this was not a great success, as we never seemed to get the cuts we wanted, so we cancelled this. For a long while we had an order of fresh vegetables being flown in by Air Pacific, lettuce, tomatoes and cucumber. Infrequently, we received fruit if it was in season such as strawberries. To hold the cost down, we shared these welcome treats fairly between households. Surprisingly, some people refused to spend money on these occasional luxuries, preferring to keep to the rice and tins in the small store. The Chinese community used to make bread and buns, and there was a bakery in Bairiki. I used to drive down to the quayside to the shop and buy lovely fresh bread daily. It was similar to the French type and had to be eaten fresh or it went stale very quickly.

There was an expansion of the Co-operative organisation in the

Fig 17.2 *Bairiki 1973: Government House.*

Islands. At first it had only been a small affair. Eventually someone was sent from the UK to set up a large Federation and main store on Betio, though he was in charge of the Co-ops on the other islands too. Coincidentally, he happened to be the same chap who was in charge in Botswana in the latter days. He was very keen for me to get involved, but I felt I had moved on from this sort of thing now. At the local Co-op store in Bairiki, where the shelves were dirty and half-filled, the staff used to sit in the back room watching Kung-Fu films on an elderly projector while the store largely minded itself. When the manageress went to order goods in Betio, even after several people had given her a list of things that were needed, she used to use the available money on bolts of cloth, embroidered silk or wools which the local women liked, rather than provisions for the expatriates. So we gave up and travelled over to the main store on Betio or shopped in the better run Bikenibeu store.

Pat was sworn in as Acting Governor for the first time and we moved temporarily into Government House. It was a very attractive house built in the local style, with a thatched palm roof (see Fig. 17.2). The central sitting room was well designed. Unfortunately, the cottage-style furniture was in poor repair and chewed by white ants and liable to collapse suddenly without warning. The dining table was enormous and could seat a vast number of people. The candlesticks, cutlery and china were always arranged tastefully by the staff and the table napkins beautifully folded. It always looked quite regal. We discovered that the Gilbert and Ellice Islanders liked the pomp of formal occasions. Our cook at Government House was very good, but had a somewhat limited repertoire. On going into to the kitchen on my first day as first lady, I was confronted by a large bare chested man putting fish into the freezer and this turned out to be the cook. The staff was so well drilled that nothing much was expected of me except to discuss the day's menu. As usual we were required to entertain quite a lot, giving several formal dinner parties, which were enjoyable. As the drinks were poured out by the Aide-de-Camp, for once Pat could relax and we enjoyed chatting with the guests. A delegation from the Japanese fisheries industry (see

Fig. 17.3) visited the islands. Pat had met them previously on a visit to Japan and was involved in the discussions setting this industry link-up to help boost the islands' ongoing economy and future prosperity.

The rest of Government House was not as fancy as the reception rooms. Our bedroom wing was more like a cell-block, with a concrete floor and walls which may well have been added much later. There were three bedrooms and two bathrooms. The master bedroom had an ensuite with a shower and washbasin. It sounds luxurious but in reality this was not the case. There was intermittent running water, but it was heated which made a nice change. Double doors led from the garden to the master bedroom, but they were always kept closed after an islander with mental health issues had rushed in one day and tried to stab the previous Governor and his wife as they lay sleeping on the bed. The garden consisted of bushes, heavy sand and coral. There was a spit of land to walk along and at the end there was the grave of a young girl. She was the niece of a former Governor, who had cut her leg on the coral reef and died of blood poisoning during the 1930s. It was badly neglected and I tried to tidy it up. I discovered that the villagers came up and used the rocks at the side of the jetty as a toilet area. After a few encounters with them, I gave up my walks in that direction. When Prince Charles had visited a year or so earlier, a summerhouse had been built near the house for him to sit in. We occasionally used to have tea served there but coconut crabs regularly fell out of the roof, narrowly missing the tea things or ourselves. The staff said it was a lucky omen as it was a special type of crab and that it brought good fortune to the house.

On one occasion we were having a dinner party at Government House, a heron suddenly flew in through the open door of the sitting room. After perching on the pelmet of a nearby window and eyeing the twelve guests seated at the large table, who were all staring back in amazement. It suddenly flew the length of the dining room just above our heads at some speed, making everyone duck down. It landed on the kitchen door which had been opened to let it through, and sat there for the rest of the meal. Later on it made its way out through an open window. It was certainly a conversation piece for a while, and of course was another 'good omen' according to the staff. On another occasion, we were not so sure about the visitors who had joined us for coffee after another dinner party. Just as the tray was put down for the maid to start pouring out into the cups, two pigs appeared at the front door, snorted loudly and chased through the sitting room and out into the garden. Everyone fell about with laughter. There was no doubt that life in Tarawa was a bit unusual.

We had two pleasant stays of three to four months in Government House during our time in the Colony. It was very nice to have efficient staff and a well-oiled household. Government House expenses were largely funded by the government, provided we did not exceed the approved budget. We were also fortunate to have the use of an official chauffeur, Teki, who drove the official Governor's vehicle which was a smart black London Cab with the Royal Arms on it. As I did not

Fig 17.3   Bairiki 1973: Patrick and Margaret officially entertaining the Japanese Fishery VIPs.

drive on the island, I found this very useful. The Governor's wife generally preferred to cycle whenever she could. They were a pleasant couple, whose ideas sometimes differed from what would have been considered the norm in these territories. Previously, more formal events such as HM The Queen's Official Birthday celebrations had local choirs accompanied by traditional chanting and dancing. On one such occasion, they decided to break with tradition and play more modern popular music at a dance where they danced along with the locals. This raised a few eyebrows amongst the elders who rather enjoyed the pomp and circumstance of the British traditions.

Our tours of duty were not too long by this time, about twelve to fourteen months. It meant that we were travelling back and forth to the UK more often and breaking our journey back by visiting many interesting countries on the way there. We were allowed to do this, provided that we paid for the additional expenses such as hotels ourselves and were always going forward to the approved destination. We also visited various other Pacific islands, including Hawaii, Samoa, Nauru amongst other places. I used to stay a little longer in the UK to see the children and to enjoy the shopping and food before returning back to the islands.

During his period of work in Tarawa, Pat made many trips overseas while I stayed behind. I always felt very safe there. He attended meetings in the Far East, London and elsewhere. Catherine was able to fly out during her main summer holiday. It was a long journey of twenty-nine hours flying with an overnight stopover in Fiji. Timothy was now married and living in the UK. We tried to see them both when we came back on leave. Suzie used to stay with friends on the island while we were away on our long leaves, which was a great arrangement. In the mid-1970s we had various visits from Members of Parliament including the then Foreign Secretary, MP James Callaghan (see Fig. 17.4), as there were concerns about the economic viability of the island group.

Pat travelled extensively to Japan, Manila, New Delhi, the USA and the Far East in the course of his duties. I accompanied him on one of these official trips to Bangkok to the ASEAN meeting where he was a

Fig 17.4 *Bairiki circa 1975: Margaret being presented to MP Jim Callaghan, then Foreign Secretary, at official Government House event.*

delegate supporting the Gilbertese Minister. We were whisked through the airport security as VIPs and then escorted in an official limousine with two police outriders on motorbikes who cleaved a way through the chaotic traffic at top speed. We went to two splendid receptions, one at the fairy palace hotel on the waterway, and then also at the President's official palace where carved ice sculptures were centrepieces on the lovely buffet tables. Afterwards the State dancers performed some beautiful traditional dances.

I visited Western Samoa with Pat, who was there on an official visit. I could really understand why Robert Louis Stevenson liked it, *Tu-si-tala* (teller of stories) was his local nickname and there is now a hotel named after him. We booked into the famous Aggie Grey's; started by a part-Samoan woman who began a club in Apia. The hotel was large and had an old fashioned air, but there was a superb swimming pool in the grounds. The system at the dining room, strictly observed, was to place you in a different place each meal to stop people getting into cliques. While Pat was involved in meetings, I was taken around to see the sights. Nothing had been done to the road infrastructure after the New Zealand administration had pulled out and the roads were in a dreadful state. My escort was related to the official in charge of the Stevenson's House 'Voilima' which is now used as the Prime Minister's official residence, so I was fortunate enough to be able to go inside and have a private tour around it. It was located in a beautiful position, high up above the sea with a magnificent view. Unfortunately, it was too slippery underfoot to visit the grave of Stevenson, which was on top of a mound. Samoa was very lush, with a good rainfall, and had plenty of fruit, vegetables, etc. We were amused to see the airfreighted crates of tinned mackerel and pilchards which were being unloaded at the airport for the locals, despite the bountiful oceans surrounding the islands.

We visited Fiji quite often en route to places and I grew to know Nadi and Suva very well and liked the people. The native Fijian peoples were outnumbered by the Indian population, who had been brought in by the British as indentured labourers for the sugar industry. Although they were forbidden by law to own land, they had nonetheless been allowed to remain in the country after the sugar industry declined. The original sugar company had brought Zebu cattle from Texas for food and to work in the fields. They were very similar to the big horned African cattle I had been used to seeing. The Fijians lived in a similar way to those on the other Pacific islands, in coconut huts which were thatched.

We always went back to the same house in Bairiki, having organised someone to move in while we were away. As usual, housing was in short supply and we would have had to give it up otherwise and simply hope for a decent replacement. This was so unlikely, that we left all our cutlery, china and personal effects in situ and had a sitting tenant. People were very grateful for the opportunity to get out of the transit hotel, so there was no shortage of takers. Having a full complement of staff helped too.

18

SEPARATION AND INDEPENDENCE
FOR THE COLONY

There was beginning to be talk of island separation. The Gilbert & Ellice Islands were not traditionally particularly integrated and had been a colonial administrative grouping rather than a natural one. The feeling grew for final separation of the two groups of islands and with it came some animosity. Up until this point many of the local main administrative public offices in Tarawa were held by Ellice Islanders, with few Gilbertese at senior level. After a period of internal self-government, the two island groups formally separated into Kiribati and Tuvalu in 1976. Thankfully, nothing sensational happened and everyone settled down to work out a constitution and train up local people for the jobs vacated by the Ellice Islanders.

The following excerpt from notes written by Patrick briefly outlines the situation.

'The Gilbert Islands achieved full internal self-government in two stages (1st November 1976 and 1st January 1977). The transition has been reported as comparatively smooth, the only major problem being the fear of the landowners of Ocean Island concerning their future.

Under the new Constitution, the Governor remains as Head of State and retains responsibility for defence, internal security and external affairs. Under the first stage of internal self-government, the post of Deputy Governor was eliminated and the Minister of

Finance replaced the Financial Secretary. The Attorney-General is now the only expatriate in the Council of Ministers. The Governor, who had presided over the Council of Ministers, no longer attends the meetings. The present House of Assembly consists of twenty-one elected members and the Attorney-General. There is also an appointed Gilbertese 'Speaker of the House'. The present House must be dissolved no later than 13 May 1978.

The separation of the Ellice Islands from the Territory provided an opportunity for a cabinet reshuffle within the Gilbert Islands and a reassignment of ministerial responsibilities. The former Ministry of Natural Resources gave way to a Ministry of Local Government and Rural Development, which has responsibility for land and agriculture, and fisheries became the responsibility of the Ministry of Commerce and Industry. According to the administering Power, the much-needed emphasis on Local Government and Rural Development has become evident in the build-up of three of the six district centres: Northern, Central and Southern.

On 1st January 1977, the Public Advisory Board was replaced by a Public Service Commission. The Commission was made up of five members. Reuben K Uatioa, former leader of Government Business and Speaker of the House, was appointed Chairman. The Commission will deal with appointments, promotions and discipline of civil servants and will have greater authority over a wider range of posts than the former Public Service Board.'

(Notes by Patrick Reardon 1977)

We lost our two Ellice Island staff as they went back to Funafuti, and we tried a couple of Gilbertese girls, one of whom was very good but rather moody around the house, so that I was relieved when she decided to go back to her own island community. The next one we tried out unfortunately had some mental health issues. When I was on leave in the UK, Pat came home to find she had drunk half a bottle of bleach. He rushed her to hospital, where she thankfully recovered and got help.

Then we found a really lovely girl called Eti Eti and she stayed with us to the end of our time in Tarawa. She was such a cheery person, helpful and worked so hard on our laundry and those miles of floors that needed constantly sweeping and polishing. She was very houseproud and enjoyed her European cooking lessons. Pat used to laugh because despite the fact her English consisted of ten words and my Gilbertese was at the same level, we used to communicate very well. I was able to tell him all sorts of local gossip which could be helpful for him at times.

The Gilbertese men did not work in the houses, with the exception of the cook at Government House. Having been brought up living off the sea and with their skills using their canoes and fishing, a lot of young men had the ambition to be sailors. The Marine Training School was always full of crews being trained. After about six to twelve months, the fully trained crew would then be flown to some foreign port to join a ship, tanker and cargo boats. After completing their tour of duty, they were flown back to the island. They arrived back festooned with presents for their families including radios.

Fig 18.1   *Bairiki 1973: Quite a few young expatriates had local wives (Margaret on right).*

In the last fifteen months or so of our stay in Tarawa, quite a devastating thing happened. The Islands had a variable rainfall, but in 1979 the rain began to fall daily and it went on raining and raining. The sand was not able to absorb it quickly and we soon all found ourselves paddling as there was no high ground, the atoll being only just above sea level. After a while, there were reports of an outbreak of serious tummy upsets and at least one death. Soon it was apparent that something graver was the cause of these illnesses. People thought perhaps Typhoid, but when the hospital rapidly began to fill up, it became clear that more outside help was needed to come. Cholera was diagnosed and the World Health Organization team flew in. Everyone was vaccinated. We were told not to clean our teeth in any water other than rainwater and to boil all drinking water. Everyone was very worried, as it was found that the water being brought up to put in the overhead tanks for houses were also contaminated and we had all been showering in it. We thought that as we had diluted our water with rain water we were less at risk, but this was not necessarily the case. In the first month or so, 580 people were admitted to hospital, eight of whom died. The local population who were very vulnerable because of their limited sanitation were most as risk. Tests of the seawater in the lagoon proved that the sea was actually contaminated too, along with the mussels which grew along the low water tide line. The *I-Nakatari* system over the sea on this side of the island was likely to be the reason. We were warned not to eat any fish unless it had been thoroughly cooked, which was a shame as we never were able again to eat the wonderful marinated raw fish again. It was frightening while it lasted, but after two to three months the epidemic died away. The relentless rains continued for several months after we left.

By this time quite a few young expatriates had local wives and we tried to include them in our various social events (see Fig 18.1). One young man had taken to labelling his drawers in the bedroom 'shirts go here' and 'socks go here' and so on to help his young wife. It must have been difficult for these young girls, who had had a very different way of life and few personal possessions before moving in with these Europeans.

We continued much the same type of life right up until our final months there and were generally very happy in Tarawa. Pat began training up someone to take over his job as Financial Secretary and travelled to various overseas meetings and conferences to support the new Minister of Finance, the Hon Roniti Teiwaki. There was political trouble over Ocean Island and the Banabans, who had been resettled in Fiji after the island was devastated by the phosphate mining. It was an emotional issue and the cause was taken up by outsiders, which eventually required a London Judge to come over to Fiji to arbitrate. Thankfully everything was eventually settled. A good account of the situation is in former Governor John Smith's book *An Island in the Autumn* details of which are listed in the Bibliography.

'First Overseas Tour of Minister of Finance

The Minister of Finance, the Hon Roniti Teiwaki and the former Financial Secretary Pat Reardon returned to Tarawa on Monday, 8th November after spending a week in Australia holding discussions with Government Officials in Canberra and Officials of the British Phosphate Commissioners in Melbourne on problems of Gilbertese employees on Ocean Island which is part of the Minister's Constituency. In Canberra, the Minister and former Financial Secretary met Mr Phillip Lynch, Treasurer of the Australian Commonwealth Government and discussed with him the question of Australian aid to the Gilbert Islands.'

(Rtetak Taburuea: November 1976)

Our final leave arrived and after arranging for our goods to be either sold or transported to the UK, we made arrangements to fly out for the final time. However, we did have one final stay at Government House to hold the fort until the new Governor arrived. While we were there enjoying the relaxed atmosphere, Pat was asked to return for a few more months to do an important job. So we put our baggage back into the house and changed our plans. We organised ourselves into a short leave trip to New

Zealand and a coach trip of South Island before returning to England. I remained in Worthing for a few weeks and Pat went back to Baraiki in time for the swearing in ceremony for the new Governor. This always took place at Government House and was performed by the Attorney General. All Senior Officers and their wives attended. It took place immediately after the Governor landed from the aircraft; a lot of signing of documents went on. Each time Pat took over as Acting Governor, he went through the ceremony, as did the Governor when he returned.

So Pat started to sort out the Gilbert & Ellice Island Development Association (GEIDA). A few years earlier someone had been sent from the UK to organise all these government departments in separate entities but this system had plainly not worked too well in the islands. First he put the electricity department on a separate footing, then the bus company and so on, until each department was responsible for its own financial and operating budgets. He also flew to Fiji for various meetings of Air Pacific, of which he was an executive member of the board. As we had to fund the rather expensive flights and hotel stay for me ourselves, I only accompanied him occasionally. By now there was an Air Pacific jet plane BA1-11 which flew to the islands several times a week with also Air Nauru flying in, together with the odd jet from Hawaii and Christmas Island. Pat made several trips to Hawaii for Pacific Islands Forum Fisheries conferences about fisheries management and an Indian expert visited the islands in this connection. Brill shrimps were also being exported, adding to the exports of Copra, which had previously been the mainstay of the island up to then, along with the aid that they received from the UK. Pat was also involved in the discussions with the Japanese Tuna Fishing Industry and made several trips in this connection, including visiting Fanning Island.

As our leave approached, Pat was formally told he was to be offered a job in Barbados. We waited for the confirmation but none came. After we arrived back in the UK, we discovered what had happened. Someone from the Foreign Office had taken this sought after posting from him, which regularly happened as part of the 'jobs for the boys' attitude that the Foreign Office took with regard to the Overseas Development Agency. They did not even have the courtesy to write and tell him, such was their guilt. So we left for the UK, stopping off in New Zealand again on the way and visiting relatives and friends there for a final time. Pat went to the Overseas Development Association, who had contacted him just after we had arrived back. They then offered him the job as Chief Secretary in the Turks & Caicos Islands in the West Indies. We decided to consider it, having never been to that part of the world before.

POSTSCRIPT: AN ISLAND ETHOS

This was certainly one of the happier postings we had. The island people were easy to get along with and Pat very much enjoyed working with them. They had always been a proud, warrior-like nation and had taken the best from all cultures; from the Missionaries, the British and other colonisers which they had adapted to suit their needs. There was a strong cultural heritage. Pat learned some Gilbertese, but as most spoke English but hardly ever had to use it. Unlike some newcomers, we respected and tried to conform to local customs to avoid causing offence to the elders and the islanders.

PART 5

The Final Posting

THE TURKS & CAICOS ISLANDS

1979–1981

FOREIGN AND COMMONWEALTH OFFICE

19

GRAND TURK

After a short leave in Switzerland, where we went to see Pat's brother and family for a few days, we returned to the flat in Worthing. Pat went off to the Foreign and Commonwealth Office to talk over his forthcoming appointment. He also received a briefing on his duties and on the political scene in the Turks & Caicos. Catherine was now working in Brighton and had a steady boyfriend.

It was a part of the world that neither of us had visited, and we looked forward to it immensely. I suppose we both thought that it would be different culturally to the other places we had been posted, and would have wonderful Reggae music and interesting local peoples. As part of our preparation, we got in touch with people who had been in the territory previously. We were warned beforehand what to expect by a former Medical Officer's wife, who clearly had been very disappointed with her first taste of West Indian life after sixteen years in the Falkland Islands.

I then got in touch with the Women's Corona Society and they sent through some helpful 'Notes on living in the Turks & Caicos Islands' which I studied. Much of what they advised was the usual basic stuff that applied for most postings, but it was helpful in forming a picture of the place. We also had a useful meeting with a former Governor and his wife. (He was also in Antigua during the riots when UK police force had to be sent in.)

After our heavy baggage had arrived back from the Gilbert Islands, we spent some time repacking it and adding more china, glass and cutlery. All these things had become rather battered and broken, so we felt that we should renew it. Then we shipped if off via Southampton, but unfortunately it then took ten months to reach us in the end, having been stopped in Florida as the official documents went missing.

As usual Pat flew out to take up his duties ahead of my arrival. The telephone system was fortunately quite modern and we were able to keep in touch, despite it being a satellite link. This meant there was a small time lag with one having to wait for the sound to catch-up, which was quite disconcerting. Later on we had direct dialling which made it much easier and we were able to speak to the children more often, but it was still quite expensive. I stayed on slightly longer in England before joining Pat. We also decided on this course of action, so that Pat could make sure that the accommodation was in good order for my arrival. There was no specific house for the job, so we had to take pot luck as usual.

Pat initially stayed with the new Governor, John Strong and his wife Janet. He was an ex-Tanganyika Administrative Officer, which meant they had much in common. This charming couple were a great asset to the islands and their house was an oasis. The letters from Pat sounded depressed, but he did not say much except to hint that everything could be better regarding the accommodation. I found out later that it was a great shock when the three uninspiring housing options were shown to him. The first, a modern house on The Ridge was stuffy and small, perched 60ft above the beach in a contoument (compound). It would not have suited us as we liked to bathe in the sea and walk along the beach each evening. The second was in a similar contoument at Corktree, which was very isolated and quite a way from the office. It was ill designed and a somewhat dilapidated bungalow, which was privately owned and rented by the Government for its staff. The paltry furnishings fell far below the usual standards. So, the one he chose was a larger bungalow, set on the beach in rather a nice location near the town and not too far from the office. It seemed to be slightly the lesser of the three evils.

A week or so later I flew to join him, via Miami. The small aircraft which flew into Grand Turk did not go out there every day, so there was always the risk of not getting a seat even when you had booked one and it was always full. The local people were regular users and many were dual nationals. So I was relieved to find myself seated for the short journey to the islands of just a few hours. I had with me the dog in its carry-on basket.

Pat was there at the airport to meet me and he was driving an automatic Ford Maverick car, which he had bought in Miami and had shipped down. This was the only way one could get a car to use on the island. We drove back to the house along the dry and dusty unmade roads. It was extremely arid and there was hardly a tree in sight. Both of us had been used to the lush tropical islands in the Pacific and this was a far cry from that. Fortunately, I was invited to stay at Government House for a few days as Pat had to fly straight off to Miami the following day to see the Federal Drug Reinforcement people there. There was a serious problem with drug smuggling on the Turks and Caicos Islands (TCI). So it was a brief hail and then farewell.

Government House on Grand Turk was an old house built in 1815, and was named after the famous battle of Waterloo. It was of mainly wooden construct. After several hurricanes and improvements carried out by various occupants, it was probably rather changed from its original form as it had several wings added at a later date. It was surprisingly limited in living space, for although the downstairs reception rooms were large and could hold a number of people, upstairs there were just three bedrooms. The master bedroom, used by the Governor and his wife, had a dressing room and an ensuite. There was an inside bedroom which was a gloomy place and the bathroom which served these two rooms was not very exciting. The larger guest room was rather nice with a ceiling fan. Given the general state of repair, I was understandably rather wary of using it. This room had a bathroom, which had been added onto the veranda and one had to be careful where you put your feet, as the boards were not too safe. Waterloo House was set in about thirty acres of land and had views over a lovely beach at the back. It was only partly fenced, which meant that both donkeys and horses roamed the grounds at will. The garden was full of beautiful trees and bushes, and the current Governor had started to construct a rather pleasant patio area just off the sitting room. Janet warned me that the house we had been allocated was not in the least like theirs. How right she was. I spent the next few days unwinding and they kindly gave a dinner party to introduce me to several key people on the island.

Pat arrived back and I went to meet him in the Governor's car, having decided that I was not going to drive the Maverick. It was a heavy car and I was not used to driving automatics. It had a tendency to roll forward quite actively and I was not at all sure I would master the technique required to control it. After coming back from Government House, we collected my cases and started off for our new home. What I saw of the small town, the capital of Grand Turk was not overly inspiring, but there were some pretty little wooden houses, placed in a higgledy-piggledy fashion around the sandy roads. It was very arid and sandy, with no trees or grass. We turned into a lane which looked quite charming and passed an interesting cottage-type dwelling with quite a nice garden with Bougainvillea shrubs in it. We then travelled on down to the bottom of the sandy lane where our bungalow was located. It overlooked the sea, with some course grass, a few bushes and one small tree. There was no veranda and nowhere to sit out in the shade, but in true island style, the beach was just 15ft away.

The house was of some strange construction largely of a pre-fab nature, but they had plastered the inside walls with a mixture of plaster and seawater which meant it continually flaked off. The state of the interior was appalling and it looked something like a condemned house ready for demolition. The lower half of the sitting room wall up to 2ft was mouldy and discoloured. Half the Marley floor tiles were missing and those remaining were broken or sticking up. It looked really awful and I could quite see why Pat was rather depressed by it all.

The only good thing was that the furniture was of quite decent quality and modern (see Fig. 19.1). There were several glass coffee tables trimmed with chrome; not ideal for a seaside area as they would be liable to corrode. A very large bookshelf, obviously built by an earlier resident, flanked one wall. There was a dining table with six chairs at the far end of the 'L' shaped room with a sideboard. The bedroom wing was down a corridor and had two bedrooms and two bathrooms. The larger bedroom had a rusted ensuite bathroom with a shower. The other, a rusted and stained bath which was not very appealing and few would have used it willingly.

After an inspection of the living quarters, Pat took me to inspect the kitchen. Despite having worked miracles with it since he got there, he had left it until last as he knew it would really upset me. The white old fashioned enamel sink was so badly rusted that the plug hole had come away from it. The large refrigerator was also badly rusted, on the outside and was similarly damaged on the inside. On his arrival, Pat managed to have the old rotten wooden kitchen units removed and some new units put in which he had found in the Public Works Department storerooms. He had them cleaned and installed. Even so, the kitchen looked so awful. He told me that he had very nearly resigned when he saw the house.

The kitchen windows had enormous, broken heavy wooden shutters, of which only one worked. During the two and a half years that we lived there we were unable to get any improvements done by the Public Works Department. Several years later towards the end of our stay and after much fighting and not giving up, we actually got a new fridge. Ironically, in Pat's office for some strange reason there were two modern kitchen units in bright orange, which were used for storage. So they were some clearly available.

We could not think how the previous occupants had accepted it in such a dreadful condition, but I suppose they too had received no consideration or help either from the British Government. It was one of the worst houses we had ever lived in; I do not say that lightly after all those years aboard in some difficult stations in Africa. Previously the Foreign Office had decided to dispense with the post of the TCI Chief Secretary with the idea of encouraging a certain amount of local autonomy. However, because of a series of issues that had arisen as a result, it had been decided to reinstate the post. The original delightful old house with lots of character in the centre of Grand Turk town, which used to go with the job, had unfortunately in the meantime been sold off.

When Pat arrived on the island he took over Blackie, an old black Labrador bitch left behind by American owners and fostered by everyone who had lived in our house. Pat loved Blackie and I think her presence helped him during those first weeks alone on Grand Turk. They used to go for walks on the beach together. He was also adopted by a young cat that adored him and followed him everywhere. It was such a sweet little thing.

When I arrived with Suzie, there were some tense moments at first between all three, but after a while everything settled down nicely and they all got on well together. Suzie had grown up with Moggy and Jess, our old Rhodesian Ridgeback in South Africa, so was happy to have company again. Unfortunately, she picked up a mite infestation which affected some dogs, but fortunately not Blackie. It was quite difficult to treat. About the same time as I arrived with Suzie, an American woman arrived with a pedigree Schnauzer. It was so badly affected, she had to return it to the USA to a vet where it was treated and sent back with a supply of pills which only worked for a time. It was a friend from Barbados who kindly solved the problem by bringing a special strong insecticidal dog shampoo for both of us to use. By that time, Suzie had lost most of the hair on her back and it took a little time before it all grew back. There was no rabies on the islands but there was a danger of it being introduced, as there was no importation control of animals from the US. The island had no official vet and had to rely on a vet who came from Miami on a diving holiday each year. All the work he did must have paid for his holiday, as there were dozens of animals that needed attention; even horses and donkeys were treated at his makeshift clinic each morning.

During this time, Pat and I had several discussions about possibly resigning. His dilemma was whether or not they would offer him another posting if he did that, and would the resignation affect his chances of promotion. Jobs were not as numerous as they had been, so on balance we decided to remain. We found the life we were leading reasonably pleasant and the location of the islands was in a new area of the world we had not yet explored. We thought perhaps we could travel on leave to South America and the other Caribbean islands quite easily from there. Apart from the Governor's wife whom I liked a lot, there were only a handful of British expatriates there. Government house was quite a distance away and I was not able to easily walk there. The other wives were at the far end of the island. There were a few miles of roads but these were not well maintained. I had thought of getting a small Honda motor scooter, but was advised against it; the islanders apparently would delight in running Europeans off the road in their huge dilapidated 1950s American cars, shouting 'Honkeys Get Out!' as they went by. The local people were unfortunately in the main not that pleasant and in my dealings with them, I found them unfriendly and largely indifferent. I decided not to get involved in any good works on this posting, as I felt that at fifty-eight years of age I had already given many years of my time to voluntary unpaid work.

The islands had had a sort of autonomy for years and were responsible for most of the Ministries, so any shortcomings in the place were largely due to neglect on their part and not lack of funding, which regularly came from the UK in the form of Grant Aid. An example of this was that an ambulance had never been purchased, despite the fact that sufficient funding had already been provided for this purpose. The sick and injured were still being conveyed to hospital in the back of a truck three years later when I left the island.

Everything was dilapidated and Pat, with his usual enthusiasm, set about trying to alter things. He found working with the local Ministers very hard going. They were obstructive, corrupt and very difficult, not only in their dealings with him, but also with the other Government officers including the Governor. It was such hard work, especially for a man of his upright character and he found the whole thing disheartening. He had always had a reputation of being always efficient, hardworking and fair. He was generally liked and respected by his office staff and those he came into daily contact with. The people he found so hard to take were the Ministers who would vote on a resolution and then decide on something else after hours of discussion; then telephone the following day and say they wanted to reverse their original decision. Hours and hours of his and everyone else's precious time was wasted. They frustrated his every effort and called him a liar, which wounded him a lot. In some ways, he realised this was not a particularly personal attack, as they gave the Governor the same treatment too. An example of this was the protracted lunches of steak and all the trimmings, they insisted on enjoying, while coming to no useful conclusions and then presenting HM Government with the bill for their meal. The Governor decided, with Pat's support, that they would only provide sandwiches in order to speed up the process of these meetings and he was castigated by them. He was an easier-going man than Pat and his contact with these civil servants was limited, which probably helped. It was only later that I realised that Pat was having such a dreadfully bad time, because he rarely if ever complained.

Having started the day at 6 o'clock with a light breakfast, Pat headed out to the office in the cool to get ahead on the paperwork, before any other staff appeared. When he could, he came home for a brief light lunch; after an hour's rest he returned to the office coming home around 6 o'clock for a relaxing drink and dinner; an evening away from it all. Most evenings we had a stroll along the beach which was quite clean, but broken up by a series of groynes, which were the islands only sea defences against the frequent hurricanes. On high tides, these were difficult to get past; either you had to climb over them or walk into the sea which was only really an option at low tide.

The water was clean and clear, but there were a lot of rocks lying below the water which made it dangerous to swim in if the water was rough. After being battered about during one of my swims, I decided to stay out of the deeper water and only really paddled in the shallows with the dogs. There were very few interesting shells, but I did start a small collection of those washed up by the tide. I also picked up smooth pieces of green or blue glass which had been washed up on the beach in their hundreds. Some may have been from quite ancient bottles. I placed them into wine carafes which I had made into table lamps as they allowed the light to shine through prettily. Sometimes larger pieces had the glass maker's marks visible and may have come from wrecks along the coast, of which there were many. Along the beach we found Tektites, black objects about the size of a base of the bottle made from a rather strangely shaped black molten material. Goodness knows how old they were, how they were formed or where they had come from; beachcombing was fascinating the world over.

I used to confine my walks with the dogs to the cooler end of the day around 5 o'clock, although it was still quite hot. The twilight came in swiftly and it was dark by 7 o'clock each night. Day biting mosquitoes were a-plenty, which carried a not very virulent strain of dengue and few seemed to be affected. At nights they were pretty busy too and some people were quite badly bitten, with the bites often getting infected as it often the case in the Tropics.

I quite often met up with donkeys on the beach, which could be unpredictable and sometimes chased people. I was walking the dogs one day when I was surrounded by several and had to retreat along a jetty. They probably were just curious, but I was not too sure. One evening I met a lone cow ambling along the beach, which was unusual. Several herds had been brought to the islands by the Southerners from the US at the time of the War of Independence; a few had survived including one magnificent bull in North Caicos. I quite often met horses or donkeys plodding along the beach too. These animals had also been brought in by early settlers or possibly the Spanish, and were now practically feral and roamed about the island freely. They were mostly Palominos with creamy manes and tails or a smaller native pony type. Around fifty horses roamed the island of Grand Turk in various herds with quite a few stallions, so foals were a regular sight and this meant that the population was always on the increase. The local solution was to ship any excess animals over to an outer island and leave them there to forage as best they could. Many must have died without adequate water and forage on these arid uninhabited outer islands. The locals were very possessive about the horses and would not allow anyone else to own any. One of the local women told me that sometimes on these islands, the mosquitoes where in such large numbers on the animals that they died. I suggested that perhaps she approach the Government for a more humane way of dispatching them, but as far as I was aware she did not follow this through as they continued to be loaded onto barges and offloaded onto the outer islands while we were there.

Pat had very keenly organised hanging baskets to put round the house containing a fern like plant; the only greenery we had apart from a few desiccated bushes and some scorched coarse grass, which managed to withstand the salt spray. Later on he brought in some exotic Bougainvillea and Hibiscus shrubs and planted them at the front of the house. It was a labour of love and he used to water them each night with a cupful of our precious non-saline water from the rain tank. This was a large concrete structure the size of a small swimming pool, but not as deep. It had a corrugated iron top onto which the rain ran and poured into the tank on the odd occasion when it rained. The annual rainfall was less than 20 inches, but I do not remember it raining very much during our three year tour at all. If used carefully, the rainwater tank was supposed to last the whole of the dry season, between rains. Pat used to inspect it regularly and one day found that the corner of the corrugated iron roofing had been pulled up. We kept watch and saw that a local family was helping themselves to it. Given there was a standpipe further down the road for the local people to use, we were not too pleased and wondered how many others had been doing it too.

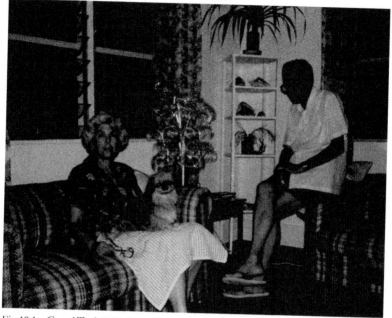

Fig 19.1   *Grand Turk 1978: Patrick and Margaret with Suzie in the house.*

Water was a precious resource in Grand Turk, so we firmly nailed down the roof and did not have any problems after that.

One of the pleasures of Grand Turk was the bird life. After the lack of birds in the Gilbert Islands, it was lovely to see the tiny brightly coloured humming birds, Flamingo and other South American and American species previously not seen by either of us. I bought a paperback guide on US birds and spent a lot of time looking through my binoculars. The dryness of the country around us was quite similar to parts of East Africa and Botswana, with its thorn bushes and scrub. There were very few trees, as the islands had been deforested to keep the rain away and dry out the *salinas* (salt pans). These pans were still evident in Grand Turk town and in the middle of the island there were more salt pans. The last big salt crop had been gathered in 1939 and production ended in 1964. The pans then lay idle and had been used by locals as latrines, as well as a dumping ground for old fridges and other unsightly rubbish from the nearby shacks. They certainly smelt bad, but despite this they attracted some migratory birds like Pelicans which settled there for a few days before heading off. Just before we were due to leave the islands, the locals were becoming aware that these Salinas were a likely tourist attraction and had embarked on a clean-up programme. They were opening up the blocked channels and letting fresh sea water in.

There was surprisingly little fish for sale, but this may have been because large scale fishing was prohibited in waters around the island which were a designated National Marine Park. The locals did not have a great history of fishing, unlike the Gilbert islanders. If they did catch any fish, they were seldom offered for sale to Europeans. There was no local produce market either, as nothing much was grown or certainly there would have been little surplus to sell. Because of the hurricanes that hit the islands from time to time, the sandy type soil was quite salty and not many things grew. The island was only just recovering from the last big hurricane Donna in 1960, which caused extensive damage to many structures on the island with its winds of over 145 mph. As most of the island was very flat with few trees to shield plants, everything became 'scorched' by the salt laden winds. We found this in our small garden, as after a particularly bad day of strong offshore winds, the Hibiscus and Bougainvillea were badly damaged by the salt spray being thrown up violently. The only solution was to place the bushes inside a native type of vegetation for protection and shelter. Pat managed to grow some paw-paw in the sandy soil at the back of the house and we did get several fruits from it, but it grew very slowly in the poor salty soil. Although the driveway was quite rocky and hard, the back garden was deep sand. Trudging round there to where the clothes line had been erected, carrying a basket of laundry was quite exhausting in the heat. During the day the temperature was around 80°F with high humidity, at night it dropped to 77°F but was still very humid.

We had ordered a twin tub washing machine from Miami, which came by airfreight. There was such a shortage of water that we had to use the same lot of water twice, having a complicated system of hoses and a big dustbin to collect it as it poured out after a rinse. Then we baled it back into the machine for the second load. The water then went onto the garden and the twice weekly wash gave us the opportunity to flush the WC properly into the cesspit system. We did all this ourselves, as we had no staff to help. The people of the TCI would not do any work that might be considered as slave work. If you asked them to hurry up a job, they would say: "Slavery died a hundred years ago!" So no one had any house staff, except at Government House.

The only people who were prepared to do any work of this type were Haitian illegal immigrants or islanders from nearby islands. Permission was not granted to import anyone suitable as it was considered that they were taking jobs away from the locals. It was an obstruction only, as they clearly did not want the jobs themselves. I managed to find a Jamaican woman who came to mop the awful floors and do the ironing. She was a bit strange, always muttering to herself and dashing off to the beach at intervals to smoke a rolled up cigarette, which could have been some sort of drug. She certainly behaved as if she was under the influence of something. She announced that she did not iron towels or underwear, so I got her to do the bed linen and Pat's shirts each time she came. I used to do the rest myself, but I was grateful that she did the basic heavy stuff. I shared the laundry maid with another lady and later discovered that she had been borrowing money, against her next week's salary, from both of us for her son's police court fines. Sadly, he was a bit of a scoundrel who did not work and constantly caused her trouble. He was a big worry for his poor mother. In the end, she disappeared to another island, owing both of us cash which fortunately did not amount to much. Like many others we would have willingly brought in a good Haitian servant and cook had we been able to.

Ironically, although Pat was now in his highest position and much better paid, we were living in quite the worst ever house of our whole career and without regular servants. Fortunately, our official entertaining was not very heavy. We had only the odd dinner party for a visitor and I mainly gave buffet parties with simple dishes and puddings. After about ten months, I was lucky to get another maid to do the ironing and cleaning. She had worked at Government House some years previously. Gladys was a very nice woman, married to a Haitian which put her beyond the pale locally. Despite being married to a local woman, he had been refused permission to get a job in Grand Turk and made a living hauling wood and water. They both left the islands regularly to work in the USA picking fruit which paid well. It was during one of their non-fruit picking seasons that they came back to the islands, so I was lucky to have her for a few months. She would come in and help when we entertained and washed up afterwards.

We had been warned before leaving the UK that the TCI was not a tropical island, so we knew what to expect. However it did still come as a shock to see how tree-less it was. The Statute Book still had a law against growing trees, even though the salt collecting was over, but I doubt that was the main reason why none were being grown now. Someone had brought in some flame trees, which lined our drive way and looked beautiful when they were in flower and also some cork trees, but these were not big trees like the coconut palms we had become used to in the Gilberts. A developer who had built some badly planned bungalows, had also planted a few trees, but these were not large either.

I found the wildflowers interesting; small flat patches of sweet pea like blooms and other pretty flowers. I would have liked a book on the subject, but none were to be had on the island. Sometimes in the evenings, Pat would drive us up to The Ridge, which was a slow climb by car to the only high area of the island of Grand Turk some 60ft above sea level. It had lovely views over the sea, but unfortunately, there were always very voracious mosquitoes there and we did not linger too long there. The island was about a mile wide and five miles long. Up on The Ridge, quite a few people had private homes being built; some were very nice and were for Government officials to rent. On the south side, they all overlooked a beach, which unfortunately was almost always covered with tar and oil from ships. The only really sandy and pretty

THE TURKS & CAICOS ISLANDS

beach was at White Sands. We did not really visit it as often as I would have liked to. Pat usually tired from the stresses of the day, preferred to relax by swimming each evening before we had dinner and watched a little TV. It was only at weekends that we explored more, if there was nothing else happening.

Given its location, the TCI have had a long connection with the USA military. In 1944 an American Air Force airstrip was built on South Caicos and in 1951 a strategic Missile Base was built in Grand Turk. In 1962 John Glenn, the US astronaut landed there when the Mercury Space Capsule splashed down nearby and the Capsule was mounted as a monument on the island. Up at the very far end of The Ridge was the US Naval Base. We did not have a great deal to do with the Naval personnel from this base, except on an official basis. They did allow us to use the PX (grocery store) though. We went onto the base every now and then to go shopping and for ice cream, but it was essentially an armed forces base. They did have a small swimming pool there too which we could occasionally use. Our relations with the US Air Force base at our end of the island were quite different however, with both US Air Force personnel and civilian employees of Radio Corporation of America (RCA) which was connected with space monitoring and exploration.

We were freely allowed the use of the base canteen and cinema, which was completely mosquito screened and we saw some of the latest films there. The programme changed several times weekly. In the canteen we could get a nicely served American style meal of steak, chicken or hamburgers with chips, together with an alcoholic drink or wine, then coffee and ice cream. It was all reasonably priced. Naturally, we dined out there often. In addition, there was a TV set with a large screen in the canteen and on this they showed videos of programmes and films from the US while we ate. It had a happy atmosphere and we made a lot of friends, eventually being asked to all the parties. Every now and then, they would have special entertainers, bands and singers, and give a special barbeque for them. By this time the Governor's wife and I had joined a Bridge class being organised by one of the American wives at her house. As people dropped out or left the island, it gradually became a group of eight people and we began to play regularly, either in my house, Government House or one of the American's homes. One of the American wives started a birthday lunch club and anyone with a birthday was invited to lunch free of charge at the hotel; the rest of us paid the bill. It grew to quite a large group of twenty-five or more people and was most successful. This friendship with the Americans from the Base was one of the things that made Grand Turk more bearable for us both, and we kept in touch for many years afterwards.

Pat's job was Chief Secretary and a very senior appointment. He was second only to the Governor and in time became Deputy Governor when the post was created. The work was much the same as it had always been. He was Head of the Civil Service there and responsible for whatever development there might be. Apart from being a choice spot for water sports including underwater diving, at that time there was not a lot you could do in the Turks & Caicos Islands as a visitor. There was at this time the start of some small holiday development on some of the other islands like Providenciales. Grand Turk had some charm, with its old buildings and pretty Front Street, but had little else to offer really. There were three small guesthouse type hotels only, so package tours could not be accommodated in those days; there being insufficient water and no local foodstuffs, cafés, restaurants or scenery to speak of. It did appeal to underwater divers, as it its seas were a protected National Marine Park and were teeming with wonderful fish, sponges and corals. Catherine and her fiancé trained as PADI open water divers there and said the diving was fantastic. Someone had spent a great deal of money building a hotel half way up the road to The Ridge, but had abandoned it part way through. It was quite a large, well built one with air conditioned rooms. When we arrived it was slowly being vandalised and everything portable had already been stolen. I did learn later that it had been subsequently refurbished and re-opened.

Pat had to travel quite frequently, either to the USA on anti-drugs work or to the UK or Washington for briefing, as the islands came under both their jurisdiction. It must have added to the stress he was feeling. He was always nervous of leaving me alone, but the two dogs kept me company and the neighbours were all warned to keep a watch on things. I was not aware of any direct attacks on Europeans there apart from several incidents at the High School, where the pupils had been known to attack the teachers. The Headmaster had also been menaced by a student with a piece of broken glass.

There was a public library in the town, rather an old fashioned place with ancient books. One day the librarian had a bonfire of quite a lot of the books from the store cupboard down on the beach. Passing Europeans going over the pile said there was some interesting stuff there, some of which should have been in the National Archives. The archives were under the Post Office and subject to flooding at certain times of the year. I asked if I could browse and was given a noncommittal answer. A European lady who had lived on the island for many years told me that she had once been allowed in, but that things were in a shocking state, and she had not been allowed access for many years subsequently. All the Government documents, bound in volumes from a hundred years earlier should have been stored there. One of these interesting volumes was in a glass case in the foyer of Government House, the pages being turned over to a new page each week. I read it from cover to cover. Subsequent enquiries regarding these volumes suggested that they were being sold off secretly to private collectors and museums by persons unknown. This was another example of the corruption at senior level, but at least they would be preserved through this and would not form part of a random bonfire.

While we were there, the Tall Ships pulled into Grand Turk harbour. They were a wonderful sight and Catherine and her fiancé who were visiting at the time, were able to join us as we sailed close by these vessels. We also had several visits of British Warships and were invited on board, having to climb up via a net rope or straight up ladder. After getting myself up to the Bridge via some more perpendicular stairs, I swore that if I ever got back off safely I would never do it again. The ship we visited was the HMS Ardent, which was sadly destroyed in the Falklands War with considerable loss of life. We had some of the officers over for a buffet supper and they were also more formally entertained at Government House. Everyone gave them hospitality around the island.

In the middle of our term there was a general election and this was predicted to be a difficult and unpleasant time. During an earlier one, the Governor had been imprisoned in Waterloo House for four days by a mob. So Pat suggested that I go to the UK for a short leave until things calmed down. I flew home to Worthing to the flat and waited. A British warship stood ready off the island, just over the horizon, supposedly on a friendly visit to the area but in fact ready to evacuate British subjects if necessary. In the end, all went quietly and the more moderate opposition party of Norman Saunders came to power. There were high hopes of this man and his government, but sadly a few years later it all came to a sticky end when Norman Saunders and one of his ministers, Strafford Misick, were arrested in the USA on drug smuggling related charges; two other ministers were implicated and there were other incidents of corruption at the time. I flew back to the islands via Miami, staying there to shop for a few days. Unfortunately, I had my wallet stolen and lost my money and credit cards, leaving me unable to pay the hotel bill. Fortunately Pat arranged for someone to bring me $200. I was not sorry to get on the plane for Grand Turk the next day, although up until this mishap I had been quite enjoying my time there.

20

ACTING GOVERNORSHIP

Pat met my plane at Grand Turk and when we went back to the house Suzie and Blackie greeted me happily. Nothing had changed of course; the floor tiles were still breaking up and the walls were still crumbling, but all of my friends were still there as were the Bridge mornings and dinner parties at the Conch Club at the Base. Pat was very happy to have me back and he had some good news. The Governor was off on leave for two to three weeks and we were to take over. This time we did not move into Government House as it was such a short period, but we did have some of our lunches there several times a week as there were official visitors to be entertained. Government House had a cook, wash-maid, house-maid and gardener, to say nothing of the lovely garden and pleasant surroundings. So even for just a couple of weeks, it was worth enjoying the different lifestyle up there. The Governor's car would collect me before lunchtime from our house, picking up Pat and visiting VIPs from the Governor's Office on the way. We would decide on the menu prior to lunch and a messenger would be sent across to let the cook know. It was just like another leave for me.

As part of his role as Acting Governor, Pat was required to go on an official tour of the other islands by air and I was fortunate in being able to accompany him officially as acting first lady. Our first visit was to Providenciales, known locally as Provo, and was the nicer of the islands with lovely beaches and a few green hills. Originally it was settled by plantation owners from the Southern States during the American war bringing their cattle and slaves. Several lovely houses were built, but only ruined foundations remained. A big development project was underway to make a new marina and Club Med was interested in building a place there. They had dug a deep water channel from the sea through the reef for the yachts to come up. The sea was crystal clear and so inviting. This was eventually developed as an upmarket holiday resort island, which Catherine and her family visited many years later. We had lunch at the Third Turtle Inn, a well-known landmark on the island. There was a sort of grotto at the back where the ADC said the Dramatic Society from Grand Turk had staged The Pirates of Penzance a few years before; obviously quite successfully, as he remembered it with some fondness.

We did not spend the night on the island, but flew onto Pine Cay in a small plane. It was a delightfully small island just 850 acres and was quite flat with few trees, but plenty of sand and beaches. We stayed at the Meridian Club, a sort of upmarket club cum guest house right on the beach, in a lovely room. The hotel, a popular diving centre, was full. While Pat attended talks with officials, I was able to explore with the help of a local guide. Pine Cay was one of the places PRIDE (Protection of Reefs and Islands from Degradation and Exploitation) worked in. It was an organisation started by the Hesses, who were marine biologists. They were building a geodisic building while we were there to house themselves and the students who were coming from American Universities. They were also breeding conch. I found it all very interesting.

I was then taken to a beach, where you could beachcomb for Lucayan Indian pottery shards. There was so much still unexplored on these islands, but an archaeological dig had been in progress earlier on another island seeking to find the remains of these settlements. At Pine Cay the settlement seemed most probably to now be underwater because of the quantity of pieces of broken pottery and tiny fragments which were scattered everywhere on the tideline. There were several nice houses built on the island; summer houses belonging to Americans who came for long holidays there. It was a wonderful spot for children with no traffic and masses of sandy beaches. The only form of transport was by electric golf carts. However, they would not have stood much of a chance in a hurricane on this low lying island.

After that interesting and lovely day at Pine Cay, we flew to North Caicos and stayed at the hotel which was called The Prospect of Whitby after a London Pub. It was built and owned by the UK building magnate, Peter Prowting and his wife, who kept a suite there for his family and visited several times a year. We had a comfortable room facing the sea, and near the sandy beaches. The hotel was managed by an English couple and they were busy trying to build a yacht harbour at the side of the hotel by dredging the sand. The road from the airport was bone-shaking and in need of some major repairs. Poor Pat was most unwell from this journey and was quite sick by the time we arrived at the hotel. Not for the first time I wondered why the headquarters of the TCI had been placed on the most unattractive and most hostile of islands. The people, as I have already mentioned, were very strange and one of their oddities was that so many of their policemen were recruited from other West Indian islands. Our very nice young Government House driver, a police constable, was from Trinidad. Another of the drivers was from Montserrat.

The people of North Caicos were descendants of slaves who were in a ship intercepted by a British Man of War after the abolition of slavery. The slaves were taken to the nearest suitable island and freed. What the poor things must have thought about being dumped there, I cannot imagine. At any rate, they built some houses and settled down. The island is dotted with little stone cottages, similar to Scottish crofter cottages. They addressed me as 'Mistress' and did a bob curtsey when they met me. Their English seemed rather quaint, with quite a few old-fashioned words in it. The soil was quite fertile and fruit and vegetables could easily be grown there. There were however a great number of small stones in the soil, which had to be sifted out in order to work the soil. We travelled around the island visiting schools; the adorable children sang us songs at the primary schools. We also visited the caves where Indian artefacts had been found. It had been several years since there had been an official visit from a Governor. We stayed three days and relaxed for a weekend, before going back to the airport to catch the flight back to Grand Turk. Unfortunately, the aircraft failed to arrive and we were left on the airstrip, fortunately one of the hotel cars was waiting for deliveries and the ADC went back to the hotel to telephone Grand Turk to find out what was going on. We had to return to the hotel and five hours later we went back to the Airport as a small private aircraft had been diverted to pick us up.

At this time there had not been that much research about the peoples and history of the islands, except for that done by Bertie Sadler, a Jamaican living on the island with his wife. His findings had been printed in several pamphlets, but were not in general print. I managed to borrow a copy of them from him. He had done a lot of research in London and New York. One of the retired Government Lawyers on the island told me that when he had first arrived some fifteen years earlier, he had sorted out all the files family by family so that one could see immediately the ancestry of each person, which was a very valuable piece of work. However, since his departure he said everything had been muddled up again and some of it lost. This is something which may well be very much regretted in the future when people want to know their past. One old gentleman in Provo took me to see his family home which was just foundations and two gun emplacements. He produced some wonderful photographs of his great-grandmother, a black lady dressed in a floor length black dress with a high collar in the manner of the early 1800s. Her husband was clearly of European descent.

I tried to get people to start a preservation society on Grand Turk and to record the memoirs of the old people before they were lost forever. The old people were always keen to talk about the past, so it would have been an easy job. I would have quite liked to have done this myself, but these things were always interpreted wrongly in these islands; if the Europeans tried to do such work they were viewed suspiciously in case it was a government tax scheme or some other such trickery. I did hear later that an American had shown an interest in this work and I do hope he managed to get the project started at least.

The first island inhabitants were thought to be Arawak Indians and the islands were rediscovered by Ponce de León in 1512, but some think it was the first landfall of Columbus on his search for the East in 1492. They were a natural hideout for pirates plundering the Spanish ships and Lord Nelson anchored there. In 1678 Bermudan salt rakers arrived in Grand Turk to work in the *Salinas* and then the Spanish invaded the islands. In the 1700s the Bahamas tried to annex the islands and the French invaded at regular intervals over the next forty years. In 1787 American loyalists settled in the Caicos Islands as cotton planters but these largely failed when the abolition of slavery took place. The Bahamas annexed the TCI, which then had seats on Bahamas House of Assembly. In 1848 the islands separated from the Bahamas and were subsequently annexed by Jamaica thirty years later. Eventually, when Jamaica became independent, TCI became a separate British Colony in 1962 and several years later the first Governor was appointed.

21

LIFE ON GRAND TURK
AND THE END OF AN ERA

Among the facilities in Grand Turk were the Post Office and a Bank. There was also a pretty basic Hospital facility with several doctors. The matron was English and most of the nurses were trained in the UK.

I mentioned earlier that we watched TV. This was an entertainment that arrived on the island soon after we did. An islander who had been working in the US came back to Grand Turk with the equipment to start up a TV Station. He took over the old lighthouse and installed it there. We all rushed to buy aerials and TV sets (ours was a small black and white one), and when the service started broadcasting we were given a day or so of programmes to whet our appetites. We were then expected to have a de-scrambler put on the back of the sets so that we could receive the programmes. We paid a monthly rent of $15. The programmes were all copied from American TV and were quite entertaining, if a little odd at times. Sometimes they finished before the end of the programme, or the reel ended and the owner had gone to bed in the lighthouse. Sometimes, he would rush back half an hour later and finish showing the programme, or it would be shown the following day. This was fairly haphazard, and usually a few phone calls were made between us all once someone spotted the rest of the programme being shown.

There was a radio station run from the American Air Force Base; tapes played all day, no disc jockeys or other programmes. We could receive BBC World Service news and always listened to the

6 o'clock news broadcast, just as we had always done. In 1980, Pat officially opened the first live broadcast of the Turks & Caicos Islands Government Radio Station.

There were one or two shops selling groceries in a small way and not long after we arrived, one of these expanded to quite a sizeable store. It was owned and run by an Englishman, with his local born wife. They made a good job of ordering frozen goods and vegetables from the US. It arrived by freight plane once a week and within an hour was on sale. We got everything we needed and some quite novel items form the US like frozen scones, pancakes, hash browns and unusual sausages. Later on another small supermarket also opened up which was well stocked. So we did well for food thank goodness. One small store sold laces, cottons, materials and wools, and there were others that sold similar products. There was also a shop that sold chemist items. I used to walk into Grand Turk to do some shopping now and again, and then have a coffee at one of the hotels and perhaps meet a friend. But generally speaking, it was too hot to do much. I missed having a hairdresser, until I discovered that one of the American women was one, so after that I could have my hair cut properly. We washed our own hair several times each week and did our own hair curler setting. It was easy to dry it in the sun.

The driving skills of one of the ladies on the island left something to be desired. One day she came to collect me for tea and while she reversed the car, I closed the house up; the next thing there was a terrifying bang. She had collided with the huge dog kennel which someone had built for Blackie the Labrador. Poor old Blackie was asleep inside it. The kennel was propelled up the garden about 10ft, and Blackie shot out of it like a rocket, howling and disappeared up the beach at speed. She only returned home that evening. I am afraid; we both then had the giggles. Another time when I was in the car with this same lady, she swung round a corner only to come face to face with a local bus. We all managed to stop abruptly. The bus was painted in flamboyant colours and had flashing coloured lights on it rather like a mobile Christmas tree. On the front written in large letters were the words: 'Put your trust in God!' She was a very popular lady and very much liked by all, but her driving prowess was a source of some amusement. When she left Grand Turk with her husband and went to live in California for a year with her daughter and family, she wrote to me saying that her American driving licence had been granted and that she was now driving happily on the left – I could not bear to think about it.

Pat was a keen churchgoer, so he attended the local Church of England services in a lovely old stone building in the centre of town. It was large and could hold 150 people. I only went a few times on special feast days. I remember one time over Christmas we went to a carol service there. Unfortunately, next door to the church they had a disco band with full amplification. No attempt to modify the sound during the service was made, so we barely heard any of the words of the service. The old timers were very religious and attended church regularly wearing hats and gloves. Some of the younger people were non-conformists – Baptists, Methodists, Seventh Day Adventists, Church of God of Prophecy, New Testament Church of God. There was also a Roman Catholic Church. Some of the more informal churches had clapping and rather jolly type West Indian singing. I went to one service where everyone stood up at will and said: 'Praise the Lord!' loudly as and when they felt like. The Governor's wife and I had been invited to the tea party that followed the service. It seemed much friendlier than our Church of England services.

While the Governor and his wife were away on leave, I was invited to open a bazaar at the Church of England Church over Christmas. I was asked to arrive at 4 o'clock. I duly arrived in my hat and best dress, with a short speech prepared, only to find that they had been unable to control the crowd and had to open the doors earlier than anticipated. So I walked into a crowded hall to be met by an agitated organiser, who took me onto the platform. Below me I could see a milling mob fighting for the goodies displayed on the stalls. After some difficulty, they managed to get some notice taken of the situation and the lady in charge introduced me in the lull of the din. I realised that the speech would never be made, so I simply said loudly: 'I declare this bazaar open!' The noise broke out again and I was handed a cup of tea and some cake. I sat on the platform and chatted to one of the helpers. Earlier in the month I had worked for days with some American friends quilting a patchwork quilt for this bazaar. I visited the table where the quilt was being raffled and asked for two raffle tickets. She looked up and asked who I was; so much for my moment of fame.

Various amusing things happen to me at Grand Turk which still make me smile. Not long before the opening of the bazaar, I was asked to officially switch on the Christmas lights. These consisted of a 30–40ft cable, strung with coloured lights, and draped over two trees in a square at the back of the town near the Methodist Church. The ceremony took place at dusk. As luck would have it, there was also a near gale blowing, which was whipping up the sand. The Naval Base had produced a dais on which I was to stand and two officers represented the US Navy. These two young men were very formal and serious in their duty. Representing the Air Force Base was the Commander and his wife. In addition to Pat and myself, there were two local officials and a boy on a bike. Everyone gave a speech, the weather grew worse and rain began to threaten, so it was suggested that we move into the Methodist Church for the short service. At this, one of the locals revealed himself as a Church of England lay preacher and said that he was not on good terms with the Methodists who might be annoyed. He was over-ruled by two women who by now had appeared on the scene. We filed into the church and sat down. Hymn sheets were handed round and one of the women went to fetch a young man called Arthur, who would supply the music. Arthur turned out to be a boy of eleven years with a trumpet, who played it extremely well too. About 6ft behind the official party, he belted out the carol 'Hark the Herald Angels' and nearly deafened us. The noise of the trumpet seemed to arouse the neighbourhood and when we came outside to mount the dais again, there were six snarling dogs, a handful of adults and lots of children milling about. I wished them all a 'Happy Christmas!' and switched on the lights.

Life went on as usual during 1980, but later that year we were burgled while out at HM The Queen's Birthday Parade. The CID dusted for prints, but no one was charged and it was generally thought to be the work of youngsters. All our drawers and cupboards had been gone through. They had shut Suzie our Pekinese in the bathroom, as she could be quite fierce and disliked youngsters. Poor Blackie had been hit with a stick, as we found this on the veranda and she went missing for hours. Apart from a pile of small change taken from the dressing table, they had taken steak, frozen vegetables and other items from the freezer. Probably the most annoying thing of all though, was that they had used our latest copy of *The Daily Telegraph* to wrap it all up in. Only the middle pages remained on the floor. We used to have to wait at least a week for our newspapers to arrive and this was considered to be a serious loss. Children used to call at the house asking for sugar and bread and we wondered if this was how they looked the place over.

We had a barbeque table and bench in the front garden and braved the mosquitoes to sit out there at times. Tim and his wife came to visit us that year and we used to sit there watching the sun go down. Pat took them with him to Haiti when he went on business for a short visit by a small plane, which they enjoyed a lot.

During the following hurricane season, severe category 5 Hurricane David hit the region with winds of 175km. It devastated the Dominican Republic and parts of Cuba nearby. We had the first reports that the hurricane was heading our way in the afternoon of 1st September. The Miami weather centre was monitoring it and planes were being sent to plot the direction of the hurricane. At first no-one seemed to be doing anything about checking the storm shutters, some of which had not been used for years. We had these huge wooden shutters at the back of the garage, and decided to bring them out to check them and put them on. We struggled to lift them but they were too big and heavy. Eventually the Public Works Department sent some men round to re-fit them all. Luckily they all fitted, and we decided to put them all on just in case. It made the place pitch black and stifling.

Accurately tracking the storm was difficult, as initial reports indicated that the hurricane was headed straight for Grand Turk, then only the Caicos Islands, then back to Grand Turk. On the particular night it was due to hit Grand Turk, we lay fully dressed on the beds waiting for news. Earlier we had packed the car with essentials including food and water and it was now parked ready by the back door, to drive up to The Ridge ready for me to stay with friends. Pat was on duty and was ready to go to the US Base to direct operations if the storm hit the island. The telephone rang all night with reports and updates. Then the weather suddenly became extremely oppressive and hot. At this point, the local people started to panic and piled up The Ridge in their cars. A high pitched wind began blowing at the island constantly, but fortunately the eye of the storm passed just 20 miles away and completely missed the islands. For a further four days, we waited while it veered all around us, before it passed over Florida, Georgia and New England and beyond. It did terrible damage to all things in its path. Afterwards, there was a strange feeling of anti-climax and relief in the island. We all calmly took down our heavy shutters and got on with our normal lives again.

One day while Pat was in the office, a local man came in to see him about a wage grievance. This was not really Pat's remit, but he was always prepared to assist people if they needed him. As the man entered the office, he locked the door behind him and after a few minutes he proceeded to try and attack Pat with a steel rod. Luckily there was a very wide desk which Pat was seated behind, at an angle which afforded him some protection. However, he brought the bar down hard several times onto the desk in an attempt to hit Pat's hands which were on the desk. The assailant then wrecked the bookcase and broke all the windows. By this time, the staff had sent for the Police who broke the door down and arrested him. He was sent for trial, but not before he was bailed and so he was at liberty that same night. An armed guard was put around the house and we both had a big stick by our beds to defend ourselves with as well. We brought all the dogs inside the room. In the end, nothing untoward happened. The noise of the guards patrolling made the dogs bark regularly which was unnerving. Then the Police Land Rover bringing in the relief guards early in the morning also woke us up. So, we were quite pleased to be left alone once the situation was considered to be safe again for us. In Court a few weeks later, the assailant was let off on a technicality.

The event shook Pat up and fortunately we were granted some leave to come back to the UK for our daughter's wedding in August 1980. While there, Pat's mother went down with a very bad attack of Shingles, so I remained in Worthing to ensure that she was alright and to ensure that Catherine was settled in her new home in Windsor, before returning home in time for Christmas. Our Christmas festivities were always very quiet in Grand Turk; everyone seemed to keep to themselves at this time. However, there were a number of parties to which we were invited for the New Year. Someone built a disco some 100 yards down the slope at the back of the house and it operated every night, except Sunday, until 1 o'clock. The noise was dreadful, so we bought an air conditioner which drowned it all out and we could sleep at last.

Just about this time, we decided not to try and return to the Turks & Caicos Islands when our tour officially ended later in the year. Hard on the back of this decision came an offer of an appointment in the British Virgin Islands (BVI) – were we interested? Pat sent a cable saying 'Yes!' Within a week, a formal letter arrived saying he would be appointed Governor of the BVI at the end of 1981. We were thrilled with this – the ultimate appointment probably and a wonderful one to go into retirement on.

Our happiness was dulled then, because Pat suddenly developed Shingles all over his face and mouth. The poor man was in such pain and discomfort. There was nothing anyone could do to help him, except give him painkillers. He lay in his bed for a week and when he was able to get up and sit in the sitting room, he had a string of people arriving with papers to sign, decisions to make, phone calls to take asking for advice – he could barely cope. Gradually the Shingles receded and he was able to face the office after about six weeks. He was far from cured and still in quite a lot of pain for a number of months later. At this point, sadly we had to put Blackie the Labrador down as she became terminally ill.

We were cheered up when the Governor said he would like us to take a short leave, before we finally departed from the islands for the BVI and we came back to the UK for a short visit. In London Pat had his medical and briefing about his new job in BVI. I accidentally broke my left wrist which meant it was in plaster for six weeks and at this time it was also decided that I should have a hysterectomy as I had been having issues. I returned to the flat after my operation just 48 hours before Pat was due to fly out again to Grand Turk. My kind neighbour prepared lunches for me and old friends from the Tanganyika days were over from New Zealand, so they stayed and helped too. Eventually, I was signed off from the hospital and was able to re-join Pat in Grand Turk.

He was back in Government House, as Acting Governor. We returned home to pack up our stuff, so that it could be shipped out to BVI. Some crates of ornaments, china and cutlery were being shipped directly home to the UK. There was no one to help pack up or nail boxes down so we did it ourselves – which was not great given both our weakened states. It was hard work in the hot weather for both of us, especially as I had not long come out of hospital after a major operation and had been instructed to avoid doing anything strenuous for several months.

Once more we enjoyed ourselves in Government House. The cook produced good lunches and prepared the evening snack. None of the Government House staff worked after 2 o'clock. It meant that Pat and I had to get our own supper and wash up. If there were official guests we had to look after them ourselves or pay the staff overtime to stay on, although they were reluctant to come in to do this extra work. The staff was well paid and a taxi collected them to bring them to work at 8 o'clock. This was far too late for Pat, who liked an early breakfast and set off to work in the cool of the day, so he made his own morning tea and breakfast. I had mine in bed when the staff arrived.

The first thing the staff did was to prepare their own full cooked breakfast, and then they baked their own bread and prepared their own food for lunch, having brought in their own ingredients. After that, the washing maid would collect the laundry (regulation shorts, shirt and vest for Pat and dresses for me) and linen. She then sat and watched the washing machine until its load was finished and hung it out, and sat outside waiting for it to dry. It was ironed the following day. Apart from this, she did no other duties except get the lunch on the cook's day off. Why the cook needed a day off, I had no idea, given she only worked five and a half days at most. There was no staff on duty on Sundays either. The housemaid did only limited cleaning. I discovered that the carpets were only vacuumed once a week, which in that dusty, sandy atmosphere was far from adequate. Apart from a little light dusting, laying tables and serving the lunch, those were her total duties.

As usual, we were required to entertain quite a lot, having a number of lunch parties which we enjoyed. We always tried to get everyone together for some sort of meal at least once. People would get big chips on their shoulder if they were not invited to Government House regularly. We tried to balance the guest lists to ensure that there was a good variety of people attending, and to honour various VIP guests who had travelled to the islands. If for some reason we had not finished before 2 o'clock the staff simply left, leaving me to do all the clearing up. Official visitors to the islands could not believe the set-up.

Sometimes we had cocktail parties in the evening, under the coloured lights in the mature patio garden at the back. It was easy to forget the dry old dusty area beyond it. The staff always did very well on these occasions. The cook made lovely cocktail snacks, the ADC dispensed the drinks and the other servants helped serve them. I was always pleased with them on those days. These parties were much enjoyed by everyone. We had, however to keep the Government House liquor stocks under lock and key otherwise it was taken by the staff. This was particularly important as it was in Bond and not subject to customs as it was for official use at Government House. We also had to keep our own drink supplies locked up, as they were pilfered too. Similarly with the flour and spices, these had to be locked up in the store. I discovered the gardener helped himself to a beer or two from our fridge whilst on duty each day and put a stop to it.

In the grounds of Government House there was a small herd of horses of around fifteen mares with foals. The foals were quite curious and a little tame. We used to put buckets of drinking water outside the back door in the late evening, for these beautiful Palomino type horses to come and drink. Because there were some young stallions amongst the herd, there were several outbreaks of fighting which caused the rest of the herd to canter past the house at some speed, whinnying and stamping. The sound the hooves made beating on the drive, used to bring Pat and I to our feet to watch them as they streaked off down the drive as though on a race course.

The donkeys used to visit the water buckets during the day. One afternoon, one of them came right onto the veranda and kept standing by the open front door. When I closed it, she came to the window and stared in at me. It was such unusual behaviour that I went out, collected the gardener and then followed her to where she was leading us. It was a spot in the back garden where her stillborn foal lay. We buried it for her and she watched us and then went quietly away down the driveway.

Pat was having various major international difficulties; a group of fifty-nine Cubans had decided to sail from the US in a wreck of a ship to invade Cuba and start a Government in Exile, using the US Naval Base. They became shipwrecked on Providenciales. Fighter aircraft from Cuba swept over the TCI, making the locals very nervous and rumours began about an imminent invasion by Cuba. Many of the Cubans on the ship were illegal immigrants to the US with no re-entry permits, so it was touch and go whether the TCI would be stuck with them. There were many problems to solve. In the end, after two weeks of serious negotiations with the US, the Americans agreed to have them back if the TCI paid the fare ($50,000), so finally we were able to repatriate them to the US.

At the same time, a boatload of Haitians was trying to land on the other side of the island as refugees. There were worries that this might spark a political issue and a flood of more refugees. With the Governor away on leave and having to do two jobs already, Pat did not need any further problems. Unfortunately, the Attorney General came to Pat and said that he had to leave immediately for the UK on compassionate grounds, so there was not much Pat could do but don a third hat.

On Sunday, 12th September 1981, Pat told me had a severe pain in his head during his afternoon rest in the armchair in the upstairs study. I suggested getting the doctor over to see him straight away, but Pat just got annoyed, so I asked him to see the doctor the next day. I know why he resisted sending for the Medical Officer, as a few days earlier it had been officially confirmed that he was to be the new Governor of the British Virgin Islands in October. Already the papers giving us all the details of our meeting with HM The Queen had arrived, and other important documents detailing *dos* and *don'ts* for Governors, together with letters for the makers of the official Governor's plumed hat to have one made up. We were over the moon about it all. This would be our last overseas appointment and we were going to retire in style. Financially, unfortunately it would not have made any difference as his pension was fixed at his Colonial level, which not very good. However, while in office he would have been paid a good salary for the three year tour which would have helped. With luck, he would have retired with a Knighthood or similar high decoration to reflect his many years in service and his dedication to the Crown on some tough assignments like the TCI.

On Monday 13th, he went to see the doctor who increased his blood pressure tablets. He seemed quite well again and did not complain of any discomfort, so I relaxed. During the week, one of the other doctors had a heart attack and sadly later died. We continued to make plans for the future and talked about possible trips to South America and North America and were looking forward very much to the next three years in BVI.

On Sunday, 19th September we had our lunch as usual, lobster mayonnaise, which was Pat's favourite. Afterwards we went upstairs to rest in the cool as it was a very hot afternoon. I fell asleep and woke up with Suzie clawing at the side of the bed. She did not do that usually, so I followed her downstairs and I could hear the TV on in the sitting room. As I joined Pat in the sitting room, he said he was feeling unwell and then he suddenly had a seizure and stopped breathing shortly afterwards. I tried to revive him and then called the hospital to get help. They quickly responded but could not revive him either. So our dream was over and our thirty-seven years of happily married life had ended. They led me into an anteroom while particulars were taken down and death certificates issued. Senior Officers from all departments were sent for. Pat's body was gently put into a black body bag and removed by two orderlies from the American Air Force base, where he would lie in the refrigerated mortuary. I could not believe it was happening to us.

With everyone senior away, the only person eligible to act as Governor now was the young Deputy Attorney-General, newly out from the UK and in post. He was hastily fetched and sworn in. No one knew where the Governor was, except me and the address was with secret documents in the Government House safe. Fortunately, I was privy to this as we had our personal money and documents stored here too. Unfortunately, in the emotional state that I was in, I could only remember the first two numbers. I was given a brandy, while someone rang our children, Timothy and Catherine, to tell them the terrible news and to ask them to tell Pat's poor elderly mother too. The Foreign Office was informed and two people sat down and composed notices regarding his death for *The Daily Telegraph* and *The Times*. Someone else got onto the UK Quarantine Authorities to have the forms urgently faxed through for Suzie's departure. Fortunately, the rest of the safe numbers came back to me, although one seemed to be wrong and it took a bit of experimenting to get it all in the correct order for the safe to open. The Governor and his wife were on holiday in the US visiting the Jasper National Park in the Rockies. They had just arrived back from a day's outing when we telephoned and were shattered by the news. They got the first flight out to Miami and came in by chartered plane the following day. Pat had died just before 4 o'clock and by 6 o'clock I was being taken to my friend's house for the night. I was quite numb and kept going for long walks on the beach. Pat had never wanted to discuss what would happen if he died suddenly, always saying that it would not happen; so I felt quite unprepared for a future without him. In the middle of the night I got up to make a cup of tea and found my friend sitting in the sitting room sewing. The poor woman was fighting a desperate losing battle with cancer and the drugs she was taking made her sleepless. The next day, many people called round to see me and express their sorrow and sympathy, so many of them local people. A memorial service had been arranged to take place as soon as Catherine and her husband arrived from the UK to fetch me. When they arrived they stayed at the Deputy Attorney-General's house.

The following extract is from a letter to me from our friend Roy Halstead, Senior Engineer, Public Works Department who explained the process.

'Following Pat's death, Captain Dale Little of the USAF offered the facilities of the Base and Pat's body was taken care of by the personnel there. On the following day the coffin, draped in the Union Jack, was taken from the Base and placed aboard a TCNA aircraft and taken to Miami. Present on the flight were the Governor's ADC and Mr and Mrs Derek Wright. The Wrights stayed on in Miami to represent the family at the cremation which took place on Tuesday, 22nd September. The announcement of Pat's death was made on Radio Turks and Caicos early on the Saturday evening and shortly afterwards the regular programme was replaced by solemn music. On the Sunday, flags were flown at half-mast and prayers were said for Pat and family at St Mary's church. In the emotional setting of the Memorial Service on Wednesday, you may not have been aware that the church was almost full. In addition to His Excellency the Governor, the Chief Minister and Ministers and a full turn out of the Ex-Servicemen's League, there were some two hundred of Pat's friends and colleagues in the congregation. It was pleasing to see the Methodist Minister taking part in the service along with Canon Jones and the Reverend Howard Williams. Everyone agreed it was a lovely and moving service and we felt that the lusty singing of the Islands was a fitting tribute to the splendid work which Pat had done in many parts of the world.'

Roy Halstead: 24th September 1981

I worried about how I would pay for all this, but knew he would never have wanted to be buried on Grand Turk. In the event, I was thankfully not asked to pay for such things as it was considered that, 'as Governor – he was given his final privilege'. Before I was able to leave Grand Turk, I had to settle various bills and organise my money at the Bank and close the accounts. The joint account was frozen, but fortunately they arranged for some payment of Pat's salary to be diverted into an account in my name and I was able to settle bills and get some travellers cheques for the journey.

The memorial service was held at the church where Pat had been a regular worshipper. It was attended by preachers from all denominations. The building was packed full of mourners. His death had been such a shock to everyone and he was well liked and respected by a great many people. Afterwards, we went to a friend of ours for the funeral tea.

We tried to relax and waited while the formalities went on. We were also waiting for Suzie's permit to enter the UK. It was to come via a British Airways plane, to be handed over to the freight plane which arrived from Miami a few hours before our own departure. Something went wrong of course and the UK plane was late with the precious packet. We arrived in Miami and went straight to the airport freight division only to find the package had been loaded on the plane to TCI which was now ready to taxi down the runway. In our hired taxi, we raced after it and got the pilot to stop and managed to get the packet back. It was a thrilling end to an awful day – saying goodbye to friends and what had become a way of life.

We stayed at the airport hotel overnight and caught the plane home the following day, after first handing Suzie over in her transport cage to the right office. I checked with the stewardess that she was loaded safely and this was confirmed before we took off. Catherine and her husband had Pat's ashes in a box with them in second class. I was flown back first class by the Government, as I was a Governor's wife. On arrival at Heathrow, we were escorted to a back area in the airport and met by a Foreign Office official who was carrying flowers for me. So ended what had been a most interesting period of my life, covering thirty-seven years of happy marriage.

I received a great many wonderful letters and telegrams of condolence from the various countries in which Pat had served including these from:
• The Private Secretary of Her Majesty The Queen
• First President of The Republic of Kiribati (formerly Gilbert Islands) Sir Ieremia Tienang Tabai
• Lord Carrington, Secretary of State for Foreign and Commonwealth Affairs
• John Edwards, Head of West Indian and Atlantic Department
• Andrew Antippas, American Charge d'Affaires, Nassau
• Michael Palliser and Dick Clift (Hong Kong and General Department) of the Foreign and Commonwealth Office
• Acting Chief Minister and Government of British Virgin Islands
• James Davidson, departing Governor of the British Virgin Islands

I believe the last word should go to Roy Halstead, who added at the bottom of his letter that:

'On a personal note, we shall miss Pat greatly. He was ever a tower of strength in the Civil Service and it was a privilege to know the warm-hearted, humorous man who did not always reveal this side of his nature in the office. Pat had a particularly difficult task to perform here and he rose to the occasion admirably – a fact which did not go unnoticed by Her Majesty's Government.'

Roy Halstead 24th September 1981.

ACKNOWLEDGEMENTS

I wish to thank my daughter Catherine for typing up and editing the original memoirs and papers and managing the project on my behalf, and my granddaughter Phyllis for finding the time to also help with the researching and referencing aspects of the book during her undergraduate degree course. A conversation a long time ago with my granddaughter, Victoria, spurred me on to write the memoirs in the first place and for that I am most grateful to her.

For taking the time to explain the book creation process, for her help with the initial design ideas and advice on photograph choices, my thanks go to Jackie Taylor. Thanks also to Lucy Llewellyn and her very helpful and professional team at Head & Heart Publishing Services, who managed the project and enabled me to realise my dream of publishing my memoirs.

August 2015

FIGURES

with the milkman who regularly called with fresh milk with debris floating on top.

Chapter 5

5.1 Keren 1952: Captured Shifta with Eritrean District Officer.

5.2 Agordat 1951: The staff wearing white djellaba and turbans (left to right).

House boy El Amin; Askari; Mohammed the Cook; Houseboy; Nanny Lulu; Safari Cook.

5.3 Keren 1951: Timothy with his nursemaid outside Mohammed, the cook's family home with goats.

5.4 Halhal 1952: Elections had to be held in readiness for self-government and Pat and teams of fellow officers toured the area carefully explaining the concept to the local population.

5.5 Halhal 1952: British Military Outpost.

5.6 Halhal 1952: Margaret and one of the staff on official visit with Patrick.

5.7 Asmara 16th September 1952: Notables, Foreign Officials and South Wales Boarder Regiment at the lowering of the British Flag and Handing over of Eritrea to a Federation with Ethiopia.

5.8 Keren October 1952: Ethiopian Emperor HE Haile Selassie and Empress touring.

5.9 Keren October 1952: Mounted welcome for the Emperor and Empress.

Postscript: The Eritrean Legacy

• Four Power Commission – Front Cover picture.

• Signed letter of appreciation from Moslem League of the Western Province Eritrea to Patrick (in Arabic with translation).

Chapter 6

6.1 Kisiriri House 1953: This was rather oddly constructed with bedrooms 20 metres away.

6.2 Central Province 1953: One of the better official Rest Houses with vehicle and office staff.

Chapter 7

7.1 Kilosa March 1957: Pre 1918 German house structurally condemned.

7.2 Kilosa 1957: Princess Tai-Lu balancing on PWD issue furniture in poor repair.

Chapter 8

8.1 Bagamoyo 1957: Boma. Upstairs Apartment in Arab House with grand facade but interior was showing signs of imminent collapse.

8.2 Bagamoyo 1957: Boma. Miles of beautiful floor tiles all needing to be polished.

8.3 Bagamoyo 1957: Visit of Governor, Sir R Turnbull, with Patrick at Court House.

8.4 Bagamoyo 1957: Patrick taking the march past on HM The Queen's Birthday Parade supported by Margaret.

8.5 Bagamoyo 1957: Patrick talking with local school children as part of HM The Queen's Birthday Parade.

Chapter 10

10.1. Mafeking House 1961: A nice bungalow with a lovely garden and a green lawn.

10.2 Shoshong 1961: Church Mission Society Centenary and Pageant re-enacting bloodthirsty attacks.

Chapter 11

11.1 Mochudi 1962: At one time the garden had clearly been lovely.

11.2 Mochudi 1962: The 50ft *Kopje* gave good views of surrounding plains and the village.

11.3 Mochudi 1963: The government oxen, used to pull the 'scotch-cart'.

Chapter 12

12.1 Gaberones House 1965: Ellen Mpeti outside the dining room, one of our two wonderful maids.

Front cover: Keren Eritrea February 1950: United Nations Four Power Commission.

Back cover: Asmara Eritrea 1947: The author and her husband in the Officers' Mess.

APPENDIX

PATRICK WILLIAM REARDON, O.B.E. (1924–1981)
CHRONOLOGY

Born Kasauli, British India
Educated at Wanstead County High School

MILITARY SERVICE
1942   Enlisted in the Essex Regiment
1943   Commissioned
1944–45 Europe Campaign WWII
        Essex Regiment Battalion served with the First Canadian
        Army in D-Day invasions and subsequent battles
1945–48 British Military Administration, Eritrea
1948   Demobilised with rank of Major

**FOREIGN OFFICE ADMINISTRATION
OF AFRICAN TERRITORIES**
1948–52 Eritrea
        Civil Administrator

COLONIAL SERVICE
1953–60 Tanganyika
        District Officer and District Commissioner (Class III)
1960–61 Tanganyika
        Acting Deputy Provincial Commissioner
1961–65 Bechuanaland Protectorate
        Assistant Secretary in the Secretariat
1965–71 Botswana
        Permanent Secretary
        Ministry of Commerce, Industry (Mines) and Water Affairs

1971   Retired voluntarily upon localisation

FOREIGN & COMMONWEALTH OFFICE:
OVERSEAS DEVELOPMENT AGENCY
1972   Gilbert & Ellice Islands
        Development Secretary
1973   Gilbert & Ellice Islands
        Financial Secretary
1974   Gilbert Islands
        Acting Governor
1977   Gilbert Islands Development Authority
        Administrator
1979   Turks & Caicos Islands
        Chief Secretary
1981   Turks & Caicos Islands
        Acting Governor
1981   British Virgin Islands
        Governor Designate

Died: 19 September 1981
Thus, his immensely rewarding career of thirty-seven years in the
service of Her Majesty's Overseas Civil Service ended.

BIBLIOGRAPHY

The original diaries, memoirs, official documents, photographs and supporting papers are stored in the collection of Margaret Reardon in The Bodleian Library, Weston Library, Broad Street, Oxford OX1 3BG. Tel: 01865 270911 http://www.bodleian.ox.ac.uk/weston

Le Breton, David, ed., 'I Remember It Well: Fifty Years of Colonial Service Personal Reminiscences', *The Overseas Service Pensioners' Association*, (Kinloss: Librario Publishing Ltd, 2010)

Swaisland, Cecillie, ed., 'A World of Memories', *Worldwide/Women's Corona Society: A Millennium Project for Corona* (Sept 2000)

TANGANYIKA
Lewis-Barned, John, *A Fanfare of Trumpets* (Witney: John Lewis-Barned, 1993)

Lumley, E. K., *Forgotten Mandate: A British District Officer in Tanganyika* (London: C Hurst & Co Ltd, 1976)

Tugendhat, Julia, *My Colonial Childhood in Tanganyika* (Gloucester: The Choir Press, 2011)

BECHUANALAND
Read-Lobo, Susan, *Lollipops of Dust: Memories of an African Childhood* (Bognor Regis: Woodfield Publishing Ltd, 2011)

Lees Price, E., *The Journals of Elizabeth Lees Price: written in Bechuanaland, Southern Africa* (London: Edward Arnold Ltd, 1956)

GILBERT & ELLICE ISLANDS

Butler, I. E., *Ghost Stories and Other Island Tales: A Colonial Officer in the Gilbert Islands* (Washington DC: Tom Butler, 2014)

Grimble, A., *A Pattern of Islands.* (London: Eland Publishing, 2012)

Mackay, M., *The Violent Friend: The Story of Mrs Robert Louis Stevenson 1840–1914.* (London: J M Dent & Sons Ltd, 1969)

Siers, J. *Taratai.* (Wellington: Millwood Press 1977)

Smith, John, *An Island in the Autumn* (Kinloss: Librario Publishing Ltd, 2011)

Smith, R., *The Lap of Luxury (Part 2) in The Overseas Pensioner* (OSPA Newsletter, 2002)

Printed in Great Britain
by Amazon